Praise for Patti Teel and *The Floppy Sleep Game*

"A must-have for kids three to ten who refuse to snooze."

—*Good Housekeeping*

"Kids won't sleep? California singer Patti Teel crafts songs designed solely to make 'em slumber."

—*People*

"Patti Teel's recording encourages children to open their hearts and minds to let good thoughts and love flow. In a childlike manner it teaches children to go inside themselves to discover love, gratitude and reverence."

—Deepak Chopra

"You're getting sleepy. A new album will make you yawn. . . . Here's the secret: Teel uses a soft voice and techniques from a gentle form of exercise called yoga."

—*The Washington Post*

"If nightmares, fear of the dark or just plain restlessness make bedtime a battle, help has arrived. Patti Teel, a special education and music teacher, has come up with a soothing mix of yoga exercises, guided imagery, storytelling, and sweet, soft music and vocals to ease youngsters to sleep."

—*Los Angeles Times*

THE
FLOPPY
SLEEP
GAME
BOOK

PATTI TEEL

PERIGEE BOOKS, NEW YORK

THE BERKLEY PUBLISHING GROUP
Published by the Penguin Group
Penguin Group (USA) Inc.
375 Hudson Street, New York, New York 10014, USA

Penguin Group (Canada), 90 Eglinton Avenue East, Suite 700, Toronto, Ontario M4P 2Y3, Canada (a division
of Pearson Penguin Canada Inc.) • Penguin Books Ltd., 80 Strand, London WC2R 0RL, England • Penguin
Group Ireland, 25 St. Stephen's Green, Dublin 2, Ireland (a division of Penguin Books Ltd.) • Penguin Group
(Australia), 250 Camberwell Road, Camberwell, Victoria 3124, Australia (a division of Pearson Australia
Group Pty. Ltd.) • Penguin Books India Pvt. Ltd., 11 Community Centre, Panchsheel Park,
New Delhi—110 017, India • Penguin Group (NZ), cnr. Airborne and Rosedale Roads, Albany,
Auckland 1310, New Zealand (a division of Pearson New Zealand Ltd.) • Penguin Books (South Africa)
(Pty.) Ltd., 24 Sturdee Avenue, Rosebank, Johannesburg 2196, South Africa.

Penguin Books Ltd., Registered Offices: 80 Strand, London WC2R 0RL, England

Copyright © 2005 by Patti Teel
Text design by Stephanie Huntwork
Cover art and design by Ben Gibson

PRINTING HISTORY
Perigee trade paperback edition / October 2005

PERIGEE is a registered trademark of Penguin Group (USA) Inc.
The "P" design is a trademark belonging to Penguin Group (USA) Inc.

Library of Congress Cataloging-in-Publication Data

Teel, Patti.
The floppy sleep game book / Patti Teel.—Perigee trade pbk. ed.
p. cm.
ISBN 0-399-53200-5
1. Sleep disorders in children. I. Title.
RJ506.S55T44 2005
618.92'8498—dc22
2005051532

PRINTED IN THE UNITED STATES OF AMERICA
1 3 5 7 9 10 8 6 4 2

Most Perigee Books are available at special quantity discounts for bulk
purchases for sales promotions, premiums, fund-raising, or educational use.
Special books, or book excerpts, can also be created to fit specific needs.

For details, write: Special Markets, The Berkley Publishing Group, 375
Hudson Street, New York, New York 10014.

**I would like to dedicate this book to my mother—
Jeanette *Grace* Jones.**

My mother's middle name is very befitting. Never have I met anyone who is more appreciative of life's small graces. The sound of a
bird's song or the soft shade of a blooming rose would stop her in her
tracks. "Look," she'd say in awe, "have you ever seen such a glorious
shade of yellow?" Alerted to the rose that I'd been oblivious to, I'd
admire its delicate beauty. But what really touched my heart was the
loveliness of the rose reflected in the glow of my mother's radiant
face. In my eyes, my mother's soft beauty rivaled that of the rose,
which so enthralled her.

I'm fairly certain that my mother has never read a book about
"living in the moment," but then, she didn't need to. She never lost
the wonder of a child, nor does she long for what most people would
consider a grander life. Her flower garden or a newly ripened tomato
are the things that bring her joy. My mother has lived a humble life,
but it is no less worthy than that of a prophet or a saint. By simply
being in her presence, those of us around her will catch a glimpse of
the world through her eyes—and see the beauty in what we fool-
ishly think of as "the little things in life." Thank you so much,
Mom, for teaching me that the small graces in life are more than
enough.

ACKNOWLEDGMENTS

Thank you from the bottom of my heart:

Gary—After all these years, you're still the one for me. Your adventurous spirit and belief in my ability have allowed me the freedom to spread my creative wings. I am so grateful to share my life and my love with you.

Nicole Diamond Austin (The Creative Culture)—My lucky stars must have been in perfect alignment. You are an agent extraordinaire with a rare combination of professionalism and warmth. Not only did you envision this book, you helped me through it each step of the way.

Michelle Howry—I am grateful to you for your wonderful editing and for having an intrinsic understanding of the message that I wanted to convey.

Dr. Anthony Allina—You embody the essence of integrative medicine and I am so honored that you did the vetting on this book. Thank you for helping me with any medical questions that came up and for your insightful opinions. In yoga, "beginner's mind" refers to an open-mindedness to new ideas and a willingness to always learn more. Although you have extensive medical knowledge, I appreciate that you have a "beginner's mind" and are more than willing to look at things from different angles.

Marty—Your charm, tenacity, and faith can move mountains, and the word "impossible" is not in your vocabulary. If it had been, my sleepy little recordings would not be helping children around the world. People are drawn to you as flowers are to sunshine, and like the sun, you provide warmth and sustenance to everyone you meet. Thank you for warming my heart with your love, encouragement, and friendship.

Dr. Kaye—Thank you, my dear friend, for opening up my mind and soul to a world that I never knew existed. I am so thankful and honored to have you as my friend and mentor.

I want to also thank Dr. Peter Claydon, Nancy Hewitt, and Dr. Tim Tupper for sharing their knowledge and insights. And thank you, Andriana, for enthusiastically helping me with each of my recordings.

FOREWORD

I have known Patti for the last twenty years. We met under delightful circumstances.

Patti and her mother attended a yoga class that I was teaching. This began a very long and intense friendship between us. I admire Patti's gifts as a singer/songwriter. Patti can compose songs with the ease that most people can carry on a conversation. She has a gift for touching children and adults with her beautiful voice and melodies.

When Patti said she wanted to share her knowledge of sleep problems I was thrilled. She has such a keen understanding of what it takes to address this very major problem among children. This comprehensive book was written with love, compassion, and understanding. Patti has presented a complete guide for parents whose children are plagued with this disorder.

I am so very proud of my dear friend and her insights. She speaks from long experience as a special education teacher and the challenges of being a mother. I too am a mother and a grandmother. Professionally I have a doctorate in clinical psychology and over the years have counseled many families. I have also taught yoga to children who have been challenged with special needs. Patti consulted me regarding the application of yoga to sleep disorders and I was happy and honored to have participated in this section of the book.

I hope that you find this book as delightful and informative as I have. Pleasant dreams to you and yours.

—**Dr. Gloria Kaye, Ph.D.,** is in private practice in Santa Barbara. She has been teaching and using yoga as a therapeutic intervention since the late sixties. She was the principal investigator on a project funded by the National Institute on Drug Abuse in the seventies. It investigated the effects of yoga on anxiety levels and psychosomatic components of anxiety. At the present time, her proposed research through the Sansum Diabetes Research Institute evaluates the effects of her work on diabetic neuropathy.

CONTENTS

INTRODUCTION What Is the *Floppy Sleep* Game?   *1*

PART ONE
THE PROBLEM WITH SLEEP TODAY

CHAPTER ONE Why Kids Are Sleepier Than Ever   *7*

CHAPTER TWO How the *Floppy Sleep* Game Can
Help Your Child   *25*

PART TWO
UNDERSTANDING YOUR CHILD'S SLEEP

CHAPTER THREE The Most Common Sleep Disturbances Kids
Face Today . . . and How Parents Can Help   *43*

CHAPTER FOUR Eating Right for Sleep   *73*

CHAPTER FIVE Your Child's Sleep Journal   *90*

PART THREE
GIVING YOUR CHILD
A GOOD NIGHT'S SLEEP

CHAPTER SIX   Establishing a Healthy Bedtime Routine   *121*

CHAPTER SEVEN   The Four-Week *Floppy Sleep* Game Program   *140*

CHAPTER EIGHT   Overcoming Anxiety and Maintaining Sleep
Success   *233*

CONCLUSION   *253*

APPENDIX A   Bedtime Activities and Rituals   *256*

APPENDIX B   Relaxation Techniques   *288*

what is the *floppy sleep game?*

TO MY CHILDREN

In my arms you were so small, before I knew it you could crawl
Later hand in hand we'd walk, I marveled as you learned to talk
Then I watched you skip and run, playing freely in the sun
You were confident and strong, and felt nothing could go wrong

When the cloudy days brought rain, I would kiss away the pain
Then I'd gently dry your tears and I'd help you face your fears
But some journeys we can't share, go forth bravely, know I care
As your new adventures start, I will hold you in my heart

HOW IT BEGAN

It seems like only yesterday when I'd hear my youngest daughter's little feet running lickety-split down the hallway and into our bedroom in the middle of the night. While each of my three children slept in bed with their father and me when they were babies, my oldest two children easily made the transition into their own beds. In contrast, when I decided that it was time for my youngest daughter to start sleeping on her own, she had other ideas.

And who could blame her? She was a snuggler and had grown accustomed to sleeping next to a warm body. To appease her, I would lie down next to her in her twin bed and try not to fall asleep myself. When I knew she was asleep I'd try to tiptoe out of her room. I was "as quiet as a mouse," but Brittany's radar was fine-tuned to pick up my escape; she'd beg me to come back . . . and I would. My husband would make a few appearances and wonder if I was ever going to come to bed with him. Eventually, I'd leave her room undetected . . . but she would find me later, in the middle of the night. When I was too tired and sleepy to care, I'd let her join us in bed. Other nights, I'd walk her back to her own bed and lie down with her again. No amount of cajoling, bribing, rewarding, or punishing improved the situation.

After playing musical beds for several exhausting months and making every imaginable mistake, I finally realized that my daughter didn't know how to relax and fall asleep on her own. Inspired by more than a decade of yoga lessons, I finally began teaching my little girl to soothe and relax herself to sleep. The progressive relaxation and breathing techniques were so simple and effective that I was stunned. Brittany's behavior and mood improved—and so did mine. I began sharing the yoga-inspired relaxation techniques with other parents and at local preschool and elementary schools. Everywhere I went, I discovered other sleep-deprived parents whose nighttime scenario was all too familiar. Parents were enormously relieved to reveal their "secret" and realize that there truly was an effective solution.

During this time period, I had already recorded *Kids World*, a collection of my own original children's songs. Upon the urging of many parents and teachers, I put the children's relaxation techniques on a recording, which I called the *Floppy Sleep Game*. At first, I only shared it with my own family and a few friends. Later, I took a booth at America's largest yearly book fair to showcase my recordings, and I brought the *Floppy Sleep Game* along, almost as an afterthought. To my surprise, my sleepy little recording garnered the most interest and enthusiasm. In response, I decided to have it duplicated and available through my Web site. The results were overwhelming.

It received a tremendous amount of attention from the media—major newspapers and magazines began to sing its praises; I was interviewed by *People*, *Good Housekeeping*, and the *Wall Street Journal*; and "The Floppy Sleep Game" recording was even featured on an episode of *48 Hours* in a segment about children's sleep problems. My little sleep CD really touched a nerve in parents nationwide. It was sobering to contemplate the enormity of children's sleep problems.

Although I was pleased by the success of the recording and grateful for all the unexpected attention bestowed upon me, I still wasn't convinced that I wanted to focus exclusively on sleep and relaxation. Each of us wants to feel as if we are making a "meaningful contribution" to the world. Like most parents, I see the need to improve the unhealthy aspects of our society that have a negative impact on the well-being of children—their heightened stress, and related sleep difficulties. But when *People* magazine dubbed me "the Dream Maker," it dawned on me that teaching children to fall asleep and nurture their own spirits by quieting and relaxing their bodies and minds is a meaningful contribution—perhaps the *most* meaningful contribution. I instilled this sentiment in my next sleep/relaxation recordings, *The Inside-Out Blessing Game* and *The Christmas Dream*.

"Baby" Brittany is now in high school, and before I know it she'll be graduating and beginning her life as an adult. I can't help but be nostalgic as I remember the precious days when she and my other children were little. Unfortunately, it's hard to treasure each precious moment with your children when they are irritable and sleep deprived. Brittany's sleep difficulties provided the catalyst that motivated me to come up with a solution that did not entail forcefully making her stay in her bedroom until she cried herself to sleep.

I believe that the subject matter of this book chose me and that for each of us, every experience in our lives prepares us for those yet to come. Who am I to teach parents about their kids' sleep? I'm *not* a doctor, although this program has been read and vetted by doctors. What I am is a parent who has been there and survived, a teacher who has seen the dramatic effects of a good night's sleep on my young students, and a musician who knows that the best way to reach kids is not to yell but to lull them. My experience as both a teacher and a parent have given me an insight that contributed to my recordings and to the content of this book.

I am so gratified by the phone calls, letters, and e-mails that I have received from parents who have made it a point to let me know that my recordings have had a positive impact on their children's lives. I am humbled when I hear their stories and imagine their children falling asleep as I remind them that they are safe, loved, and blessed. I feel privileged to write this book and talk to you parent to parent, as someone who makes her share of mistakes, but like all of us, continues to learn from them. This book picks up where the CDs leave off. It contains a step-by-step program for you to follow so that you can teach your children to relax and fall asleep independently, while choosing and adapting solutions to meet their changing needs. In addition, I've included a great deal of additional information on the subject of sleep and on ways you can use the techniques from the *Floppy Sleep Game* program to help your children cope with fear and anxiety in a healthy way. I am so very grateful to have the opportunity to share this book with you.

—*Patti Teel, 2005*

PART ONE

THE PROBLEM WITH SLEEP TODAY

CHAPTER ONE

Why Kids Are Sleepier Than Ever

If your child has always had trouble sleeping, you may be understandably skeptical that there could actually be a simple solution. However, I'd like to restore your optimism by telling you about Jason. His mom, Cindy, called me on the phone, desperate for some advice and help. Jason had always had trouble sleeping, but now he was nine years old and she was at her wit's end. The entire family had been struggling right along with Jason for *much* too long. As a baby, Jason had been colicky and would cry at bedtime unless Cindy held, nursed, or rocked him to sleep. As he grew older, Cindy continued to help Jason fall asleep by rubbing his back or lying down next to him. Now, he was in the third grade and each night, it took him several hours to fall asleep. Jason's parents were both concerned that his mood and ability to do well in school were being compromised. Cindy also expressed frustration at having to spend her evenings running back and forth to Jason's room rather than having time alone with her husband. While most parents expect to have some sleepless nights when their child is a baby, Jason's sleep problems had been going on for nine years!

I recommended that Jason begin learning the basic relaxation skills that will be outlined in the *Floppy Sleep Game* program, while Cindy and Jason's dad gradually gave Jason less and less attention at bedtime. Within a few weeks I received a letter from Jason's mother, expressing her relief. She wrote, "Jason has been able to transition himself into a deep enough relaxed state to fall asleep for the very first time in his life. My husband and I finally have some time in the evenings that does not require running back and forth to our son's room until midnight! Keep up the good work and thank you from the bottom of my heart!"

Even though Jason's sleep difficulties had gone on for a long time, the basic problem was a simple one—he did not know how to relax and fall asleep on his own. Often, children who have trouble sleeping need to be taught to be good sleepers. Once your child becomes a good sleeper, everything will be a little easier. You are likely to notice that your child is more agreeable and that his health and ability to focus has improved.

Since you are reading this book, it's obvious that you want your child to become a good sleeper and you are already aware that sleep is very important. However, you may not realize just how severe the ramifications of inadequate sleep can be, seriously affecting a child's health, behavior, and ability to learn. While past studies have consistently reported that 25 to 30 percent of all children have some sort of sleep problem, that figure continues to skyrocket. In March 2004, the National Sleep Foundation reported that a whopping 69 percent of children have sleep difficulties. Obviously, something is terribly wrong when more children than not are having trouble sleeping. I'm often asked why so many children have sleep problems today. Actually, there are a number of factors contributing to children's sleep difficulties.

WHY ARE MORE KIDS SUFFERING FROM SLEEP PROBLEMS?

Lax Rules

No doubt, most parents are less strict about enforcing their rules. In fact, in our era of "democratic parenting," children are often given the leeway to bend or eliminate the rules that they don't like. However, certain rules, such as when a child goes to bed, should be nonnegotiable. We can't always expect our rules to be popular, and there are some decisions that we must make for our children. While it's a good idea to give children choices when it's appropriate, there are many instances when it is foolhardy to do so. Kids are not miniature adults who are capable of managing their own lives. We would not allow our child to play in the street, because we know it is hazardous. Similarly, we should not endanger our child's physical and emotional health by allowing him to stay up too late.

The Family Bed

In previous generations, except in cases of hardship, it was almost unheard of for American children to co-sleep with their parents. Today, the family bed has become more and more acceptable. I'm not against co-sleeping for a period of time if it's agreeable to all concerned. The problem arises when either you or your spouse is no longer happy with the situation, but your child resists sleeping alone. Many children find it difficult to fall asleep on their own after having become accustomed to assistance at bedtime or co-sleeping with their parent(s). This is certainly not an insurmountable problem; however, parents should realize that to make a smooth transition from co-sleeping to "solo sleeping" their child may very well need to be taught to relax in order to begin falling asleep independently.

Stress

Most of us remember our own childhood with nostalgia and want to believe that our children are as carefree as we were. It is only wishful thinking, however, for us to believe that although our own lives have become frenzied and stressed, our children's lives have not. Like adults, today's children have busier, more scheduled lives; they often don't cope well and have a difficult time unwinding and falling asleep. Children frequently replay the day's events in their minds or worry about tomorrow, when they should be sleeping. The adultlike pressure of their nonstop lives also puts kids at risk of becoming sick, angry, anxious, and depressed.

Overstimulation

Probably the most important reason kids are sleeping less is a simple one—overstimulation.

There is an unrelenting buzz today. The never-ending sounds and the pace can be unnerving. There seems to be too much of everything—too much mail, too much homework, too many toys, too many clothes, too much to do, too much traffic, too many people, too much information, too much news, too much noise, too many choices! Sometimes there seems to be too much of everything, except time to relax.

Think about the noises and images your young child is likely exposed to in any given evening, just hours before he goes to bed. The aftereffects of television, video games, and household commotion can make it difficult for a child to unwind and relax. It has become so commonplace for kids to be bombarded with all kinds of sights and sounds that we have become unconscious of its negative effects—and therefore complacent about protecting our children from it.

Yet, this early overexposure to all kinds of stimulation is the very thing that is causing our children to become overly anxious, stressed, and sleep deprived. We cannot continue to be oblivious to the sights and sounds that we're exposed to, and we need to realize that everything we see and hear affects us. The sounds of modern technology can be particularly injurious. Several studies have shown that children who live or attend school under the flight path of airports have significantly increased blood pressure and stress hormones. In addition, their speech perception, reading, and long-term memory is also adversely affected.

It's important to become vigilantly aware of what your child sees and hears, whether in the form of television, noise, words, or music. That way, you can protect them from negative noises and images that saturate our environment—and replace those negative images with positive, reassuring, calming sights and sounds that promote relaxation.

Growing Up too Soon

Even diligent parents are finding it impossible to completely protect their children from being exposed to too much too soon, especially by the media. But in addition to the overstimulation caused by a constant barrage of media exposure, there are other ramifications. The problems that stem from this overexposure begin to snowball. In addition to becoming anxious and having sleep problems, children are often precocious and knowledgeable regarding adult topics and begin participating in grown-up activities much earlier than they should. It's really no wonder that children think that they are grown up long before they are.

As caring, compassionate adults, we need to work together to make our society healthier for all children. In the meantime, in lieu of moving to the wilderness, there are small things parents can do to help their children thrive.

HOW PARENTS CAN HELP

Teach Kids to Relax

If you enjoy the benefits of yoga, prayer, meditation, or quiet reflection, I don't need to convince you of the importance of teaching your children to turn inward, away from society's frenzied pace and its narcissistic fascination with image, possessions, and accomplishments. Being purposefully relaxed and quiet helps children to know who they are and gives even young children a sense of calm, enabling them to deal with stress and fall asleep at the end of a busy day. By creating a "family quiet time," your child will learn that having a quiet space in life is important for everybody. Such a time could include drawing, reading, stretching, listening to soothing music, or just looking up at the stars.

Unfortunately, today's families are so overscheduled that quiet family time is a rare commodity. With only the best of intentions, many parents have become overzealous about providing structured activities for their children, filling every moment with lessons, team sports, or other organized activities. Children absorb their parent's stress as they are frantically driven from one event to another. While it's true that safety issues don't allow us to let our kids play as freely as in bygone days, it's important not to overschedule your child. Of course, it's wonderful to support and celebrate your children in ways that are meaningful to them. However, cut out the extra activities that are not particularly enjoyable or important to your child.

Many children have become so accustomed to their structured lives that they don't know what to do with themselves when no one is directing them. When I was a child, my siblings and I went to school, came home, changed our clothes, and then went outside to play with the other kids in the neighborhood. Although my mother had us keep her informed of our whereabouts, we were expected to occupy ourselves—and we did just that. Today, we do our kids a disservice when we don't give them the time and space to daydream and play freely. Don't think of it as wasted time. By entertaining themselves, children will use their imagination and become more creative, self-sufficient, and independent.

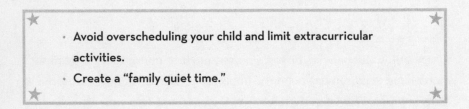

- Avoid overscheduling your child and limit extracurricular activities.
- Create a "family quiet time."

Teach Kids to Be Active

Physical activity is one of the simplest and most effective ways to help reduce stress and ensure that a child gets a good night's sleep. It releases both physical and emotional tension and has a positive effect on the neurotransmitters in the brain that affect mood. Unfortunately, the rise in childhood obesity is a telltale sign that many of our children are not getting adequate exercise. Children should have at least thirty minutes of moderate-intensity activity every day.

You can't assume that your child is getting an adequate amount of physical activity at school. Many schools have eliminated or cut back on their physical education programs, and children who prefer more sedentary activities may not be physically active during recess. Some children are naturally active and get a great deal of exercise just by running around with their friends, riding their bikes, and playing various games such as tag or kick ball. The very children who enjoy running around and playing actively are also likely to be interested in team sports and extracurricular sports lessons. While your child doesn't need to take formal lessons or be on a sports team, it is important that he takes part in physical activities that are enjoyable to him.

If your child is a reluctant exerciser, be a role model for an active lifestyle and find activities that you enjoy doing together. Use your imagination and try out a variety of activities such as bike riding, hiking, in-line skating, or dancing. If you jog and your child is old enough, have him ride his bike alongside you so you can both get your exercise. If you don't feel it's safe for your child to walk to school and your schedule allows it, plan to walk to school together in the morning or home in the afternoon. Young kids usually enjoy having a few extra minutes to spend walking and talking with Mom or Dad. It's also a good way to teach safety lessons about crossing the street and watching for cars that may be coming out of driveways.

Be sure that your child has the opportunity to play outdoors. Exposure to daytime sunlight has been shown to help children (and adults) sleep better at night. If you don't have a big enough space for your child to play outdoors, take him to the park. At the end of an active day, you and your child will both be more likely to get a good night's sleep.

Although vigorous exercise is important, it should not be done within several hours of bedtime. Boisterous activites, or vigorously exercising too late at night stimulates the body and raises the metabolic rate, making it difficult for many children to relax. However, slow, sustained stretching and yoga is great to do before bed because it aids relaxation and prepares the body for a good night's sleep. It also helps kids to get out of their heads and into their bodies after a day of riding in cars, reading, being on the computer, and watching TV.

> ⋆   ⋆
> - Try to ensure that your child has at least thirty minutes of
>   moderate-intensity exercise each day.
> - Be a role model for an active lifestyle.
> - Find fun, outdoor activities that you can do together as a family.
> - Do slow, sustained stretches in the evening before bed.
> ⋆   ⋆

Teach Kids to Turn It Off

Time that children spend watching television takes away from time that could have been spent creatively. It's also a concern that the ready-made pictures on television may rob children of the ability to make pictures in their own minds. Many teachers are convinced that this accounts for many of their student's reading difficulties. Children who don't enjoy reading or find it difficult often have trouble "picturing" what they read.

In addition, children are very vulnerable to the effects of television violence. Research has shown that watching it can cause children to behave more aggressively, become desensitized to the pain of others, and fearful of the world around them. Remember, things that may not be frightening to an adult could be terrifying to a young child. Frightening images and sounds can trigger bedtime fears and nightmares, especially for young children who are still learning to distinguish make-believe from reality. But there is yet another compelling reason why we should be cautious about exposing children to excessive amounts of television, video, and computer games.

Many of us who work closely with children have begun to suspect that today's technology may be changing the wiring in our children's brains and contributing to the rise of ADHD and other neurobiological disorders. Although more studies are needed, preliminary research seems to indicate that television viewing and other forms of video have the potential to affect the brain and related learning abilities. A study published in *Pediatrics* in April 2004 suggested that TV viewing in very young children contributes to attention problems later in life. According to D. A. Christakis, the lead author of the study, "Each hour of television watched per day at ages one through three increases the risk of attention problems by almost 10 percent at age seven." A television programming tactic that is often used to keep children's attention focused on the show may be particularly harmful. Both Christakis and Jane Healy, author of the book *Endangered Minds*, warn that programs that use rapid scene changes may have a particularly harmful effect on brain chemistry. They believe that exposure to this type of high-intensity, unrealistic action conditions a child's mind to expect that level of stimulation and that after adjusting to it, they become bored and inattentive without it.

You may not want to completely eliminate television from your household but be sure to limit viewing time and turn it off when it is simply running in the background. Carefully monitor the shows that your child watches, and keep in mind that for young children, slow-paced shows are preferable to fast-paced ones. Video games are known to provoke high levels of stress so limit the amount of time that your child is allowed to play them. Have a quiet time each evening and turn everything off at least an hour before bed.

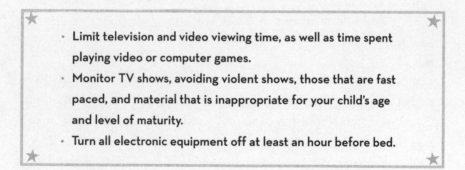

- Limit television and video viewing time, as well as time spent playing video or computer games.
- Monitor TV shows, avoiding violent shows, those that are fast paced, and material that is inappropriate for your child's age and level of maturity.
- Turn all electronic equipment off at least an hour before bed.

THE IMPORTANCE OF SLEEP

For years, our culture has underestimated the importance of sleep in adults as well as in kids. It's not uncommon to hear adults brag about how little sleep they get as if it's a badge of honor. It's hard to understand why the

tragic consequences of inadequate sleep haven't gotten the serious attention that they deserve. For instance, although driving while intoxicated is
a serious problem, so is driving while drowsy, and yet the dangers have received a fraction of the attention. According to the U.S. National Highway Traffic Safety Administration (NHTSA), being sleepy behind the
wheel can have the same effect as being drunk—and fatigue and drowsi-
ness are the principal causes for approximately 100,000 reported crashes
a year.

We have also seriously underestimated the role that sleep deprivation
plays in children's behavioral, learning, emotional, and health problems.
But as research continues to emerge, we are finally beginning to realize
that a good night's sleep is as important as proper nutrition—affecting a
child's mood, immunity, and the ability to learn. While the number of
children who have sleep problems is staggering, by improving sleep hygiene and teaching children to relax, the majority of them are relatively
easy to solve.

THE CONSEQUENCES OF SLEEP DEPRIVATION

Sleep deprivation does not discriminate; it is an extremely common problem that affects children, teens, and adults. America is not the only country with sleep problems; insomnia is a modern-day malady that affects
people in every industrialized country. In the following section we'll look
at the consequences of inadequate sleep so that you will understand why
it's vitally important for you to make the commitment to solve your child's
sleep problems.

Sleep Deprived Parents Are Overwhelmed

You probably know firsthand that parents are among the most sleep-
deprived segment of the population. It's very common for parents to sacrifice

sleep and stay up too late to try to catch up on their backlog of obligations or to be too stressed to unwind, relax, and fall asleep.

Recently, I picked up a popular parenting magazine where moms were asked, "What goofy things have you done while in a sleep-deprived stupor?" The reader's responses included packing cat food in hubby's lunch, making a grilled cheese sandwich without the cheese, getting kids dressed for school on Saturday, and driving the baby to work instead of dropping her at Grandma's. Although we can all laugh at these silly, sleepy mistakes, it's important to realize that sleep-deprived stupors can have serious consequences. A sleep-deprived, spacey mom or dad cannot adequately protect or parent their child. Patience wears thin and humor evaporates when a sleep-deprived parent has to deal with a cranky, overly tired child.

> Set an example. Try to get enough sleep yourself. "Do as I say, not as I do" is generally not very effective with children. If you want your children to value sleep, make it a priority in your own life.

Today, adults average ninety minutes less sleep per week than 100 years ago and, with the exception of Starbucks, we're *all* paying the price. Car accidents, absenteeism, decreased productivity, road rage, and health problems can all be consequences of adult sleep deprivation. For your children's sake, as well as your own, it's important to *make sleep a priority*.

Sleep-Deprived Children Have Difficulty Behaving

Of course, it's not just Mom and Dad who are suffering from sleep deprivation—often kids aren't getting enough sleep, either, and it can have big consequences for their behavior. Sleep-deprived children are likely to have trouble getting along with their friends and families. Unfortunately, many parents, teachers, and even doctors are still not trained to recognize the symptoms of sleep deprivation in children and it is frequently either undiagnosed or misdiagnosed and therefore mistreated. Although there is some variance in the amount of sleep a child needs, parents are likely to underestimate their child's sleep needs because they often misread the signs of sleep deprivation. Although everyone recognizes that when toddlers have tantrums they are overly tired, parents and teachers often forget to take sleep deprivation into account when older children misbehave. Insufficient sleep often shows itself as irritable, frustrated, inadaptable, or angry behavior. When Northwestern University studied 500 preschoolers, they found that those who slept less than ten hours (including naps) were 25 percent more likely to misbehave. They had more behavioral problems such as aggression and oppositional or noncompliant behavior.

As a former special education teacher, when I talked to parents about their child's inappropriate or hyperactive behavior, I would often discover that their child wasn't getting enough sleep. That's exactly what happened when I met with James's mother.

I first met James when I was a resource teacher. His second-grade teacher asked me to observe James in his classroom because he was exhibiting behavioral and learning problems. As I watched James, I soon realized that he took more of his teacher's time and attention than the other nineteen children put together. He was always moving about the classroom when he was supposed to be seated and it was very hard for him to wait his turn or remember to raise his hand before blurting out the answer. When he did raise his hand, he would immediately become frustrated if he wasn't called on. My heart went out to James. It was obvious that he desperately wanted to please his teacher but with nineteen other children to attend to, she often couldn't respond fast enough to prevent James from having a meltdown. I referred James to the school psychologist, and not surprisingly, he was diagnosed with ADHD and a learning disability that involved an auditory processing deficit. The classroom teacher, psychologist, and I met with James's mother to set up his individualized educational plan. During our meeting, I asked James's mother if her son got enough sleep. She said that James always waited up for her until she came home from work at 11:00 P.M., but she didn't think it was a problem. Because James had so much energy late at night, she assumed that he didn't require a lot of sleep. I wasn't surprised that James's mother didn't realize that he was sleep deprived, even though he was getting less than seven hours of sleep a night. Over and over again, I've had parents tell me that their child becomes supercharged at night and doesn't require very much sleep. I explained to James's mother that extreme fatigue often shows itself as "wired" behavior and this usually indicates that a child needs more sleep, not less. Often, the more tired a child is, the harder it is to fall asleep, stay asleep, or both. I convinced James's mother that he needed more sleep, and in addition to receiving remedial help in the resource room, James began to consistently go to bed at 8:30. He also practiced relaxation techniques both at home and at school. These skills helped him to fall asleep at night and "keep his cool" by day. Within a month's time, James's behavior had radically improved, and his meltdowns were a thing of the past. I'm convinced that most of the improvement in James's behavior was because he was no longer sleep deprived.

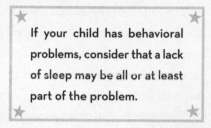

If your child has behavioral problems, consider that a lack of sleep may be all or at least part of the problem.

Sleep-Deprived Children Have Difficulty Learning

Sleep affects our children's ability to learn. Tel Aviv University administered tests to fourth and sixth graders and found that by adding just one hour of sleep, children's attention span and memory improved dramatically, often by several grade levels. A good night's sleep benefits logical reasoning skills and helps children to organize their brains, process information, and remain alert in class the next day.

I don't believe it's a coincidence that as the number of children with sleep problems has gone up, achievement and test scores have gone down. Children who are sleep deprived are frequently inattentive and spacey, have trouble concentrating, and run the risk of being mislabeled as ADHD. In the July/August 2003 issue of *Psychology Today*, a Brown University study suggests "sleep deprivation in normal children can lead to symptoms of attention-deficit hyperactivity disorder (ADHD)." Researchers found that several days of sleep deprivation resulted in the development of ADHD symptoms, and that children's hyperactivity levels escalated with each additional night of poor sleep. Other studies report that even when children have been diagnosed correctly, their ADHD symptoms are likely to improve when they get more sleep.

But even though research shows a clear link between sleep and school performance, many teachers and schools are slow to get the message. Federal law mandates that special education students have IEPs (individualized educational plans). I have taken part in countless IEP meetings and can tell you that the subject of sleep deprivation is generally overlooked by school psychologists who fail to take it into account when making their assessments.

Teachers are often unaware that a lack of sleep is what keeps many of their students from remembering what they've been taught during the day, jumping to the conclusion that a child has a learning problem when the real culprit may very well be insufficient sleep. I often conduct workshops at teachers conventions and conferences and am on a mission to let every educator know that a full night's sleep is one of the most important factors for learning. In fact, bedtime is probably the most vital period of the day for processing new information. When a child is taught

> ★ If your child has learning problems, consider that a lack of sleep may be all or at least part of the problem. ★

something new, but then doesn't sleep long enough or deeply enough for the information to move from temporary to long-term memory, it can be lost forever. I tell teachers that encouraging their students to go to sleep at an appropriate time is the best homework they can assign because kids really do wake up smarter when they've had a good night's sleep!

Sleep-Deprived Children Have Health Problems

Every function in the body is affected by sleep. For a child, the risks of sleep deprivation are much more serious than simply waking up in a grumpy mood. Research shows that children with sleep disturbances have more medical problems—such as allergies, ear infections, and hearing problems. They are also more likely to have social and emotional problems.

There is a whole host of health problems that have consistently been associated with inadequate sleep.

1. Sleep loss is linked to obesity and diabetes.

Sleep loss can contribute to weight gain and obesity by triggering the hormones that regulate appetite and hunger. In other words, inadequate sleep may cause children to overeat. University of Chicago researchers reported new evidence in the December 7, 2004, issue of *Annals of Internal Medicine*, that a lack of sleep changes the circulating levels of the hormones that regulate hunger, boosting appetite and a person's preference for high-calorie, high-carbohydrate foods.

Many physicians believe that sleep loss can also affect the ability to metabolize sugar and trigger insulin resistance, a well-known factor for diabetes. At the American Diabetes Association's 61st Annual Scientific Session, new evidence was presented that inadequate sleep may prompt development of insulin resistance. (In recent years, there has been a dramatic rise in the incidence of childhood obesity as well as type 2 diabetes.)

2. Sleep loss is associated with anxiety and depression.

Insomnia is a significant risk factor for depression. It also contributes to anxiety by raising cortisol, the stress hormone. We have known for some time that depression and anxiety can contribute to insomnia; however, recent research has shown that insomnia often precedes the first episode of depression or of a relapse. Physicians are looking more closely at the importance of solving sleep problems in order to eliminate or decrease the severity of anxiety or emerging depression.

3. Sleep loss may impede physical development.

The highest levels of growth hormone are released into the bloodstream during deep sleep. Because sleep deprivation results in a decrease in the release of growth hormone, height and growth may be affected by a lack of sleep.

4. **Sleep loss affects immunity.**

During sleep, interleukin-1, an immune system–boosting substance, is released. Several nights of poor rest can hamper a child's immunity.

5. **Sleep-deprived children are more accident-prone.**

A lack of sleep has an adverse affect on motor skills. Dr. Carl Hunt, director of the National Center on Sleep Disorders Research at the National Institutes of Health, says, "A tired child is an accident waiting to happen." Bicycle injuries and accidents on playground equipment are more likely to occur when a child is sleep deprived. And unfortunately, the stakes get continually higher when poor sleeping habits continue and the accident-prone child becomes the teenager who is driving while drowsy.

> ★ If your child has frequent health and/or emotional problems, consider that a lack of sleep may be all or at least part of the problem. ★

6. **Sleep loss may affect the response to vaccinations.**

A study published in the *Journal of the American Medical Association* (September 25, 2002) reported that sleep deprivation limited the effectiveness of the flu shot.

HOW THE *FLOPPY SLEEP GAME* CAN HELP

There are a number of parenting books on the subject of sleep, and some of them are very popular and include some sound advice. Basically, there are two schools of thought: one believes it's essential for children to fall asleep on their own and the other thinks that co-sleeping is the best option.

By far, the majority of American physicians and sleep experts advise parents that babies and children should be left to fall asleep by themselves. Accordingly, they should not be held, rocked, or join the parent in bed. Some of them take a hard line and recommend leaving babies and young children to "cry it out" for unthinkably long periods of time.

The problem is that once a child is no longer sleeping in a crib, he will be up and out of his bed when he is upset. Most authors don't seem to realize that many parents are buying their book and looking for advice after having shared their bed or assisted their child to fall asleep for months or even years. When they decide that it's time for their child to fall asleep alone, reassuring, compassionate advice is not forthcoming. Instead, parents are made to feel as if they are failures—and that their child is doomed to continually have sleep problems because he didn't learn to fall asleep independently as a baby. Let me offer you some reassurance. Even if your child has never fallen asleep without your assistance, it's not too late for him to become an independent sleeper and *The Floppy Sleep Game* program will show you how your child can do so.

The second, less popular school of thought encourages parents to sleep with their babies and young children. Proponents believe that it promotes bonding and a strong attachment that helps a child to feel safe and secure. This approach is generally called *attachment parenting* and experts who advocate these principles generally advise parents to let their child decide "when the time is right" to begin sleeping on his own. Although this approach works for some children, others will continue to want to sleep with their parents long past the time when Mom and Dad are happy with the situation. Unlike the *Floppy Sleep Game* program, proponents of this approach generally provide very little information and advice to help a child transition safely and happily into his own bed.

Both approaches completely ignore or give scant attention to the most useful, long-term solution: teaching children the self-soothing skills that will enable them to relax and fall asleep independently. And while most parenting books on the subject of sleep focus on babies, the *Floppy Sleep Game* program is devoted entirely to children, their unique needs, as well as their capabilities. Kids are very receptive to relaxation techniques and are ready to learn to fall asleep by consciously relaxing their bodies and minds. The *Floppy Sleep Game* program will help you teach your child to do just that.

In order for your child to be physically and emotionally healthy as well as a successful student, it's essential for him to get a sufficient amount of quality sleep. The consequences of inadequate sleep have serious ramifications and can be extremely detrimental to the overall quality of your child's life. Lax rules, difficulty transitioning from the family bed, stress, overstimulation, and the media are all factors that contribute to the sleep problems that children face today. It's important to simplify and slow down the pace of your child's life so his world doesn't feel like it's spinning out of control.

Admittedly, we cannot control all the issues that contribute to stress and sleep problems in our modern society. However, your child's reaction to stress is something that he *can* learn to control by purposefully calming and relaxing himself. In the following chapter, I will describe the three simple relaxation techniques that your child will be learning in the *Floppy Sleep Game* program. Although the techniques are simple, their benefits are profound, and very soon, your child will be using them to de-stress, relax, and independently fall asleep.

CHAPTER TWO

How the *Floppy Sleep Game* Can Help Your Child

Sharon was a hardworking hairdresser, a single parent whose only time to spend with her daughter, Melissa, was in the evening after work. Melissa slept in bed with her mother, but when she turned seven, Sharon decided that it was high time for Melissa to sleep in her own bed. Melissa was understandably opposed to the idea; she had gotten used to sleeping in her mother's bed and couldn't seem to fall asleep alone.

Sharon tried everything she could think of to try to get Melissa to sleep in her own room. She thought that if she redecorated Melissa's room, it might solve the problem. A room befitting a princess was created for her—complete with soft colors, a new canopy bed, 400-thread-count sheets, and a cozy new comforter. But Melissa still couldn't fall asleep unless she was in her mother's bed. Sharon was beginning to get irritated with her "little princess" and confided to friends that she felt more like a "royal subject" than a mom!

But the problem was not that Melissa was spoiled. She just had not learned how to relax and fall asleep without assistance. Finally, a client of Sharon's recommended the *Floppy Sleep Game* and Sharon purchased it the same day. To Sharon's surprise and delight, Melissa learned to do the relaxing exercises and fall asleep on her own. Night after night Melissa relaxed her body and mind, and fell asleep in her own bed. Soon, you too will be able to tell a similar success story about the little prince or princess in your life!

As loving parents, we want to help our children in any way we can. Sometimes we help too much. With only the best of intentions many parents "train" their children to need assistance by giving back rubs or lying down with them at bedtime. It's easy for a child (or an adult for that matter) to become accustomed to these indulgences. At this point, it is a matter of debate as to whether a parent has trained their child or a child has trained their parent. Like a puppy that gets fed or picked up when he barks, a child will learn that whining and complaints of not being able to sleep will be rewarded with back rubs and warm snuggly parents to cuddle up with. Maybe I'm making children sound very manipulative. But the truth is that many kids have a difficult time falling asleep without assistance because they have learned to associate sleep with being in their parent's presence. As much as we'd like to be there for our kids, we also want them to grow into independent young people. That's where the *Floppy Sleep Game* program comes in.

No More Bedtime Tears or Tantrums

I am bemused when authors nonchalantly advise parents to be sure that their child falls asleep independently in his own room, without telling parents how they should accomplish this remarkable feat. On the rare occasion that the author expands upon his recommendation, the "stricter" sources sometimes advise parents to go so far as to put a latch on their child's door so he can't get out. Now, let's put ourselves in the child's place. Imagine that every night for weeks, months, or even years, you've been falling asleep while being lavished with attention from someone that you love more than anything in the world. Suddenly, it all changes and you are expected to fall asleep on your own, without any attention. I don't doubt that after weeks or months of feeling forsaken, if your loved one continued to ignore your anguished pleas for attention, you would eventually begin to fall asleep on your own. However, it's not necessary for a child to be traumatized in this way. The *Floppy Sleep Game* program is a gradual process that ensures your child will be successful. Rather than being upset, your child will be proud of the fact that he is learning to relax and fall asleep independently.

Many sleep experts warn you to *expect* your child to be upset for a period of time when you follow their program. Since the majority of them advise you to abruptly withdraw your attention at bedtime, with no mention of teaching a child self-soothing skills, being upset is certainly an understandable reaction. But learning to independently fall asleep does not have to be upsetting. However, expecting a child who has a sleep problem to fall asleep without first teaching him to relax is like expecting a child to read before he has learned the alphabet.

In progressive steps, the *Floppy Sleep Game* program will teach your child to relax himself to sleep while you gradually and systematically decrease your attention. You teach your child many things and one of the most important is to relax and fall asleep independently. The *Floppy Sleep Game* program will empower your child, as little by little, he takes charge of one more thing in his life, falling asleep. Best of all, this will be accomplished without *trauma, tears, or tantrums*. With the *Floppy Sleep Game Program*, this step toward independence does not have to be a painful process for you or your child.

The *Floppy Sleep Game* program will solve children's two most frequent sleep problems: not being able to fall asleep and awakening during the night unable to fall back asleep. Brief night wakening is normal; however, once kids learn to fall asleep independently at bedtime, they will be able to fall back asleep when they briefly awaken during the night. In contrast, children who have difficulty falling asleep by themselves at bedtime usually have the same problem when they awaken during the night.

The relaxation skills taught in the *Floppy Sleep Game* program will be beneficial for all children: those who have always been good sleepers, others who may have slept well as babies but developed sleep difficulties later on, as well as children who have continually struggled with sleep. In addition to enabling your child to fall asleep, the relaxation skills that he learns will help him to become more resilient and capable of calmly dealing with stressful situations.

The *Floppy Sleep Game* Program: An Overview

Before beginning the *Floppy Sleep Game* program, you will be keeping a sleep journal to help you sort out why your child is having trouble sleeping. For one week, you will be carefully observing when and how your child sleeps, his eating habits, and other factors that might be contributing to sleep difficulties. Let me give you an example. Your observation alerts you to the fact that on the weekends, your child is staying up nearly three hours past his usual bedtime. You determine that this is contributing to his sleep difficulties. Before beginning the *Floppy Sleep Game* program you would correct this problem by adjusting his bedtime on the weekends.

When you begin the program, it's important to take a few minutes each evening to have your child practice the relaxation techniques that he will be using in the program. Either you will direct your child or he will follow the directions on one of the first seven tracks of the corresponding CD. Don't let the playful approach of the relaxation practice fool you. While the activities on the CD and those in the book are presented in a fun manner, they were carefully crafted to review and teach important relaxation techniques. Each night, after the relaxation practice, your child will be ready to begin the program.

The three steps of the *Floppy Sleep Game* program consist of guided relaxation, focused breathing, and visualization. The order of the program is very important. The guided relaxation portion is first because it will help a child to wind down and become calm, physically relaxed, and quiet enough to focus on his breathing. In step two, as your child focuses on his breath, he will continue to become more and more relaxed. In this dreamy, relaxed state, he will be ready for step three, which is visualization.

Each week, your child will be getting less and less direction from you as he follows the three steps of the program and becomes more capable of relaxing himself to sleep. During week one you will read the guided relaxation routine, the focused breathing instructions, and visualization process to your child, assisting him with the directions and guiding him through the process. However, even during week one, you will begin to give less assistance as your child becomes familiar with your instructions and more adept at relaxing. During week two, you will remain in your child's room but rather than reading the guided relaxation and focused breathing instructions (that is, the Flop Game), you will be playing it on track eight of the CD. After listening to the CD and following its directions, your child may be drifting off to sleep. However, if your child is still awake, you can either read him a visualization or have him listen to the visualization on track nine. During week three, your child will be falling asleep without you in the room. He will either listen to tracks eight and nine of the CD or a personalized tape that you will be making—consisting of a guided relaxation exercise, focused breathing instructions, and a visualization. By week four, your child will be getting used to falling asleep on his own and will have the choice of doing so with or without the recording.

This system is designed for parents who want their children to fall asleep independently, in their own beds. If your child has been co-sleeping with you, be sure you are committed to this change before starting the program. If you waffle back and forth, letting your child sleep with you at times and other times not, you will probably not be successful. Start the *Floppy Sleep Game* program when you're well rested and dedicated to helping your child take one more step toward becoming self-reliant.

As parents, one of the most ineffective things we do is say things to our children such as, "You're going to be really tired tomorrow if you don't get to sleep!" This only causes kids to be worried about falling asleep as well as how tired they will

> **Tip:** Don't start the *Floppy Sleep Game* program when you have guests in the house, and make sure your entire family is healthy before beginning.

be if they don't. A much better approach is to teach children to relax. Even before your son or daughter is completely asleep, the state of thorough relaxation is very restful; in fact, studies show that it is almost as beneficial as sleeping. Eventually, when it occasionally takes a few minutes longer than usual to fall asleep, your child will enjoy the opportunity to relax and explore the wonder of his own imagination.

> Tip: Don't put stress on a child who complains of not being able to fall asleep.

As previously mentioned, there are three basic techniques that you will use over the course of the next month to teach your child to relax and fall asleep. Below is a brief overview of each of them.

Guided Relaxation

Children are wonderfully receptive to guided relaxation. It often helps if children are first taught to tense and then relax each of the muscle groups, a technique known as progressive relaxation. By first tensing their muscles, children are able to feel and understand the contrasting feeling of relaxation. Each night during "relaxation practice," your child will practice progressive relaxation in a number of fun ways: tensing and relaxing his muscles by making fists with his hands, holding his eyebrows up, or curling himself up into a tiny ball. Children will hold the tension in their various muscle groups for five to ten seconds before releasing them and relaxing.

Step one of the program is the progressive relaxation routine called the Flop Game. Children will be tensing and then relaxing their arms and legs by holding them up straight, before loosely relaxing them and letting them "flop" down on their beds. Then, your child will tense and relax other muscle groups in his body. By the end of the Flop Game, your child's body will be thoroughly relaxed and he will be ready to do step two of the program, which is focusing on the breath.

Focusing On the Breath

It has been said that the breath is the life of the soul, connecting and calming the body and mind. Children are naturally fascinated by their own breathing, just getting quiet and paying attention to it is extremely soothing. Rather than thinking about the events and worries of their day, as children focus on their own breath, their minds will become quiet. Their breathing will also automatically slow down and deepen, bringing more oxygen into their bodies and helping

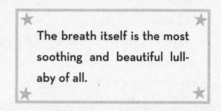

The breath itself is the most soothing and beautiful lullaby of all.

them to relax. For several seconds, at the end of each of the CD's relaxation practice sessions (tracks one through seven) children are directed to quietly listen to their own breath.

In the *Floppy Sleep Game* program, kids will practice being very quiet and simply watching their breath. They don't need to try to change their breath in any way. In fact, they don't have to *do* anything. They will just be watching the breath as it breathes itself. It will be a time of undoing, allowing, and letting go—a time to gather the senses that are usually focused on the outside world and turn them inward.

Throughout the program, children will continue to get quiet and focus on their breathing. After a few days of this simple yet valuable activity, children will be introduced to belly breathing (that is, diaphragmatic breathing) and will continue to use it regularly throughout the program. If you watch babies breathe, you will notice that they breathe deeply and that their entire belly rises and falls with each new breath, however, by age six, most children have already become shallow breathers. Diaphragmatic breathing, or "belly breathing," is a wonderful way to release

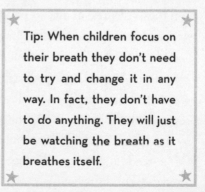

Tip: When children focus on their breath they don't need to try and change it in any way. In fact, they don't have to *do* anything. They will just be watching the breath as it breathes itself.

mental and physical stress and tension. It calms the mind and induces a state of relaxation in children's bodies.

Visualization

Most people have used creative visualization their entire lives, long before they knew there was a name for it. Children have vivid imaginations and creative visualization usually comes quite naturally to them. However, because we have so many ready-made images from such sources as TV, computers, video games, and so forth, it is more important than ever to encourage and provide opportunities for our children to use their imaginations.

There are two main types of creative visualization that will be used in this program. One type is a fixed scene where the narrator provides the structure, taking the listener on an imaginary journey. I think of it as interactive storytelling; your child experiences the story as if he or she is truly living it. In the second type, children come up with their own ideas and pictures, seeing or imagining them in their "dream minds." Visualization skills are enhanced through practice, and before you know it, your child will be effortlessly visualizing scenarios of his own choosing as he drifts off to sleep.

Some people think that visualization is ineffective for them if they don't actually "see" images in their minds. Most children are able to actually see images; however, even if they don't, the process is still useful. If children (or adults) can remember events that have already happened, then they have the ability to visualize, creating something in their imaginations that is not happening in the here and now. It's conjuring for the sheer purpose of making yourself feel good.

I call the blurred time between awake and asleep "twilight time," a perfect time to use creative visualization. We give our sons and daughters a precious gift when we teach them to treasure this magical time. During "twilight time," the conscious mind is relaxed enough to be carried away with a freedom not typically experienced in a totally awakened state. At this point children have actually entered a meditative state; their brain waves are operating at a slow enough rate (often called the theta state) to facilitate creative visualization and sleep. As a child, long before I'd heard of the term "visualization," I would move seamlessly from my nightly visualization into a dream; in effect choosing the opening scene of the first evening's dream. As children thoroughly relax and the line between asleep and awake fades, their visualizations may gradually transform into dreams. This is also a time when positive affirmations and thoughts can be extremely powerful as they more easily enter a child's subconscious mind. It is very effective to intersperse positive thoughts and affirmations throughout a visualization. Be sure to focus the attention of these statements and affirmations on what you want for your child, rather than what you don't want. For instance, if your child has been sick, naturally you hope he gets well. It's important that the statements and affirmations that you choose focus on wellness, rather than on not wanting to be sick. This may seem inconsequential; however, by focusing on what is not wanted, rather than what is wanted, you may inadvertently be inviting it into your life.

We help our children to create their own experiences by encouraging them to visualize or imagine themselves obtaining their heart's desire. By imagining that they already have what they desire, children will be allowing it and welcoming it into their reality. Pure desire is a wonderful thing; it is a feeling of expectation and anticipation. Parents sometimes ask me if visualizing the attainment of goals teaches children to expect them without putting forth the necessary effort. In fact, the opposite is true. By focusing on what they want, children will be drawn to the opportunities and experiences that will bring them closer to their goals. People often confuse desire with yearning, which focuses on not having what we desire. One of the easiest ways to differentiate yearning from desire is to pay attention to how it feels. Desire brings forth joy, eagerness, and expectation while yearning is likely to be associated with feelings of discouragement and pessimism.

Because it's so much more fun for children to learn when imagination and fantasy are involved, visualization is interwoven into your child's relaxation practice on tracks one through seven of the corresponding CD.

AFFIRMATIONS SHOULD FOCUS ON WHAT IS WANTED, RATHER THAN THE LACK OF IT.	
FOCUSING ON WHAT YOU WANT:	FOCUSING ON THE LACK OF IT:
You will fall asleep easily.	You won't have trouble falling asleep.
You feel happy.	You're not sad.
You will wake up feeling refreshed.	You won't wake up tired.
You will feel well.	You're not sick.
Sweet dreams.	Don't have nightmares.

In the *Floppy Sleep Game* program, visualization is the third and final step. The visualizations in the program will take children to a magical place called Dream Land, where anything and everything is possible. There, they will attend a school for dreaming children, called the Dream Academy. The kindly Dream Maker is the school's headmaster and she will teach "the dreamers" the very essence of visualization, that their thoughts are powerful tools for manifesting their desires and that in their dreams they are free to go anywhere and do or be anything.

Visualization is a wonderful way to drift off to sleep, but it provides other benefits as well. For instance, children can use visualization to promote healing and wellness. Our minds and bodies are not separate entities—they are connected. When a child creates positive pictures and self-suggestion, it can have a beneficial effect on both his physical and emotional health. It sounds simplistic; however, children who picture themselves as happy and healthy will be taking an important step toward becoming happy and healthy. Happiness and improved health are gifts that each child can give himself through the power of his own imagination.

> ★ Visualization is wonderfully liberating because reality places no constraints on a child's imagination. ★

THE FAMILY BED—YES OR NO?

The family bed, also called co-sleeping, is a practice in which babies and young children sleep with one or both of their parents. It's estimated that approximately one-third of American families frequently sleep together during all or part of the night. While some parents wouldn't dream of letting their babies and young children sleep with them, others couldn't imagine letting their babies and young children "cry it out" and sleep alone.

Many sleep experts are not open-minded on the issue. In fact, according to some experts co-sleeping will have fostered an unhealthy dependence, harmed marriages, and increased the probability of sleep disorders. Dr. Ferber says in his book, *Solve Your Child's Sleep Problems*, "Sleeping in your bed can make your child feel confused and anxious rather than relaxed and reassured." He also insinuates that parents who believe in the family bed have emotional problems and says, "If you find that you actually prefer to have your child in your bed, you should examine your own feelings very carefully."

I recently read another article that used almost the exact same words, but had the opposite message. It stated that if you resist having your child in your bed, you should examine your feelings very carefully. What's a parent to think?!

I don't feel that there is one right way to parent a child. It is important for parents to decide for themselves whether co-sleeping is an option that suits their lives and that they are comfortable with. Although some babies may prefer to sleep alone, I disagree with Dr. Ferber and others who believe it is harmful for babies and very young children to co-sleep with their parents. It can make your baby and toddler feel loved, secure, and comfortable. Of course, it is not for everyone, but it is a viable option. Let's stop the finger-pointing and acknowledge once and for all that we are all individuals who have different temperaments, opinions, and approaches to parenting.

The La Leche League International, the world's leading breast-feeding organization, recommends co-sleeping from birth. The baby can nurse more easily and both mothers and babies get more sleep than those who sleep apart. Throughout most of the world, co-sleeping is a way of life; it is the norm for 90 percent of the world's population. There has been a great deal of research suggesting that it is *normal* and *healthy*.

After co-sleeping with their parents, many children decide on their own that it's time to start sleeping in their own beds; however, a great number of them will need to be taught to relax and fall asleep by themselves. My rule of thumb is that when anyone in the family bed is uncomfortable, it's time for the child to sleep on his own. I assure you that it is never too late for your child to learn to sleep independently and when you decide that the time is right, the *Floppy Sleep Game* program, will help your child make an easy transition from the family bed into his own bed.

How to Use This Book

I hope that this chapter has given you a basic understanding of what the *Floppy Sleep Game* program entails. In addition to solving the two most challenging and common sleep problems, falling asleep and staying asleep, it will be a fun adventure for you and your child to embark upon. At the end of your monthlong adventure, you will have a well-rested, independent sleeper who will proudly be able to say, "I can go to sleep by myself."

If this book consisted solely of the *Floppy Sleep Game* program, it would still be very beneficial. I understand that you may be eager to begin the program, and of course, if you want to skip directly to the program itself in chapter 7, you can. However, in the chapters that precede the *Floppy Sleep Game* program we'll be covering a lot of important information. In chapter 3, we'll cover health issues and sleep disorders that can contribute to a child's sleep difficulties. Then in chapter 4 we'll discuss the importance of diet and foods that can either detract from or aid a good night's sleep. And, since the behavior demonstrated by a sugar-sensitive child can look a lot like sleep deprivation, you'll learn how to determine if this is a problem for your child. Chapter 5 contains the sleep journal that will help you to pinpoint unidentified factors that may be contributing to your child's sleep difficulties, and chapter 6 has tips for a successful bedtime routine along with activities to help rid your child of bedtime fears and worries.

By waiting and starting the *Floppy Sleep Game* program after you keep a weeklong sleep journal, you will be able to integrate any changes that you deem necessary before beginning the program. However, there is no disadvantage to starting the sleep journal in chapter 5 right away, while continuing to read chapters 3, 4, and 6.

You can choose to continue with the book in the following ways:

1. You can continue with the book in the order it is written.
2. Start the sleep journal in chapter 5 right away—while reading or referring back to chapters 3, 4, and 6.
3. You can immediately start the *Floppy Sleep Game* program in chapter 7.

Option One: Continue with the book in the order that it is written.

Step 1:   Read chapters 3 and 4.

Step 2:   Begin the weeklong sleep journal in chapter 5, identifying factors that are likely to be contributing to your child's sleep difficulties. Leisurely read chapter 6 on bedtime rituals during the week.

Step 3:   Analyze the sleep journal, making changes to correct any behaviors that are contributing to your child's sleep difficulties.

Step 4:   Start the *Floppy Sleep Game* program in chapter 7.

Advantages:

- Before beginning the sleep journal, you will read about sleep disrupters and the bedtime routine, helping you to identify potential problems.
- The sleep journal may identify undetected factors that are contributing to your child's sleep difficulties.
- You will be able to correct any behaviors that are likely to be contributing to your child's sleep difficulties, as you begin the *Floppy Sleep Game* program in chapter 7.

Disadvantages: None.

Option Two: Start the sleep journal in chapter 5 immediately.

Step 1: Start the sleep journal in chapter 5 *now*, while continuing to read about sleep disrupters and the bedtime routine in chapters 3, 4, and 6 or refer back to them, as needed.

Step 2: Analyze the sleep journal, making changes to correct any behaviors that are contributing to your child's sleep difficulties.

Step 3: Start the *Floppy Sleep Game* program in chapter 7.

Advantages:

- You can move everything along by starting the sleep journal immediately.
- The sleep journal will identify undetected factors that may be contributing to your child's sleep difficulties.
- You will be able to correct any behaviors that are likely to be contributing to your child's sleep difficulties before you begin the *Floppy Sleep Game* program in chapter 7.

Disadvantages: None, as long as you continue reading chapters 3, 4, and 6, or refer back to them, as questions arise.

Option Three: Begin the Floppy Sleep Game program in chapter 7 immediately.

    Step 1: Begin the *Floppy Sleep Game* program in chapter 7.

Advantages: You can start the program without delay.

Disadvantages: You may be unaware of factors that are contributing to your child's sleep problems and without keeping the sleep journal, they may remain undetected.

In the following chapter, after a discussion of sleep cycles, we'll discuss sleep disturbances as well as health and emotional problems that have associated sleep problems. Some of the disorders and health problems are quite serious, while other disturbances are quite typical, such as sleep talking or occasional nightmares.

If your child has one of the more serious problems or disorders that we'll be discussing, it will be necessary for you to work with your physician. But whatever the problem, whether serious or mild, it will be more pronounced when a child is stressed and overly tired. A consistent bedtime and the relaxation techniques from the *Floppy Sleep Game* program will be extremely beneficial for a child who is struggling with any type of sleep disturbance, health problem, or neurobiological disorder.

PART TWO

UNDERSTANDING YOUR CHILD'S SLEEP

CHAPTER THREE

The Most Common Sleep Disturbances Kids Face Today . . . and How Parents Can Help

Up until now, I've told stories involving children whose sleep difficulties were behavioral. However, though less common, there are other sleep problems that are indicative of a more serious problem. Such as Lauren's . . .

Lauren and her mother, Peggy, were looking forward to the mother-daughter fashion show that would be taking place at an upscale department store at 8:00 A.M. the following morning. Peggy had hesitated to have her daughter take part in the event because she knew how difficult it was for Lauren to "get going" in the morning. But Lauren's friends were going to be there and she was so excited about it that Peggy finally relented. Lauren and her mother would both be modeling an outfit from the store, and in appreciation, the store was letting them keep the clothes. Lauren spent the day practicing her turns as well as her "model stance."

That night, Peggy tried to get Lauren to go to bed early, but as so often happened late at night, Lauren was a "ball of energy" and didn't actually fall asleep until well after midnight. In the morning, Lauren's mother had a very difficult time waking her. Knowing that Lauren would not want to miss the fashion show, Peggy persisted. Lauren awoke with a glazed look in her eyes and reacted with a seizure-like rage that lasted well over two hours. Of course, they missed the fashion show.

When Lauren finally calmed down, she was heartsick. In addition to being disappointed, she felt guilty for the way she had acted, said she hated herself, and plunged into the depths of despair. Lauren's mother felt awful for her daughter. She understood that Lauren hadn't planned on starting her day by raging uncontrollably. The raging was due to a disorder that so often affected their lives. Lauren has been diagnosed with bipolar disorder. While the *Floppy Sleep Game* program had been beneficial for Lauren, she and her family also need to work with a physician to find the right medications or supplements to stabilize her mood. Until stabilization occurs, she and her family are likely to continue dealing with wild rages and tough times.

Toward the end of this chapter, we'll look at sleep problems that are associated with neurobiological disorders, such as bipolar disorder. But first, we'll review the stages of sleep, common sleep disorders, health issues, and parasomnias. (Parasomnia means "around sleep" and includes abnormal events during sleep such as sleepwalking and night terrors.) Some of the sleep disturbances that we'll discuss are very serious while others are not. After reading this chapter, the information can also serve as a reference guide that you can refer back to as you keep your child's weeklong sleep journal.

Our brains are on a bit of a roller-coaster ride as we go through the different stages of sleep. For children who experience nightmares, night terrors, sleepwalking, and sleep talking, it can be quite a wild ride! Knowing the stage of sleep when disturbances are prone to occur will help you to identify them. For instance, knowing that nightmares usually occur in the second half night's sleep, but that night terrors generally take place within a couple of hours of falling asleep will help you to differentiate the two.

A Normal Night's Sleep for Your Child

Healthy sleep follows a regular cycle each night. For babies, each sleep cycle takes about sixty minutes; by the time we are adults a sleep cycle is completed in approximately ninety minutes. We all progress from stage one, a light sleep, through stage four, the deepest stage of sleep. Then it's back up again through stages three and two, then a period of REM sleep (the stage where most dreams occur) then down and up and down again. So, a normal sleep cycle has this pattern: waking, stage one, two, three, four, three, two, REM.

The first and second cycles of the night are primarily made up of deep sleep, and if your child is prone to sleepwalking and night terrors, this is when they are most likely to occur. Children move rather quickly through the lighter stages of sleep and are likely to have entered a deep sleep within fifteen minutes of falling asleep. As the night progresses, they spend more of the sleep cycle in light sleep (stages one and two), and also experience more REM sleep, when most dreaming takes place. While the REM sleep during the first sleep cycles of the night is only a few minutes long, during each of the last two sleep cycles it lasts close to an hour and is interspersed with light sleep. It's normal for children to briefly awaken during the night, especially when a stage of sleep is coming to an end. Children who have not learned to relax themselves back to sleep are likely to come looking for Mom or Dad during these brief awakenings. The *Floppy Sleep Game* program will help with this problem because once children are able to independently fall asleep at bedtime, they will be much more likely to be able to fall back asleep when they briefly awaken during the night.

Just as our breath and hearts have

> The techniques in the *Floppy Sleep Game* program will not only help your child fall asleep, they will also help him fall back to sleep if he awakens in the middle of the night.

a rhythm, so do our brains. When children are fully awake and alert their brains produce small, high-frequency waves called beta waves. The relaxation techniques from the *Floppy Sleep Game* program help children to become more and more relaxed. This causes beta activity to decline as a child's brain begins producing alpha waves, which are slightly less frequent and lower in amplitude. Alpha waves reduce anxiety and are good for a child's health. They are also useful for creativity and can be thought of as the "bridge" from wakefulness to sleep. As children relax their muscles and focus on their breath they become more and more relaxed—and theta waves are likely to appear. By the time they are listening to the visualization in step three of the *Floppy Sleep Game* program, they are probably in what I call "twilight time," that wonderfully relaxed state between awake and asleep. During this state of reverie, children are likely to begin to see spontaneous images in their minds and are also especially receptive to positive affirmations.

Sleep is categorized into two basic types: REM sleep and non-REM sleep. Our bodies need both types of sleep to be fully rested. There are four stages of non-REM sleep that take us from a light sleep to a deep sleep.

REM sleep, or rapid eye movement sleep, is so named because the eyeballs make fast lateral movements under the lids. In REM sleep, the slow brain wave patterns of non-REM sleep are replaced by fast, low-amplitude waves. Because the brain waves are similar to those when we're awake, REM sleep is also called *paradoxical sleep*.

REM Sleep

Children spend more time in REM sleep than adults, and it's the stage of sleep when the information encountered during the day is processed. Although children can also dream during other stages of sleep, the most vivid dreaming, including nightmares, takes place during REM sleep. Children who wake up or are aroused during this phase of their sleep cycle are usually coherent and can talk about their interrupted dream. When children are deprived of REM sleep, their bodies will try to make up for it by spending more time in REM sleep on subsequent nights.

Because REM sleep is so important, losing even an hour of sleep can have a profound effect. Studies show that the more REM sleep we get, the more likely we are to wake up in a positive and upbeat mood. When children are deprived of REM sleep, their memory and mood is adversely affected and they are likely to become irritable, moody, and fatigued. There are some sleep disturbances that occur almost exclusively during REM sleep; two of the most common are **nightmares** and **REM sleep behavior disorder**.

Nightmares

Nightmares are very real to young children and can be extremely disturbing. After a nightmare, your child may wake up and call out to you. Give your child assurances that you're there and that you won't let anything harm him. Children may be fearful after a nightmare and have trouble falling back asleep, remembering the troubling dream. As soon as your child is calm, encourage him to go back to sleep. If your child finds it reassuring, you may wish to leave a night-light on. Talking over worries and concerns earlier in the evening may be helpful in reducing nightmares. Occasional nightmares are common; however, if they occur frequently and persistently for more than a month, seek professional assistance.

REM Sleep Behavior Disorder

Normally while dreaming, muscles are inhibited or nearly paralyzed. However, we act out our dreams in our minds, but not in our bodies. REM sleep behavior disorder causes people to physically "act out" their dreams. Often the dreams are violent in nature, which is usually in direct contrast to the dreamer's waking personality.

This disorder can occur in children, although it is even more common in adults. I have firsthand knowledge of this sleep disorder because from time to time, my husband has this type of dream enactment. Once, while dreaming he was being mugged, he took a swing at his stalker and hit me! Another time, while dreaming there was a swarm of bees stinging him, he got out of bed and began yelling and wildly swatting at them. When people with REM sleep behavior disorder wake up, they will vividly recall their dreams. The diagnosis for REM sleep behavior disorder should be made by a sleep specialist. Medications may be effective; however, for occasional incidents they are probably not advisable, especially for children.

Non-REM Sleep (Also Called Slow Wave Sleep, or Orthodox Sleep)

Many of the restorative functions of sleep occur during non-REM sleep. Non-REM sleep is also called slow wave sleep (SWS) or orthodox sleep because our muscles and brain waves are doing just what we would expect them to—slow down and relax. While the brain waves in REM sleep are very similar to those when we're awake, during non- REM sleep the brain waves that are associated with wakefulness are replaced by increasingly slow, deep brain waves. There are four stages of non-REM sleep, which will be described briefly in the following section.

STAGE ONE: BETWEEN AWAKE AND ASLEEP (THE HYPNAGOGIC STATE)

During stage one, children are vaguely aware of what is happening around them; it is the stage between awake and asleep. The alpha brain waves become interspersed with the slower theta waves, which are associated with both light sleep and deep meditation. Children may feel a sudden jerk of their entire body (called a hypnagogic startle), have a sensation of falling, or begin to see vivid, spontaneous images. We can encourage our children to enjoy this magical time between awake and asleep by explaining that the "pictures in their minds" are inviting them into the wonderful world of dreams.

STAGE TWO: LIGHT SLEEP

Children are lightly sleeping, but they can still wake up easily and often don't think that they have been asleep at all. Brain waves continue to slow down and are intermixed with occasional rapid bursts of rhythmical brain

activity, called sleep spindles. The heart rate slows and the body temperature decreases in preparation for deep sleep.

STAGES THREE AND FOUR: DEEP SLEEP

During stages three and four, children move into a deep sleep. The first
third of the night's sleep is mostly made up of stage four, the deepest level
of sleep. Children enter a deep sleep quicker than adults and within fifteen
minutes of falling asleep, they are usually in a deep sleep. The delta brain
waves during deep sleep are large and slow and the heart rate is stable.
Deep sleep is the *most* essential stage of sleep and it can occupy up to 40
percent of a child's total time asleep. A growth hormone is secreted during
deep sleep and repairs to the body and brain take place. It is usually very
difficult to awaken children during stage four sleep and if you do, they are
likely to feel disoriented. Night terrors occur during deep sleep as does
sleepwalking, which is sometimes accompanied by urinating in inappropriate places.

While nightmares and REM sleep behavior disorder would usually occur
during REM sleep, other sleep disturbances such as sleepwalking and night
terrors are more likely to occur during non-REM sleep.

In the following section, we'll discuss the most common non-REM sleep
disturbances such as sleepwalking and night terrors. If your child is prone to
sleepwalking and night terrors you may not be able to eliminate them completely; however, getting more sleep and the relaxation techniques from the
Floppy Sleep Game program may diminish their occurrence.

SLEEP TALKING

Sleep talking is often a muttering of jumbled words or phrases that generally occurs in light sleep. Unless it's associated with a night terror, I hesitate to even call it a disturbance, because it is more normal than not.
Don't be overly concerned if your child talks in his sleep, it is extremely
common. In fact, when you talk to children during light sleep most of

them will talk back, although their reply is likely to have nothing at all to do with what you said to them.

Sleepwalking (Somnambulism)

Sleepwalking usually occurs during deep sleep. It is fairly common in childhood and is often hereditary. Most sleepwalking episodes last from five to fifteen minutes and take place during the first two hours after a child falls asleep.

Sleepwalking children often look as if they are awake. Many sleepwalkers just wander around the house, returning to bed on their own with no memory of the episode. Sometimes, during sleepwalking, a child will urinate on the floor (nocturnal bedwetting enuresis). Unfortunately, parents sometimes misinterpret the situation and think that their child is being disobedient when he is really sleepwalking.

Confronting and awakening a sleepwalking child is likely to cause emotional distress or an outburst, which can be mistaken for a tantrum. Rather than awakening a sleepwalking child, calmly guide or carry him back to bed. If your child is prone to sleepwalking, it can be triggered by stress, anxiety, sleep deprivation, a full bladder, environmental noise, or being awakened within a couple hours of falling asleep. Sometimes, but not always, more sleep can reduce its occurrence. If your child is known to sleepwalk, for safety's sake, remove toys and other objects from the floor. Put a string of bells on your child's door so you will know if he leaves his bedroom. Usually sleepwalking stops on its own but if your child does not grow out of it by the age of ten, or if there are nightly episodes, consult with a physician and/or a sleep specialist.

Night Terrors (Also Called Sleep Terrors)

Night terrors happen during deep sleep and are often accompanied by sleepwalking and sleep talking. Sometimes parents mistake them for simple nightmares. Unlike nightmares, which usually occur during the second half of the night, night terrors usually take place earlier in the evening—one to four hours after a child falls asleep—and they usually last from five to ten minutes (although it will probably seem longer to a frightened parent).

Often, children experiencing a night terror thrash about and are confused. They also may walk or run around in an agitated, angry, or frantic state.

When my son was two, three, and four years old, he had many night terrors that most often occurred when something abruptly awakened him. Because of his propensity to have night terrors during the afternoon, I didn't have him stay at preschool for nap time. If your child is prone to night terrors, be sure to inform and educate your child's teacher or care-giver on the subject. I often speak at educational conferences and have been surprised to find that many teachers and even day-care providers are unfamiliar with night terrors.

Night terrors can be alarming for parents (or teachers) especially if they don't know what is happening. It can almost seem as if a child is pos-sessed or having an emotional breakdown. When my friend's preschooler had a night terror, she took her to the emergency room. This is not an un-common reaction.

While a child is having a night terror, don't wake him; it is likely to in-crease his agitation. Keep the lights dim. Unlike nightmares, children have no memory of their night terrors. Like many parasomnias, night terrors are more likely to occur if close family members have a similar history. My mother used to tell me that sometimes I scared her because as a youngster I would wake up, seem angry, and speak in what she called gibberish. In retro-spect, I'm sure I must have been having night terrors. All of my children had night terrors that started when they were about three years old and ended by the time they were five. They often occur in overly tired children and some-times, but not always, more sleep helps. If your child has frequent night ter-rors, try having him go to bed earlier or if it's feasible, have him take a nap.

In young children, night terrors do not signify physical or emotional problems. If night terrors continue after age six, seek advice from a physi-cian or a sleep specialist.

TOOTH GRINDING (BRUXISM)

Tooth grinding usually takes place during stages one and two of sleep and can be related to anxiety and stress. Relaxation exercises from the *Floppy Sleep Game* program may be helpful. In particular, the yoga asana Lion, is

yoga move to prevent tooth grinding

THE LION

Sit on your heels.

Put your hands on your knees and keep your arms straight.

Sit up straight.

Breathe in and open your mouth wide. Stick out your tongue, down toward your chin.

Open your eyes wide. Look at the tip of your nose.

Stretch your fingers straight out and keep your hands on your knees. Roar!

(Repeat two more times.)

Benefits: The Lion relaxes parts of the body that most stretches don't: the face, jaw, mouth, throat, and tongue.

a fun, simple way to help kids relax the face and the jaw and prevent tooth grinding. Dentists sometimes recommend the use of a night guard because tooth grinding can cause damage to the teeth as well as misalignment.

Other Common Sleep Disorders

So far, we've discussed sleep disturbances and disorders that are more likely to occur in a particular stage of the sleep cycle. However, there are other disturbances and disorders that are not associated with a particular stage of sleep.

CIRCADIAN RHYTHM DISORDER

A circadian rhythm disorder is characterized by an inability to sleep at normal times. It is a common occurrence in babies who may have their days and nights turned around. The most common circadian rhythm disorder that affects children is *delayed sleep phase syndrome*. Children with this type of circadian rhythm disorder often stay awake until late at night and then have a difficult time waking up in the morning. By consistently waking their child up earlier, parents can begin to correct this problem. Making a child wake up earlier can cause him to be even more tired and sleep deprived for a week or two; however, if you continue to firmly enforce it, your child should begin to fall asleep earlier and the sleep deprivation will slowly resolve itself. Even on the weekends, don't vary bedtime or the wake-up time by more than a total of an hour a day. Since your child may already be having behavior or learning problems due to a lack of sleep, if you can, start changing his wake-up time during a school vacation.

Another thing that you can do to reset your child's clock is to simulate the dawn by opening curtains and turning on the lights. Starting about an hour before you want your child to wake up, open the curtains (if the sun is up) and gradually turn on more and more lights until it is quite bright. Although you can try using regular lamps or lights, there are actually full-spectrum lightbulbs available. You can also purchase timers that cause the light to become brighter and brighter, simulating a sunrise. (Look on the Internet—search for "dawn simulators"—for more information.) Natural sunlight can also be helpful. Spending at least an hour outside in the sunlight, especially in the morning, may help a child to reset his body clock.

Melatonin is a hormone produced by the pineal gland in the brain. Several studies have indicated that melatonin supplements can be quite successful in the treatment of circadian rhythm disorder in children. However, its long-term effects on children have not been thoroughly studied. If your child continues to have a seriously delayed sleep phase (that is, staying up too late at night and having difficulty getting up in the morning), ask your physician about melatonin supplements. Although it is sold without a prescription at health-food stores, it should *only* be taken by children under a doctor's supervision. Ask your physician about a combination of bright light in the morning and a dose of melatonin in the evening; it can be a very effective therapy for a child who has a seriously delayed sleep phase. A consistent bedtime and the relaxation techniques from the *Floppy Sleep Game* program will also help your child to relax and fall asleep earlier in the evening.

BEDWETTING

Bedwetting can occur in all stages of sleep and it is a very common problem. It sometimes takes place during deep sleep while a child is sleepwalking. Heredity is also a strong contributing factor; it is more common if one or both parents had bedwetting problems as children. Children with ADHD also have a higher incidence of bedwetting. If your child is bedwetting past the age of five, be sure to check with your pediatrician to rule out physical causes. (Occasionally, bedwetting can be caused by physical problems such as a urinary tract infection, diabetes, epilepsy, or sleep apnea.)

It goes without saying that you must not criticize or punish children who wet themselves in their sleep. Bedwetting can be very upsetting and embarrassing to older children. If your child is disturbed by bedwetting, you will probably want to combat it by putting together a plan with your pediatrician.

Once medical factors have been ruled out there are several things that you can try:

1. Cut back on fluids after about 6 P.M.
2. Be sure that your child uses the bathroom before bed.
3. Several times during the day, when your child is urinating, have him stop, midflow, for five to ten seconds.
4. Several times a day, have your child hold off using the bathroom until his bladder is very full.
5. Try using positive reinforcement. It's human nature to wake up more easily when there is something to look forward to. With children under the age of eight, you may want to try using a star chart; give a star for every dry night and a reward after a certain number of stars. If your child does not have success with this ap-

proach, discontinue it after several days, unless you use it in conjunction with another type of treatment, such as an alarm system.

6. Try giving a hypnotic suggestion or affirmation during the evening's visualization. Tell your child that he will wake up and use
   the bathroom when his bladder becomes full.

7. There are alarm systems available that attach to your child's pajamas or to the sheets. An alarm is activated at the first sign of
   wetness, signaling your child to use the bathroom. If you consider this approach, be sure that your child is motivated and that
   it doesn't feel like a punishment. It should be used under a doctor's supervision and is generally recommended for children
   seven years of age and older.

8. There are medications that can be prescribed by a physician.
   (As with all medication, discuss the pros and cons with your
   physician.)

RESTLESS LEGS SYNDROME (RLS)

Restless legs syndrome is more common in adults, but it can also occur in
children. It is usually characterized by unpleasant sensations in the legs
and feet, although it can sometimes also occur in the arms. Relaxation exercises, stretching, and massage may relieve the discomfort. Restless legs
syndrome is often mistakenly diagnosed as "growing pains"; children describe it as a creepy, crawly, itchy, tugging, or tingly feeling. Usually, kids
feel as if they have to move their legs or walk to get rid of the uncomfortable feeling. It can make falling asleep or staying asleep difficult and contribute to sleep disturbances, daytime fatigue, and/or irritability. If it begins
to seriously affect your child's ability to fall asleep or get a good night's
sleep, check with your physician regarding treatment or medication.

Children who have a parent with restless legs syndrome are much more
likely to have it as well. It is also associated with low levels of iron, folic
acid, or magnesium. Caffeine can increase or worsen the symptoms. Studies have shown that children with restless legs syndrome are more likely to
have ADHD, but as with sleep apnea, it's hard to know what percentage

of children are being misdiagnosed due to their sleep-deprivation symptoms. If your child suffers from restless legs syndrome he may find some relief from stretching, a warm bath, and relaxation techniques, such as those in the *Floppy Sleep Game* program.

SLEEP PARALYSIS

Sometimes, upon awakening or falling asleep, children's muscles remain inhibited or "paralyzed." For several seconds up to a few minutes, children experiencing sleep paralysis are unable to move or call out. As you might imagine, this can be very upsetting for a child who then may have a hard time explaining what happened. My youngest daughter experienced sleep paralysis only once but she still remembers it as one of the scariest things that has ever happened to her. She described the experience as "like being in a coma." Oftentimes, children also experience hypnagogic hallucinations during sleep paralysis. These are auditory or visual hallucinations that can be pleasant or frightening. Most sleep researchers believe that sleep paralysis and hypnagogic hallucinations occur as people begin moving in or out of REM sleep. Remember, most dreaming occurs in the REM stage when the muscles in our bodies are suppressed, keeping us from acting out our dreams. In sleep paralysis, something has gone awry. The child is awake but the muscles are suppressed as in REM sleep, creating an inability to move (or paralysis). As the brain is either going into or coming out of the dreaming state, it may result in hypnagogic hallucinations as well. Voluntary eye movement or a soothing touch will usually bring back a child's ability to move. Many people experience sleep paralysis at one time or another in their lives; however, if it occurs regularly it's important to consult with your physician because it can be a symptom of narcolepsy. Stress and sleep disturbances increase the episodes of sleep paralysis. Good sleep hygiene and relaxation techniques, such as those presented in the *Floppy Sleep Game* program may reduce their occurrence.

OBSTRUCTIVE SLEEP APNEA

Obstructive sleep apnea is a scary and potentially dangerous disorder for children. When children have obstructive sleep apnea, the upper airway is blocked during sleep, causing pauses in breathing. Each time there is a pause in breathing, the level of oxygen in the blood falls. In response, the oxygen-starved brain partially rouses itself in order to open the throat and take a breath. After falling back asleep, this cycle continually repeats itself throughout the night. This interrupts deep sleep, increases daytime sleepiness and irritability, reduces the release of growth hormone, and can lead to poor weight gain. It is also linked to bedwetting. Sleep apnea is often unrecognized in children and some kids outgrow it. It is often seen in children ages three to six, but it can also occur in older children and adults, especially if they are overweight. Snoring is one of the main symptoms of obstructive sleep apnea, especially when it is followed by breathing pauses. Children with obstructive sleep apnea often have temporarily enlarged tonsils and adenoids due to allergies or infection. Breathing pauses can also occur when the tongue and throat relax and a child has a particularly narrow airway. Treatments include removal of a child's enlarged tonsils and adenoids or the use of a machine that blows air into the airway.

Like other sleep problems, obstructive sleep apnea is being recognized as a cause of children's learning and behavioral problems and is often mistaken for ADHD. Many children who snore do not have sleep apnea. However, if your child snores and has learning or behavior problems, he should be evaluated for sleep apnea by a physician.

Symptoms of obstructive sleep apnea include the following:

- **Snoring:** Snoring can be a sign of sleep apnea. However, keep in mind that not every child who snores has sleep apnea.
- **Mouth breathing and sleeping with an open mouth, pulling in the chest with each breath, sleeping in unusual positions:** If you notice that your child briefly stops breathing, gasps for breath, or works particularly hard to breathe while sleeping, you should have him evaluated for sleep apnea by a physician.
- **Restless sleep and trouble sleeping:** Sleep apnea seriously disrupts a child's sleep as there is an intermittent blockage of his breathing during sleep, causing him to repeatedly arouse himself to take a breath.

- **Waking with a headache, daytime sleepiness, feeling tired during the day:** Lack of a good night's sleep together with the lack of oxygen during sleep can cause a child to feel tired during the day and to wake up with a headache.
- **Behavior and learning problems that mimic ADHD, difficulty paying attention, hyperactivity:** Because children with sleep apnea do not get a good night's sleep it can have a very serious impact on their behavior and ability to pay attention and learn. Several studies have found that children who snore or have sleep disorders are much more likely to be diagnosed with ADHD. Of course, this leads us to the obvious question as to whether or not these children have been diagnosed correctly with ADHD or if the symptoms of disrupted sleep led to a misdiagnosis.
- **Weight loss or poor weight gain:** Most children with obstructive sleep apnea are not overweight; however, if your child is overweight, it is likely to contribute to sleep apnea symptoms. Paradoxically, children with sleep apnea also often lose weight or have trouble gaining weight. This may be due to the fact that interrupted sleep reduces the release of growth hormone.

NARCOLEPSY

The main symptom of narcolepsy is excessive daytime sleepiness, but it is not the same as being sleep deprived. Children with narcolepsy are prone to fall asleep unexpectedly, sometimes during the middle of an activity. They don't realize that they are sleepy and then suddenly, they are asleep. Another symptom of narcolepsy is sleep paralysis; children cannot move or open their eyes when they wake up. They also may experience cataplexy, which is when strong emotions such as anger cause muscle weakness and in extreme cases, temporary paralysis or collapse. Children may appear to have fainted but they are fully aware of what's going on. Kids with narcolepsy are also prone to have scary hypnogogic hallucinations. These are visions that appear just as they begin to drift off to sleep and are difficult to distinguish from reality.

There is often a family history of narcolepsy. While it more commonly occurs after the onset of puberty, it can also occur in younger children. If you suspect your child may have narcolepsy, check with your pediatrician and/or a sleep specialist.

Other Health Issues That Affect Sleep

Almost all health problems can interfere with a child's ability to get a good night's sleep and the subject could fill a library. However, I focused on allergies and asthma because they are so prevalent and are such a serious hindrance to a good

> Just as a lack of sleep can contribute to health problems, conversely, health problems can contribute to or cause sleep disturbances.

night's sleep. If your child suffers from asthma or allergies, you're not alone. Allergies are the most prevalent children's health problem and asthma in children has increased dramatically in the last decade. It's important to take steps to get a child's allergies and asthma under control in order to help him sleep better at night and function better during the day.

ASTHMA (REACTIVE AIRWAY DISEASE)

Asthma can seriously impact your child's ability to breathe freely and get a good night's sleep. Children with asthma usually have recurring wheezing, coughing, and shortness of breath. The muscles surrounding the airways tighten and the airway linings (mucosa) become swollen and inflamed. Asthma can occur at any age, but symptoms most commonly start when a child is between three and eight years of age. Both allergies and asthma are often inherited.

Fortunately, asthma that starts in childhood often improves with age. My son had his first asthma attack when he was only two years old. If you are the parent of a young child with asthma, it's important to fine-tune your radar because it can become serious very quickly. Early on, I noticed that my son's laughter and speech had a different sound to it before an asthma attack. I would know when he was about to have a problem even before he felt it.

It can be vitally important for a child to take prescribed medication at the first sign of troubled breathing. But be aware that many of the medications used to treat asthma can act as stimulants, delaying the onset of sleep and detracting from its quality. When young children have asthma, it may be hard for them to properly use an inhaler. Young children may need to use a nebulizer, which can prevent many trips to the emergency room. (A nebulizer is a machine that makes a very fine mist from liquid asthma medications. A face mask is attached for the child to breathe in the medication. Often it's covered by insurance.) When children are learning to use an inhaler, they often don't breathe deeply enough and most of their medication remains in their mouth and throat. If your child has asthma, show him where his lungs are located. Explain that the medicine needs to go down to the lungs and have your asthmatic child hold his breath and visualize the medicine opening the airways. Deep, diaphragmatic breathing not only helps a child to effectively use an inhaler, it builds lung power and exercises the airways. It can also help a child to remain calm at the beginning of an attack. (See belly breathing, p. 158)

A long-term preventative medication, Advair, was recently approved for children, ages four and up. Taken twice daily, it can often get a child's asthma under control. Of course, as with all medications, there are pros and cons that you need to discuss with your physician.

Nocturnal asthma is sleep-related worsening of asthma and it's extremely common. Allergens that your child is exposed to during the day may cause a reaction at nighttime, when body temperatures drop and the airways cool. In addition, the body releases chemicals during the night that may alter lung function. Many children don't have any trouble breathing during the day but experience asthma symptoms that flare up as they sleep. The breathing problems may be mild or they may be dangerous and severe, resulting in a full-blown asthma attack. But one thing's for sure—it definitely affects the quality of sleep for your child. In addition to the serious health problems caused by the asthma itself, because it can affect a child's sleep, it can lead to behavior and learning problems. Asthma accounts for more hospital visits than any other chronic illness and most of them occur in the middle of the night. Perhaps due to environmental toxins, the prevalence of asthma has increased by at least 40 percent in the last decade.

Controlling your asthmatic child's sleep and home environment is extremely important. Asthma is most often triggered by allergies; it's important to figure out what your child is allergic to so you can eliminate it from his environment. Often, if you are able to get a child's allergies under control, asthma attacks will lessen. In addition to allergies, asthma can be triggered by fumes, exposure to cigarette smoke, exercise, weather changes, colds, respiratory infections, and stress, both physical and emotional.

However, it's impossible to control your child's environment when he is away from home. If your child uses an inhaler, be sure he always carries it. When my son had sleepovers with his buddies, his asthma would consistently kick in at a certain friend's house. I realized that it was because the family had an indoor cat. Even though they kept the cat out of the bedroom, its dander was throughout the house. It was hard for my son to feel excluded from his friend's sleepovers; however, it was not worth it for him to spend the night because he would have asthma for several days afterward, usually missing school.

It's important to work with your child's doctor if his sleep is being affected by either asthma or allergies. You may need to add, change, or modify your child's medication to alleviate nighttime symptoms. (Research has also shown that acupuncture can be an effective treatment for respiratory diseases, including asthma, and swimming is often a particularly beneficial form of exercise.)

Allergies

Like asthma, allergies usually start in childhood. The symptoms of allergies—a runny nose, sneezing, watery eyes, and a stuffy nose—can affect the quality of your child's sleep. Children who have nasal congestion are likely to awaken repeatedly during the night and reposition themselves in order to try to breathe more clearly.

If you're not sure what triggers your child's allergies, you may want to make an appointment with an allergy specialist to determine if allergy testing is advisable. While a child with allergies may or may not have asthma, the number one trigger for asthma is allergens—such as dust, pollen, and dander. Once you determine what triggers your child's allergies or asthma you can try to take steps to avoid them.

To avoid an allergy or an asthma attack:

- Don't allow smoking in your house.

If your child is allergic to dust mites:

- Have wood or linoleum flooring and avoid carpeting.
- Wash sheets and bedding in hot water (130 degrees Fahrenheit or higher).
- Use pillows that are machine washable and dryable. Avoid down pillows or comforters.
- Keep knickknacks and stuffed animals to a minimum, or in closed displays.
- Wash a favorite stuffed animal in hot water or put it in the freezer for twenty-four hours every couple of weeks to kill the allergens.
- Keep the air vents clean.
- Keep the bedroom as free of dust as possible. Close closet doors.
- Use an air purifier.
- Avoid canopy beds and sleeping on bottom bunks. (Dust mites occupy upper mattresses and canopies.)
- Encase your child's mattress with vinyl covering.

If your child has pet allergies:

- Keep pets out of the bedroom and/or out of the house. Beware that if you keep your pet in the basement and have forced heating, the allergens can be blown throughout the entire house.
- If you do have a dog or a cat, wash them weekly.

If your child has mold allergies:

* Use a dehumidifier.
* Keep books in a case or out of the bedroom.

If your child has pollen allergies:

* Rather than opening windows, use the air conditioner.
* Use an air purifier in the bedroom to reduce triggers in the air.

Special Needs and Sleep Disturbances

More children than ever before are being diagnosed with special needs "neurobiological disorders" such as ADHD, clinical depression, bipolar disorder, sensory integration dysfunction, autism, and Asperger's syndrome. Children with these disorders are very likely to have sleep difficulties. In addition, the problems that characterize the disorders will be greatly exacerbated by a lack of sleep.

My years as a special education teacher have shown me that it's not easy for children with special challenges, nor is it easy for their parents. The children with these types of disorders are often very bright and appear perfectly normal, yet they are likely to have a difficult time "fitting in" and controlling their inappropriate behavior. Children are not the only ones who are likely to be judged harshly when they misbehave. Parents, especially mothers, are often criticized when their children "act out." Hang in there! Support groups with other parents may be helpful. There is still a great deal of misunderstanding regarding brain disorders.

In the field of psychiatry, especially with children, it's not easy to make a conclusive diagnosis. There is not a blood or urine test that will pinpoint the problem. Rather, the diagnosis is made based on a description of the symptoms, observable behavior, and family history. Many times, this is a long and frustrating process; it's not uncommon for parents to take their child to three different specialists and get three dissimilar diagnoses. And yet, it's important for you to get the appropriate diagnosis so that you can understand what's going on inside your child and give the kind of attention and help that is needed. As a parent, I encourage you to trust your gut feeling if you think that something is not right. You will need to be your child's advocate, educating yourself and searching for approaches and experts that will help your child.

Your child may or may not need medication, and approaches that don't involve medication should always be considered. For instance, occupational therapy may be able to help a child with sensory integration dysfunction and a modified teaching approach, relaxation techniques, and focusing skills can go a long way toward helping an ADHD child. Although there are physicians who are very knowledgeable regarding medication, the only way to truly know if a medication will work for your child is for him to try it. Although I wish it weren't so, I've often felt as if my students were human guinea pigs as they tried one medication after another. What works for one child is likely to fail miserably with another. This can be very discouraging for the entire family.

It's very likely that your child will have to try several medications before you find the one that works, and then the physician may need to carefully adjust the dosage as you diligently watch for adverse reactions and side effects. However, when you find the right medication, or combination of medications, you may discover that your delightful child has been there all along!

I *cannot* stress enough the importance of good sleep hygiene and relaxation skills. Children with neurobiological disorders are often stressed—as they struggle to control their behavior, "fit in," and try to keep up with their schoolwork. They may also suffer from sleep-related side effects of medications that they are taking. Medications to treat mood disorders, stimulant medications used to treat attention deficit/hyperactivity disorder, and some of the medications used to treat tics in Tourette's syndrome can all contribute to sleep problems.

If sleep problems continue to plague your child, work with your physician. Consider alternative therapies such as nutritional and dietary supplements, biofeedback, and Chinese medicine. This is likely to be an adjunct to the care provided by your child's primary-care physician. To ensure maximum benefits and avoid any negative interactions between traditional medication and alternative remedies, be sure that all of your child's health-care providers work together. When you find the right healing modality for your child, you are likely to see a big improvement.

All children do best with healthy sleep habits. However, everything needs to be "buttoned down" if your child has special needs. For instance, while many children would have some difficulty settling down after a stimulating evening, it might cause a child with a neurobiological disorder to be up half the night. And while a consistent bedtime is always recommended, a child with autism is likely to feel very unsafe and unsettled if his bedtime routine is disrupted. For many children, it's as if their reactions have been cranked up to full throttle. Of course, each child is different and you will know best what sets off a problem in your own child. However, in general, the same bedtime rules apply—only more so.

ADHD

Attention deficit/hyperactivity disorder is a neurological condition that is characterized by inattention, hyperactivity, and impulsivity. There are three subtypes of ADHD that are generally recognized by professionals. There is the predominately hyperactive-impulsive type (children don't show significant inattention), the predominately inattentive type (the child does not show significant hyperactive-impulsive behavior)—previously called ADD, and the combined type (a child who displays both inattentive and hyperactive-impulsive behavior). Research is finding that there is a strong genetic component. However, ADHD is not the only disorder that is characterized by attention problems, poor impulse control, and hyperactivity. Those characteristics are also likely to be displayed by children who are anxious or depressed, have a sugar sensitivity, or are sleep deprived. The sleep deprivation may be due to sleep apnea, allergies, asthma, circadian rhythm disorder, or restless legs syndrome. Not only are children at serious risk of being misdiagnosed as ADHD, if their sleep or health problem remains undetected, their health can be jeopardized. And remember, even when children are correctly diagnosed, increasing with ADHD, and improving their sleep is likely to minimize its symptoms.

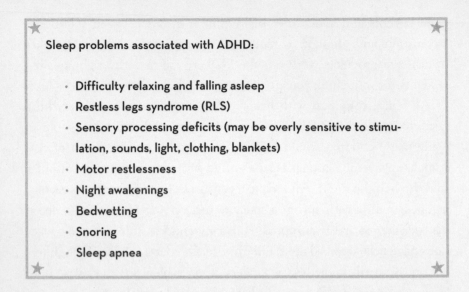

Sleep problems associated with ADHD:

- Difficulty relaxing and falling asleep
- Restless legs syndrome (RLS)
- Sensory processing deficits (may be overly sensitive to stimulation, sounds, light, clothing, blankets)
- Motor restlessness
- Night awakenings
- Bedwetting
- Snoring
- Sleep apnea

If your child has ADHD, good sleep hygiene in conjunction with self-soothing relaxation techniques may be all that is needed to solve his sleep difficulties. Children diagnosed with ADHD usually respond particularly well to relaxation techniques, such as those presented in the *Floppy Sleep Game* program. It is very beneficial for a hyperactive child to practice relaxation techniques at least twice a day. Adequate exercise during the day is also very important. If you suspect that medication is interfering with your child's sleep, meet with your physician to discuss adjusting it. Be aware that stimulant medications such as Cylert, Ritalin, Dexedrine, and Adderall may make it difficult for a child to fall asleep at night, especially if they're taken in the late afternoon.

TOURETTE'S SYNDROME

Tourette's syndrome is a neurological disorder that is characterized by involuntary movements (tics) and involuntary vocalizations (vocal tics). Motor tics are likely to involve eye blinking, grimacing, nose scrunching, head jerking, shoulder shrugging, and hand movements. Common vocal tics might include grunting, sniffing, clearing the throat, and loud sounds or words. Children with Tourette's syndrome are likely to have disturbed sleep and it may take them a long time to fall asleep because they often tic

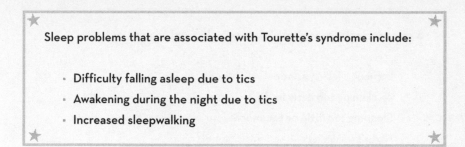

Sleep problems that are associated with Tourette's syndrome include:

- Difficulty falling asleep due to tics
- Awakening during the night due to tics
- Increased sleepwalking

vigorously when they go to bed. Tourette's syndrome is often co-morbid (co-occurs) with ADHD, increasing the likelihood of additional sleep problems. If a child is taking medication to treat his tics, it can also contribute to sleep difficulties.

Because stress can lead to an increase in tic symptoms, relaxation techniques and the *Floppy Sleep Game* program may be particularly beneficial. Some children are more disturbed by their tics than others. Often, by becoming "the observer," a child will become less stressed and his tics will lessen. If your child suffers from tics, just ask him to quietly watch his body and what it is doing, just as if it belongs to someone else. It may not seem as if a child would be able to understand the concept of becoming "the observer," but many children catch on to the idea easily.

DEPRESSION AND ANXIETY

It can be difficult to diagnose depression in children. While some children may appear to be sad and lose interest in the activities they usually enjoy, other depressed children exhibit irritable, hyper, or agitated behavior. Many children with depression also suffer from anxiety. Children who are anxious or depressed often have a number of physical complaints such as headaches or stomachaches. If you suspect that your child is depressed, be sure to seek help from a professional. Depression may be caused by a difficult situation or it could be the result of a chemical imbalance in the brain. Be aware that the use of antidepressants in children can be very dangerous and that they should be used with great caution. Recently, the Federal Drug Administration ruled that antidepressants must come with the strongest government alert—a black box warning. It states that

> **Sleep problems associated with depression and anxiety include:**
>
> · Difficulty falling asleep
> · Awakening too early in the morning
> · Sleeping too little or too much
> · Night awakenings

antidepressant drugs can cause increased suicidal thoughts and behavior in children and adolescents. While there may be cases where their use is warranted, they should certainly be used with great caution.

It's very important for children who suffer from depression or anxiety to exercise, although it might be the last thing they feel like doing. Relaxation techniques may be very helpful, especially if anxiety is a problem. Check with a physician for advice on supplements that may be beneficial. Omega-3 fish oil supplements can be an effective treatment for depression. And, tryptophan increases serotonin levels and may help with both depression and sleep problems. Have your child eat foods rich in tryptophan (p. 82) or consider having him take 5-hydroxytryptophan, an over-the-counter supplement that contains tryptophan described on page 87. (The following chapter will contain more information on the use of supplements.)

BIPOLAR DISORDER

Bipolar disorder in adults usually looks very different than childhood-onset bipolar disorder. In adults, it is characterized by extreme changes in mood, fluctuating from extreme elation and high energy to low energy and depression. In children, however, bipolar disorder is more often characterized by chronic irritability and rages. It is frequently misdiagnosed as ADHD. While stimulant medications are typically prescribed for children with ADHD, many physicians believe that these types of medications can actually trigger bipolar disorder in susceptible children. To complicate matters even further, most experts are of the opinion that a child can have both ADHD and bipolar disorder.

Bipolar children often have a seriously delayed sleep phase. They typically become more active and alert late at night but may be next to impossible to wake up in the morning. Earlier in the book, I recommended that when most children have this type of circadian rhythm disorder that parents should begin to wake kids earlier, in order to reset their internal clock. This can be very difficult to do with a bipolar child. Sleep problems are usually a very big problem for children with bipolar disorder and a lack of sleep can seriously exacerbate the problems associated with it.

HOW YOU CAN HELP

If you cannot get your child to settle down and fall asleep at a reasonable hour, work with your physician. (Consider working with a physician who specializes in childhood bipolar disorder.) Dawn simulators and melatonin supplements sometimes help to reset a child's internal clock. A dawn simulator is an electronic timer that is plugged into a lamp, causing the light to become brighter and brighter in order to create an artificial dawn.

Sleep problems that are associated with bipolar disorder:

- Night terrors
- Bedwetting
- Nightmares
- Sensory processing deficits (may be overly sensitive to light, sound, pajamas, and blankets)
- Motor restlessness
- Anxiety and panic
- Oppositional and defiant behavior
- Sleep paralysis
- Sleeping too little or too much
- Extreme difficulty waking in the morning, low energy level, and poor mood upon arising
- More alert at night leading to delayed sleep onset

Omega-3 fish oil is known to be a particularly helpful mood stabilizer. (These and other supplements will be discussed in the following chapter.) As much as you possibly can, try to have your child keep a regular sleep schedule and teach your child self-soothing relaxation techniques, such as those in the *Floppy Sleep Game* program.

Sensory Integration Dysfunction (Commonly Called DSI)

Sensory integration dysfunction is an inability to effectively process information taken in by the senses. A child with sensory integration dysfunction may either overreact or underreact to stimulation from the environment. I once had a student who would scream and overreact when she was touched lightly but if she was hit or pushed roughly by another child, she didn't seem to feel the painful sensations at all. Children with a tactile sensitivity may be overly sensitive to the feel of their pajamas or blankets and a tag that another child might not notice may need to be removed because it is bothersome. If your child is overly sensitive to sound you may notice that he covers his ears when he is around noise. Children who are overly sensitive to light often complain that the light is too bright or that it hurts their eyes. While sensory integration problems may be present by themselves they are also commonly seen with autism, Asperger's syndrome, ADHD, anxiety disorders, and learning disabilities.

Typically children with sensory integration deficits have a very difficult time calming themselves after an exciting activity. To help them settle

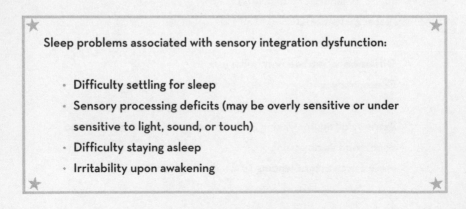

Sleep problems associated with sensory integration dysfunction:

- Difficulty settling for sleep
- Sensory processing deficits (may be overly sensitive or under sensitive to light, sound, or touch)
- Difficulty staying asleep
- Irritability upon awakening

down, it's important to have "quiet time" in the evening, long before you begin your bedtime routine. Like children with autism or Asperger's, change can be very difficult for them. It's very important to have a consistent and predictable bedtime routine. Especially at bedtime, try to protect your child from sensory stimuli that he finds disturbing. If your child is sound sensitive, lower your voice and reduce auditory distractions. If he is light sensitive, dim the lights throughout the bedtime routine. Some children are upset by a light touch but may enjoy a firm massage. Sleeping under heavy blankets or a sleeping bag is sometimes comforting. Relaxation techniques are important and the *Floppy Sleep Game* CD can be especially soothing.

AUTISM AND ASPERGER'S SYNDROME

Autism affects a child's ability to communicate, form relationships, and respond appropriately to the environment. Children with autism generally avoid eye contact and exhibit repetitive behavior and language. Children with Asperger's syndrome share many of the same traits. However, they are likely to have a normal or high IQ and do not have language or cognitive delays. Experts disagree as to whether it is a form of autism or a separate syndrome. Children with Asperger's syndrome often have a preoccupation with a favorite subject. Sensory integration problems may contribute to autistic like behaviors such as rocking, spinning, and hand flapping.

Sleep problems associated with autism and Asperger's:

- Difficulty falling asleep
- Sensory processing deficits (may be overly sensitive or under sensitive to light, sound, or touch)
- Restless sleep
- Night awakenings
- Early morning awakening

Children with autisim and Asperger's also have sensory integration difficulties—so many of the same recommendations will apply. It's important to have calm, quiet activities throughout the evening. Since many children are particularly resistant to change and have trouble transitioning from one activity to another, remember to give your child a ten-minute warning before it's time to get ready for bed. Be sure to have a consistent bedtime routine. If your child is overly sensitive to light or sounds, keep the lights dim and speak quietly throughout the bedtime routine. Teach your child the relaxation techniques from the *Floppy Sleep Game* program. You may find that the *Floppy Sleep Game* CD is an especially effective sleep aid.

In this chapter we looked at the typical sleep cycle and its disturbances, problems that are associated with allergies and asthma, as well as the most common neurobiological disorders. It's important for you to be aware of various types of sleep disturbances or disorders—if for no other reason than to rule them out. If your child is sleep deprived, it's important to know the cause so you can work on an effective solution. Think of yourself as an investigator and be determined to discover the factors that are contributing to your child's sleep problems. In the following chapter, we'll look at one more ingredient that affects your child's sleep—his diet.

CHAPTER FOUR

Eating Right for Sleep

Jordan was Becky and Jeff's youngest child, and their only son. He was slender and had always been a picky eater, even as a baby. To entice Jordan to eat, his parents would buy him almost anything he asked for at the grocery store. Jordan's favorite food was a heavily advertised, sugary, brightly colored cereal. Jordan and Becky realized that it probably wasn't the best choice, but at least he'd eat it, and it was fortified with vitamins. Every day, Jordan had his favorite cereal for breakfast, for an after-school snack, and sometimes he'd have a bowl of it at night when he didn't like what was being served for dinner.

Not coincidentally, Jordan's second-grade teacher reported that he had a hard time staying focused on his work, especially around mid-morning. At home, Jordan's mood seemed to change every few hours, but his parents didn't believe that his diet had anything to do with it. Sometimes Jordan was giggling and overly excited and a couple of hours later he'd be whiny or angry. He also had a hard time falling asleep without the television, so Jordan's mom and dad let him watch it in the family room until he drifted off to sleep. Jeff and Becky didn't think it was a big deal. They often did the same thing themselves.

Jordan's poor eating habits continued throughout elementary school and by the time he was in junior high, the once slender little boy was thirty pounds overweight. He continued to be moody and seemed to have some mild learning problems. He still couldn't fall asleep without the television, but now he had one in his room. He's presently in his first year of high school—and he continues to struggle with his bad temper and his schoolwork.

It's painful to watch when people we care about ignore the importance of a healthy diet and good sleep hygiene. It's not that Jordan's parents don't love him—they just refuse to take a look at their unhealthy lifestyle and how harmful it is.

Food has a huge impact on our child's well-being. It can energize, increase hyperactivity, or induce fatigue. Just as a lack of sleep can jumble a child's thinking or cause learning problems, so can an inadequate diet.

Each child is a unique individual, and it's unreasonable to think that "one size fits all" diet advice is realistic. Children seem to be born not only with an emotional temperament but with a food temperament. For instance, my son has always had a particular suspicion and aversion to any food that is green; however, he doesn't care much for sweets. In direct contrast, my youngest daughter has always loved vegetables and from the time she was a toddler, her favorite food was broccoli. Unfortunately, she also inherited my sweet tooth.

Diet is critical for children's health and everything that we eat affects us. However, it affects each of us a little differently, depending on our individual makeup and metabolism. Many children are highly sensitive to sugar and any form of sweets in their diet. For them, sugar consumption can aggravate many problems such as hyperactivity, anxiety, nervousness, irritability, and poor concentration—all of which can lead to sleep difficulties.

SUGAR SENSITIVITY

Those of you who have not experienced an extreme sugar craving may have trouble understanding what it's like. I'm not talking about satisfying a sweet tooth by having dessert. Children (or adults) who crave sugar are fixated on having more of it, once they start eating it. My sugar cravings began early. When I was a little girl, my father would treat my mother to a box of Russell Stover candy. The box would have lasted her for several weeks, except for the fact that I knew where she hid her stash. As a child who craved sugar, each time I'd sneak into the drawer for another piece, I'd tell myself that it would be my last. I just didn't seem to be able to stop, and I still remember how guilty I felt.

My love/hate relationship with sugar continued into adulthood. My husband would often bring home a two-pound bag of peanut M&Ms because he would enjoy having a few of them from time to time. Usually, however, he wouldn't get the chance because once I started on the bag, I wouldn't stop until every last M&M was gone. My youngest daughter and I have both been known to eat the frosting off of a cake or an entire package of cinnamon rolls and once either of us started on a container of ice cream, it was a goner.

Although "a sweet tooth" sounds innocuous, it is one of the main signs of sugar sensitivity. People whose body chemistry is overly sensitive to sugar often crave it and have an insatiable appetite for carbohydrates and sweets such as cookies, doughnuts, and ice cream. These are not simply sweets; they are a combination of sugar and fat and are the types of food that also contribute to obesity, a risk factor for type 2 diabetes. When some children eat carbohydrates or sugary treats, their blood-sugar level spikes and then drops sharply a few hours later.

Most children with this type of sugar metabolism imbalance would not meet the criteria for a diagnosis of hypoglycemia, although their symptoms, as well as the dietary solution, are much the same. **Hypoglycemia** occurs when the body is unable to regulate the amount of sugar in the blood and the blood-sugar level drops below a specific level. However, sugar sensitivity can occur when the blood-sugar level drops rapidly, even when it is well above the level for a diagnosis of hypoglycemia. The drop in blood sugar is often associated with a craving for sweets, although some children (and adults) crave starchy foods.

The brain uses glucose (blood sugar) as its only fuel and needs optimal levels to function well. When there is a dysfunction in a child's glucose metabolism it affects levels of serotonin and beta-endorphins in the brain.

This, in turn, can cause kids to become moody, difficult, and overly sensitive to stress and pain, both emotional and physical. Serotonin helps to regulate sleep and low levels of this neurotransmitter can contribute to anxiety, depression, insomnia, and headaches. In an extreme example, bipolar children frequently crave sugar and carbohydrates, suggesting that a biochemical imbalance in the brain may indeed contribute to these types of cravings.

As you probably noticed from our discussion in the last chapter, the symptoms of sugar sensitivity can look a lot like those of attention deficit disorder or sleep deprivation. In one of the school districts where I taught a self-contained special education class, several of my students had their government-funded breakfast at school. It consisted of sugary fruit punch and a frosted cinnamon roll. Looking back, I cringe when I think of how it must have affected those kids' moods and ability to concentrate and learn!

Irritability, confusion, the inability to think straight, and disproportionate anger can be signs of either sleep deprivation or rapidly fluctuating blood-sugar levels. When these symptoms take place a couple of hours after eating sugar or carbohydrates and are relieved almost immediately by eating, there's a good chance that they were caused by blood-sugar levels that have dropped quickly. Your sleep journal will help you to discern if these types of mood swings are due to fluctuating blood-sugar levels. Like sleep-deprived children, sugar-sensitive youngsters often have a difficult time waking up in the morning and are likely to wake up in a bad mood.

Some children handle sugar, while others cannot. Regarding the trend to call sugar a drug, well-known author and holistic physician Dr. Andrew Weil says, "I prefer to call sugar a food that may have a drug-like effect in some individuals." If you suspect that fluctuating blood-sugar levels are causing emotional or behavioral problems, try to balance your children's sugar metabolism by changing their diet. Have your child eat a protein-rich, low-carbohydrate diet in which the carbohydrates come from nonstarchy vegetables. This type of diet also decreases the risk of developing type 2 diabetes.

If you'd like to know which carbohydrates have the most dramatic or moderate affect on blood sugar, you may want to become familiar with the glycemic index. It ranks carbohydrates on their immediate effect on blood

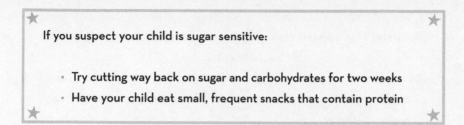

If you suspect your child is sugar sensitive:

- Try cutting way back on sugar and carbohydrates for two weeks
- Have your child eat small, frequent snacks that contain protein

sugar levels. Carbohydrates that release sugar (glucose) gradually into the bloodstream are lower on the glycemic index and tend not to cause a large spike in blood sugar. In contrast, foods that rank high on the glycemic index cause the blood sugar to rise quickly and are more likely to lead to a dramatic crash in the hours to come. There is a lot of information on the glycemic index on the Internet, including www.mendosa.com/gi.htm.

After eating a high-protein diet for two weeks, evaluate whether your child is healthier, both physically and emotionally. If your child's behavior and energy level has improved, make the diet changes more permanent. The cravings for sugar and processed carbohydrates are likely to decline dramatically after several weeks without them. Although an occasional sugary treat is not likely to be harmful, for sugar-sensitive children and adults, avoiding processed sugar is a lifetime commitment with significant health benefits.

Here are some healthy tips for all children, especially a sugar-sensitive child:

- Graze: have your child eat healthy snacks throughout the day that contain protein to stabilize blood-sugar levels.
- Have breakfast and lunch include most of your child's daily protein, which will help with daytime alertness, energy, and mood.
- Avoid sugar and sugary products including soft drinks, candy, and sweetened breakfast cereals.
- If you feel the need to sweeten something, try stevia, "the sweet herb" (available at health-food stores).
- If your child does have an occasional sugary treat, serve it after a meal when it will have less of an impact.

> Be aware! The following contain large amounts of sugar:
>
> Rice syrup, barley malt, cane sugar, beet sugar, corn sugar, date sugar, maple sugar, invert sugar, corn syrup, turbinado sugar, brown sugar, honey, molasses.
>
> Carbohydrates composed of simple sugars: sucrose, glucose, lactose, maltose, xylose, dextrose. *(Take note that these types of sugars end with "-ose.")*
>
> Chemically, the following are alcohols, but are derived from sugar molecules: maltitol, xylitol, sorbitol, mannitol. *(Note that sugars with an alcohol base end with "-tol.")*
>
> When possible, avoid artificial sweeteners; most studies conclude that there are health risks. Although aspartame has no effect on sugar metabolism, in exess it may cause other health problems such as nervous disorders.

- Avoid refined, white flour products such as white breads and crackers.

Although sugar-sensitive children usually improve dramatically on a high-protein, high-fat, and low-carbohydrate diet, some children feel best and have more energy on a moderately low-protein and higher complex-carbohydrate diet. The same is true for adults, reminding us once again that we are individuals and that metabolisms vary. Since each of us is unique, it will take some keen observation to determine which foods may be affecting our child's health, behavior, and sleep. As you begin to see the connection between what and when your child eats and whether it contributes to poor sleep, you will begin to develop your own plan. For instance, some children (as well as adults) are bothered by spicy foods before bed, while others are not. Eventually, we want each child to have his own awareness so that he can know the importance of choosing healthy foods that will make him feel good and sleep well.

FOOD ALLERGIES AND SENSITIVITIES

If a child is allergic to a particular food, the immediate reaction may be sneezing, congestion, a rash, nausea, or an uncomfortable swelling in the throat. In contrast, food sensitivities may not cause a reaction for several hours or even until the next day. This makes it quite a bit more difficult to determine if your child has a particular food sensitivity. Reactions to a food can include gastrointestinal problems, headaches, congestion, low energy, aching muscles and joints, irritability, a short temper, and mood swings as well as restlessness and difficulty sleeping.

When a child repeatedly eats the same food too often, he can actually develop a sensitivity to it. And often children seem to crave the very food that is causing the problem. My daughter loved the turkey sandwich from our local deli and, because I knew it was a good source of protein, I got in the habit of letting her eat one almost every day. When she began to experience irritability and mood swings, I took her to a holistic physician. He suspected that she was having an issue with food sensitivities and had my daughter's blood drawn and sent to a laboratory that specializes in diagnosing them. When the results came back, the doctor called me on my cell phone and told me that the only food my daughter was extremely sensitive to was turkey. At the time, I was driving to the store to buy her yet another turkey sandwich!

In his book *Chemical Sensitivity*, William J. Rea, M.D., explains that a person won't have an immediate reaction to a food that he is exposed to on a daily basis. But, he says if the substance is avoided for four days, and then taken, the patient will have an immediate reaction if it is harmful to him. Dr. Rea says: "Food sensitivity often is missed because the individual is eating the offending food one or more times daily, causing symptoms to be masked." He advises that in order to identify a food intolerance or sensitivity, you should remove the food that you suspect is causing the reaction and observe any change. Then after several days, reintroduce the eliminated food and watch for reactions.

I should mention that there are a number of physicians who do not believe in food sensitivities. Dr. S. A. Rogers, author of *The Scientific Basis of Environmental Medicine Techniques*, believes this is due to conservatism of the medical community and a few pieces of error-ridden research. To me, common sense would suggest that foods can elicit significant problems in sensitive children.

Symptoms that can be the result of food sensitivities in some children:

- Sleep disturbances, including difficulty falling asleep
- Bedwetting
- Tantrums
- Mood swings
- Headaches, including migraines
- Stomachaches
- Eczema
- Asthma
- Seizures
- Bad breath
- Gastrointestinal problems

Both food allergies and sensitivities can cause a number of health problems, including sleep difficulties. Herbert Rinkel, M.D., suggests that food-sensitive individuals are likely to be restless and inattentive by day and have a difficult time sleeping at night. According to Dr. Rinkel, insomnia at night and difficulty arising in the morning due to fatigue are frequent reactions to food intolerance. Commonly, children are sensitive to dairy products, wheat, corn, soy, and yeast.

DEALING WITH PICKY EATERS

We all know that children are healthier and sleep better if they eat a healthy diet containing a variety of foods from all the food groups. Unfortunately, some children can be incredibly picky. I don't think it's a good idea to cater to a child's every whim or to battle over food. Fill your house with healthy foods and snacks and don't get in the habit of buying junk food. That way, when your children are hungry, they will have no choice but to eat healthy and nutritious foods.

In addition, children are much more likely to be interested in eating meals that they have helped plan and prepare. Buy a healthy children's cookbook and have fun planning and preparing nutritious meals and snacks together.

Healthy Tips

- Eat a variety of foods from all of the food groups.
- Drink a lot of water during the day; even slight dehydration can cause feelings of anxiety.
- Make sure your child gets enough calcium; it enhances the synthesis of serotonin, the chemical that induces feelings of well-being. Low levels of calcium can cause irritability and nervousness. Food sources include milk, yogurt, cheese, broccoli, sunflower seeds, carob, and spinach.
- Eat organic foods as much as possible. (Many food additives can also be detrimental to sleep.)
- Eat more complex carbohydrates, rather than processed carbs. (Include raw fruits and vegetables.)
- Don't use sugary treats as a reward or to console a child when he or she is upset.

To Ensure a Good Night's Sleep

What you eat and *when* you eat can affect *how* you sleep. In the following section, we'll review the foods and bedtime snacks that are likely to help your child sleep and identify the foods that should be avoided.

- Avoid late afternoon or evening caffeine and sugar consumption. (Sodas are usually a huge source of both sugar and caffeine.)

- Eat foods rich in B vitamins: sources of B vitamins include whole grains, legumes, organ meats, raw nuts and seeds, mushrooms, deep-sea fish, eggs, meat, and dark green vegetables.
- Eat foods rich in magnesium. Food sources include nuts, whole grains, sunflower seeds, legumes, whole grains, avocados, and raisins.
- Avoid eating dinner any later than three hours before bed if it seems to energize your child. (Eating too late at night raises the metabolic rate and energizes some children.)
- Have an evening bedtime snack that contains tryptophan. Tryptophan is an essential amino acid that the brain converts into the neurotransmitter serotonin. Serotonin is then converted into melatonin, which assists in sleep. Many children find a glass of warm milk calming and it is a good source of tryptophan. Other sources of tryptophan include cottage cheese, yogurt, pineapples, plums, bananas, eggs, turkey, sesame seeds, sunflower seeds, cashews, and peanuts. It's best to combine these tryptophan-rich foods with complex carbohydrates like whole-grain cereals, bread, or potatoes; it helps the brain to absorb the tryptophan. Bedtime snack suggestions: whole-grain cereal with milk, oatmeal with milk, peanut butter sandwich with ground sesame seeds, oatmeal cookies with milk.
- If your child has a bedtime snack, have it half an hour to an hour before bed.

ALTERNATIVE THERAPIES

In the following section I've listed just a few of the homeopathic remedies, vitamins, minerals, and amino acids that are known for their calming, relaxing properties. This is a vast field and as with medications, there are contraindications that should be taken into account. Each child is unique, and just as medications can cause adverse reactions, an herb or amino acid that calms most children may have the opposite effect on another. Unfortunately, many physicians are not as well versed on the use of supplements as they could be; fortunately, more doctors are beginning to take an approach that integrates the best of both worlds. If you decide to consult with a physician regarding your child's physical or emotional health and would like to pursue these types of remedies, I suggest you choose a medical doctor who specializes in a holistic approach. A holistic physician practices integrative medicine; he is likely to use a combination of traditional medicine and alternative therapies.

For referrals to holistic MDs and osteopaths you can contact:

American Holistic Medical Association
www.holisticmedicine.org
410-569-0795

There are also naturopathic doctors, as well as naturopaths, who do not prescribe conventional medication, but specialize solely in alternative therapies such as diet, nutritional therapy, and supplements such as homeopathic and herbal remedies. However, there can be a great variation in their level of expertise and training. The difference between a naturopathic physician and a naturopath lies in the education that he has received. A doctor of naturopathic medicine (N.D.), also called a naturopathic physician, has four years of formal education from a naturopathic medical college. However, a naturopath may have received his education from a trade school or by correspondence. Even more confusing, in some states, a naturopath is allowed to call himself a doctor of naturopathic medicine (N.D.).

For more information and referrals to naturopaths in your area you can contact:

The American Association of Naturopathic Physicians
www.naturopathic.org
202-895-1392

Homeopathic Remedies

Available in health-food stores, homeopathic remedies are natural and are prepared from minerals, animal products, and small quantities of herbs. Unlike herbs, homeopathic remedies are regulated by the FDA. The goal of homeopathy is to gently stimulate the body to heal itself. Homeopathy uses highly diluted doses of natural medicines (plant, minerals, and herbs). In homeopathy, a natural medicine that would cause the same symptoms that the person is already experiencing in a large dose is homeopathically prepared and diluted. If you have chosen the right remedy, the tiny, highly diluted dose works in many cases to help cure a person. Dr. Andrew Weil talks a great deal about homeopathy in his book, *Health and Healing*. Although, scientifically, he does not feel satisfied with the homeopath's explanation for their efficacy, he believes that the remedies do work. He also reported that he himself was treated successfully with a homeopathic remedy. Dr. Weil said: "That homeopathy does work is abundantly clear from many testimonials by both patients and doctors." Children respond to homeopathic remedies for several reasons. They like the taste, the remedies come in tablets or pellets that dissolve easily, and they work very quickly with few side effects or contraindications. If you decide to try a homeopathic remedy on your own, it can be difficult to sort through the myriad of symptoms in order to decide which remedy would be most beneficial. However, because these remedies work quickly, it doesn't take long to determine if you've chosen an effective one. If a remedy doesn't bring improvement within a couple of days, discontinue it, for it's not likely to work. If a remedy works, stop taking it once the symptoms are gone. Otherwise, taken over too long a period of time, you can eventually develop the symptoms you are trying to relieve. Homeopathic practitioners consider homeopathic remedies to be safer than traditional medication. If you work with a practitioner he will take both a child's emotional and physical health into consideration and individualize the treatment depending on the symptoms. For a chronic problem, seek out a medical doctor who also specializes in homeopathy or is board certified in homeopathy. Like naturopaths, homeopathic practitioners vary widely in their level of training, experience, and expertise. Look for a well-trained, experienced practitioner who is easy for you to communicate with.

For more information on homeopathy and referrals you can contact:

National Center for Homeopathy
www.homeopathic.org
877-624-0613

Kali Phosphorous (Kali Phos)

Kali phos is a cell salt, that is, a homeopathic preparation of mineral compounds that are found in all living things. Cell salts were developed over a century ago by Dr. William Schuessler, a German doctor and homeopath. Schuessler felt that minerals were an essential part of the body. He discovered twelve mineral compounds, which he called cell salts, or tissue salts. Schuessler concluded that diseases and abnormal states in the body were due to deficiencies of these twelve mineral salts. Homeopaths explain that while the low doses of cell salts would not be able to supply enough of the mineral compound to correct a deficiency, they stimulate the body to use the minerals more effectively. Today, cell salts are available over the counter at health-food stores. Kali phos is beneficial for nervous conditions, including sleeplessness. It may be useful when a child cannot rest because of overstimulation.

Chamomilla

The chamomilla homeopathic remedy comes from the chamomilla plant, which is an annual herb. It has been used as a domestic remedy since early times. It's helpful for sleeplessness and nervous excitability. The chamomilla is also used in chamomile tea, which is listed below, under herbs.

Hyland's Calms Forté 4 Kids

This is a combination of eight botanical remedies, including chamomilla. It may provide relief from nervous tension, restlessness, and sleeplessness. Available at health-food stores, it is recommended for children ages two and up and comes in dissolvable tablets.

Vitamins

Although some physicians believe that children get all the vitamins they need from eating a balanced diet, others recommend vitamins. Many doctors believe taking a multiple vitamin is a good idea, because many children eat erratic diets, and added chemicals may deplete nutrients. Vitamins may be particularly helpful if your child seems especially stressed, or is frequently ill. They should be taken with a meal to avoid upsetting a child's stomach. Check with your physician for specific vitamin recommendations.

Minerals

Minerals come from the nonliving, naturally occurring elements of the earth. The mineral salts in the soil find their way into the chemical makeup of our foods, or in seafood from the dissolved minerals in the ocean water. Of course, the best way for children to get the minerals they need is to eat a variety of fresh vegetables. However, the mineral content of food depends greatly on the soil that it comes from and if your child doesn't eat many vegetables, it's a good idea for him to take a daily multimineral supplement or a multivitamin/multimineral supplement.

Magnesium (Taken with Calcium)

Magnesium, taken with calcium, can be a mild neuromuscular relaxant at bedtime. You can find tablets or powders that combine magnesium and calcium. This combination may help promote sleep, especially if muscle tension is causing a problem. (Too much magnesium, however, can act as a laxative and cause an upset stomach.)

Amino Acids

Proteins are made up of amino acids. Whether or not amino acids are taken as supplements or from the protein in the foods we eat, they can be very helpful in overcoming depression and anxiety. If your child suffers from anxiety or depression and you would like to try and treat it naturally, consult with a holistic physician.

Green Tea

Green tea has become very popular; it is very relaxing because it contains theanine; an amino acid that has a calming effect. Children may like green tea and find it soothing; however, be sure it is caffeine free. If your child does not like the taste of green tea, you can also buy theanine in tablet form. When children are anxious, I have found it especially helpful to use theanine in conjunction with 5-hydroxytryptophan.

5-hydroxytryptophan

This is an over-the-counter supplement that contains tryptophan, which has a calming effect on the body and increases serotonin levels naturally. Serotonin is converted into melatonin, the sleep hormone. It's best to take it on an empty stomach approximately an hour before bed. This supplement may also be useful for the treatment of depression. (Vitamins C and B_6 help your body to convert tryptophan to serotonin; however, they can be taken earlier in the day and are most likely in your child's multivitamin.)

Herbs

Some people have the mistaken belief that because herbs are plant materials that come from nature, they are harmless. Just as traditional medicine can have adverse reactions and interactions, so can herbs. In fact, the active ingredient in plants provides the structural basis for many of our modern pharmaceuticals. However, unlike traditional medication, herbs are not regulated under federal law and legal standards for their processing, harvesting, and packaging are not applied. Although herbs can be very useful medicinally, I *don't* recommend you use them without the advice of a knowledgeable health professional, such as a holistic physician, naturopathic physician, or an herbal physician. He will be able to advise you on just how to use the herb and will recommend how much to use.

CHAMOMILE

A cup of chamomile tea can help a child relax and sleep. Many children prefer it with a little bit of honey and it can be used safely, even with very young children. *Warnings: with all herbs it's important that it is pure and comes from a reliable source. Chamomile is made from the chamomile flower. If your child is prone to allergies, start with only a sip or two and watch for any allergic reactions.* (Chamomile is also available as the homeopathic remedy chamomilla.)

VALERIAN

It has a calming effect on the nerves and sedative qualities. It is available as an herbal tea and also comes in tincture form. The taste is rather strong but can be mixed into a glass of juice to make it more palatable for a child. Valerian should not be used every night.

PASSIONFLOWER

Passionflower is a fast-growing vine with purple and white flowers and sweet fruits. The flowers and leaves have a long history of use for easing anxiety and insomnia. It is available as a bulk herb or a concentrated liquid extract and it is also included in some sleep and relaxation tea formulas. (Note: It is not recommended for expectant mothers because it can cause contractions.)

Essential Fatty Acids

OMEGA-3 (FISH OIL)

It has numerous health benefits and is used by the nervous system to create calming neurotransmitters. Food sources include cold-water fish, especially salmon, mackerel, and trout. If your child doesn't eat much fish, supplements may be beneficial. However, just as fish can contain high levels of mercury, so can fish oil capsules. Be sure to choose a brand that tests the levels of mercury and other heavy metals. *The following companies sell fish oil that has been tested for heavy metals such as mercury: Carlson, Ethical Nutrients, and Oceana. (Oceana also makes a liquid fish oil with a mild lemon flavor that can easily be mixed into a child's drink.)*

CHAPTER FIVE

Your Child's Sleep Journal

When I spoke to Leslie, she couldn't wait to have her five-year-old daughter begin the *Floppy Sleep Game* program. She said that her daughter, Chloe, relentlessly called out to her after being tucked into bed and didn't fall asleep until after 11:00 P.M. Then in the morning Chloe usually woke up in a bad mood, complaining of a headache. I was fairly confident that the *Floppy Sleep Game* program would help Chloe to fall asleep without needing constant reassurances from her mother. However, I urged Leslie to keep a sleep journal first for a week, to determine if anything else was contributing to Chloe's headaches and poor mood in the morning.

When the week was up, she took a close look at her observations. Leslie realized that Chloe did not have a consistent bedtime routine and that her bedtime varied by as much as an hour on any given night. More worrisome was Chloe's snoring. Although Chloe had been known to snore lightly from time to time, Leslie realized that it was occurring much more frequently and that it had gotten quite a bit louder. She also noticed that Chloe's blankets were twisted and off her bed in the morning. Leslie was concerned because Chloe had three of the symptoms of sleep apnea: snoring, restless sleep, and a headache upon awakening in the morning. She took Chloe to her pediatrician for an evaluation and was relieved when sleep apnea was ruled out. However, the examination revealed that Chloe had a great deal of nasal congestion, which contributed to her snoring. The physician advised Leslie to take steps to keep Chloe's room as free of allergens as possible. Leslie did a thorough cleaning of Chloe's room, took out the carpeting, washed her bedding, and packed away most of her stuffed animals. Leslie began to enforce a regular bedtime and set up a consistent bedtime routine as Chloe began the *Floppy Sleep Game* program. Chloe began to look forward to her familiar and comforting bedtime routine and enjoyed learning to "flop" her arms and legs. Her allergies began to subside and she stopped snoring. Chloe began to fall asleep on her own and she no longer called out to her mother after being tucked in. She was happy in the morning and no longer woke up with a headache.

While the *Floppy Sleep Game* program would have been helpful on its own, the sleep journal revealed important problems that otherwise may not have been recognized or addressed.

Why Do I Need to Keep a Sleep Journal?

Keeping a sleep journal is the best way to pinpoint your child's sleep problem. It is very possible that your child's primary sleep problem is that he has not learned to fall asleep on his own and has become accustomed to assistance, making it difficult to fall asleep without it. Even if that ends up being the case, your sleep journal is likely to be revealing and you'll probably become aware of things that you never noticed before. For instance, you may notice that your child's bedtime routine is not as consistent as you'd like it to be or that your child's diet should be healthier.

In a small percentage of children, the problem is more serious and a sleep disorder or underlying medical condition is causing or contributing to the sleep problems. The sleep journal will help you determine if you should consult with a physician, and if so, your observations will be invaluable in helping your doctor make an accurate assessment.

WHAT AM I LOOKING FOR?

Think of yourself as a scientist. You will not only be identifying a problem, you will be trying to pinpoint the cause so that you can take steps to solve it. For instance, if your child is frequently upset, you would analyze the information gathered in the sleep journal to try to determine the cause. Among other things, you would examine whether your child is consistently upset a few hours after eating sugary foods, or if your child is getting enough hours of sleep for his age. If you discover that your child is not getting enough sleep, then you have to figure out why. The problem could simply be behavioral or it could be due to a sleep disorder or a health problem, such as asthma. Once you've identified the problem(s) you will begin to take steps to solve them.

For one week, you will be carefully observing your child's sleep habits. Among other things, you will be recording the time your child goes to bed and rises in the morning, the amount of time it takes him to drift off and his total hours of sleep and energy level throughout the day. Watch for hyper, moody, or inattentive behavior as well as learning difficulties and illnesses, all of which may indicate that your child needs more sleep. You will also be paying attention to the ways your child tries to elicit your attention and assistance at bedtime. Not to worry, the *Floppy Sleep Game* program in chapter 7 will solve this issue. This week, just be aware of what it is your child does—and whether your response is rewarding. For instance, if your child calls you back into his bedroom and you rub his back, that would most definitely be rewarding.

Start keeping your sleep journal on a "typical week" when you are not planning to be out of town or have houseguests. Before beginning, read through the observation portion of the sleep journal so that you'll know what to watch for and record. You can record your observations whenever you'd like during the day. The sooner you record them, the more accurate they are likely to be. If you notice something important that occurs during the day and you don't have the sleep journal with you, jot down a little note for yourself. For example, perhaps your child has a complete melt-

down and you realize that it occurred about two hours after he ate
some caramel corn. You would want
to write this down in order to determine if it's a pattern. Minimally, record your observations twice a day,
while they're still fresh in your mind.

> If you work outside your home, have your child's care-taker assist in observing and recording the information.

Some parents jot down their day's observations after their child goes to
sleep at night. Then, in the morning they record what happened during
the night. In order to get a true representation of the factors that may be
affecting your child's sleep, it's important to keep the sleep journal for all
seven days; it's best if they are consecutive.

What You'll Be Watching for Throughout the Day

In the Morning
* You will be watching to see if your child seems well rested when
he wakes up in the morning.

In the Afternoon
* You will be watching for signs of fatigue and mood problems late
in the afternoon.

In the Evening
* You'll be paying attention to your child's bedtime routine and
noticing if it's consistent.
* You'll observe whether or not your child needs your assistance to
fall asleep.
* You'll record how long it takes your child to fall asleep.

Throughout the Night
* You will watch for any incidents where your child gets out of bed
or calls out to you during the night.

- You will watch for any nighttime disturbances such as sleepwalking or night terrors.
- You will watch for signs of snoring or restless sleep.

THROUGHOUT THE DAY AND EVENING
- You will observe what your child eats and its effect on his mood.
- You will be watching for health complaints.
- You will be watching for hyperactivity, fatigue, mood, or behavior problems.

HOW MUCH SLEEP DOES MY CHILD NEED?

As you can see by looking at the sleep chart below, there are variations in the amount of sleep that a child needs. If your child wakes up easily and is not tired, overly active, moody, or inattentive, then he's probably getting enough sleep. Conversely, if your child needs to be awakened in the morning and is tired, overly active or lethargic, moody, and inattentive, there's a good chance that he needs more sleep.

Sleep Chart

The following recommendations come from the National Sleep Foundation:

AGE	AVERAGE HOURS OF SLEEP NEEDED
three to five	ten to thirteen
five to twelve	ten to eleven

At the end of the week, carefully review your observations and the analysis below each section. Refer back to chapters 3 and 4 as needed, for more detailed explanations. Compile and list any changes you plan to make on your "plan of action," which is located on the last page of the sleep journal.

SLEEP JOURNAL

WEEK ONE OBSERVATION : MORNING WAKE-UP CALL							
	DAY 1	DAY 2	DAY 3	DAY 4	DAY 5	DAY 6	DAY 7
Wake-up time:							
Awakened on own?							
If not, was child difficult to awaken?							
Mood upon awakening:							

Notes or observations regarding early morning mood; include any health complaints such as headaches or stomachaches:

_____

_____

_____

_____

ANALYSIS: MORNING WAKE-UP CALL

PROBLEMS AND SOLUTIONS:

• **Problem: Does your child wake up too early in the morning?**

This can occur when a child has had enough sleep, or paradoxically, when more sleep is needed. Block early morning sunlight with dark shades or curtains. Set an earlier bedtime.

If you determine that your child has had enough sleep, seems well rested, and is getting the recommended amount of sleep but wakes up earlier than you'd like, try the following options.

Make bedtime a little later. If your children are old enough, encourage them to play quietly until you get up. Get up earlier yourself and enjoy the morning with your children.

• **Problem: Is your child's wake-up time inconsistent?**

Be sure that your child's bedtime and morning wake-up time is consistent. Even on the weekend, it should not vary by more than an hour a day or a total of two hours for the weekend.

• **Problem: Is your child unable to awaken on his own, or does he suffer from a poor mood upon awakening?**

This is usually a sign that your child needs more sleep. Set an earlier bedtime, a later wake-up time or both. Add an afternoon nap if age appropriate and schedule permits. If your child is a "night owl," but tired in the morning, gradually set an earlier wake-up time.

Not every illness or health issue is due to sleep deprivation; however, inadequate sleep affects immunity and children who lack sleep are more frequently ill and prone to get headaches and stomachaches.

List any changes you plan to make:

_____

_____

_____

_____

WEEK ONE OBSERVATION : BREAKFAST AND MORNING SNACKS							
	DAY 1	DAY 2	DAY 3	DAY 4	DAY 5	DAY 6	DAY 7
Breakfast consisted of:							
Mood after breakfast:							
List of morning snacks:							
Snacks effect on mood:							

Notes or observations regarding morning food consumption and its effect on mood:

_____

_____

_____

_____

ANALYSIS: BREAKFAST AND MORNING SNACKS

PROBLEMS AND SOLUTIONS:

• **Problem: Did breakfast consist of sugary/processed carbohydrates that caused increased energy followed by fatigue and/or irritability later in the morning?**

• **Problem: Does your child have increased energy after sugary snacks or carbohydrates followed by fatigue or irritability a couple of hours later?**

• **Problem: Does your child crave or binge on sweets and carbohydrates?**
  Avoid processed carbohydrates and sweets such as doughnuts and/or sugary breakfast cereals. Have frequent, small, high-protein snacks (cheese, nuts, seeds, etc.). Cut down on sugar and carbohydrates.

Note: It's important to determine what triggers a child's fatigue and mood problems. While sleep deprivation may cause fatigue and irritability, if mood is immediately improved by eating, sugar sensitivity may be a contributing factor. (See pp. 74–78.)

List any changes you plan to make:

_____

_____

_____

_____

WEEK ONE OBSERVATION : LUNCH AND EARLY AFTERNOON MOOD							
	DAY 1	DAY 2	DAY 3	DAY 4	DAY 5	DAY 6	DAY 7
Time of lunch:							
Mood before and after lunch:							
Lunch consisted of:							
Did your child take a nap?							
If yes, at what time?							
How long did your child sleep?							

Your child may be at school during lunchtime. If so, note his mood after school and how the after-school snacks affect it.

Note on naps and observations regarding lunch and its effect on mood:

_____

_____

_____

_____

ANALYSIS: LUNCH AND EARLY AFTERNOON MOOD

PROBLEMS AND SOLUTIONS:

• **Problem: Is your child's lunch time erratic?**
  As much as possible, eat lunch at the same time each day.

• **Problem: If your child's lunch is high in sugar content and/or processed carbohydrates, does it cause hyper behavior followed by fatigue or irritability within a couple of hours?**
  Have a nutritious lunch high in protein. Cut down on sugar and carbohydrates. (See pp. 74–78.)

• **Problem: Is your child napping too late and/or more than two hours?**
  Nap should be completed by three P.M. and shouldn't last more than two hours or bedtime is likely to be affected.

List any changes you plan to make:

_____

_____

_____

_____

WEEK ONE OBSERVATION : LATE AFTERNOON MOOD

	DAY 1	DAY 2	DAY 3	DAY 4	DAY 5	DAY 6	DAY 7
Late afternoon mood: (fatigue, irritability)							
Any physical complaints? (headache, stomachache)							
Late afternoon snacks and beverages:							
Snacks effect on mood and/or physical complaints:							
Did child unintentionally fall asleep?							
If so, what was child doing? (riding in the car, watching TV)							
What time was it?							
How long did child sleep?							

Notes or observations regarding afternoon mood:

_____

_____

_____

_____

ANALYSIS: LATE AFTERNOON MOOD

PROBLEMS AND SOLUTIONS:

• **Problem: Late in the afternoon, is your child's mood poor? Is he inattentive or fatigued?**

• **Problem: Did your child unintentionally fall asleep? (See narcolepsy, pp. 58–59.)**

• **Problem: Did your child complain of not feeling well?**
    Increase total sleep. Set an earlier bedtime and/or later wake-up time.
    Reinstate nap if age appropriate and schedule permits.

• **Problem: Was your child irritable and/or inattentive a couple of hours after lunch and did his mood and energy level improve by eating? (See pp. 74–78.)**

• **Problem: Did your child have increased energy after eating carbohydrates or sugary foods, followed by fatigue and/or irritability after a couple of hours? (See pp. 74–78)**
    Cut back on carbohydrates and provide frequent, high-protein
    snacks. Reduce or eliminate sugar consumption.

List any changes you plan to make:

_____

_____

_____

_____

WEEK ONE OBSERVATION : EVENING MOOD							
	DAY 1	DAY 2	DAY 3	DAY 4	DAY 5	DAY 6	DAY 7
Mood before dinner:							
Time of dinner:							
Evening snacks and drinks:							
Mood before bed:							

Notes or observations regarding evening mood:

_____

_____

_____

_____

ANALYSIS: EVENING MOOD

PROBLEMS AND SOLUTIONS:

• **Problem: Is your child in a poor mood before dinner?**
This is usually a sign that your child needs more sleep. Set an earlier bedtime, a later wake-up time or both. If age appropriate and schedule permits, reinstate the afternoon nap.

• **Problem: Is your dinner time inconsistent and/or late, causing bedtime to be pushed back?**
As much as possible, have dinner at the same time each night. Plan ahead for an earlier dinner so that you can have a relaxed evening and bedtime routine.

• **Problem: Did your child have snacks or drinks that contained caffeine, such as sodas or chocolate?**
Be sure your child stays away from caffeine or chocolate in the evening. Stock your house with healthy snacks. Tryptophan, an amino acid, can help children sleep. Tryptophan sources: milk, turkey, chicken, bananas, yogurt, pineapple. (See p. 87.)

• **Problem: Was your child supercharged or cranky before bed?**
Set an earlier bedtime or reinstate afternoon nap if age appropriate and schedule permits. Have quiet time before bed.

List any changes you plan to make:

_____

_____

_____

_____

WEEK ONE OBSERVATION : BEDTIME ROUTINE							
	DAY 1	DAY 2	DAY 3	DAY 4	DAY 5	DAY 6	DAY 7
Time you started bedtime preparations:							
Note bedtime routine: (bath, brushing teeth, story, prayers)							

Notes or observations regarding bedtime routine:

_____

_____

_____

_____

ANALYSIS: BEDTIME ROUTINE

PROBLEMS AND SOLUTIONS:

• **Problem: Are you rushing through the bedtime routine or starting it late?**

Allow adequate time for a relaxed bedtime routine. (See chapter 6.)

• **Problem: Is your child's bedtime routine inconsistent?**

Children do best when their bedtime routine is consistent. Try to follow the same order regarding your choice of activities. (See chapter 6.)

List any changes you plan to make:

_____

_____

_____

_____

WEEK ONE OBSERVATION : FALLING ASLEEP AT BEDTIME

	DAY 1	DAY 2	DAY 3	DAY 4	DAY 5	DAY 6	DAY 7
Was child reluctant to have you leave his room?							
Did your child express fears or worries?							
If so, of what?							
Did you assist your child to fall asleep?							
If so, how? (lying down with child, rubbing back)							
Did you leave child's room while he/she was still awake?							
Did child call out or get out of bed after you left the room?							
If yes, how many times?							
Did he/she give a reason?							
If so, what was it?							
Your response:							
Time child actually fell asleep:							

Any other notes/observations regarding bedtime:

_____

_____

_____

_____

ANALYSIS: FALLING ASLEEP AT BEDTIME

PROBLEMS AND SOLUTIONS:

• Problem: Is your child reluctant for you to leave him alone?

• Problem: Does your child need your help to fall asleep?

• Problem: Do you stay with your child until he falls asleep or does he protest when you leave the room?

• Problem: Does it take more than thirty minutes for your child to fall asleep after you leave the room?

• Problem: Did your child call out to you or get out of bed after being tucked in?

> Teach your child to fall asleep independently with the *Floppy Sleep Game* program in chapter 7.

• Is your child fearful or worried at bedtime?

> Address fears as much as possible in the daytime. For example, if your child is afraid of dogs, read stories about dogs, sing songs about dogs. Make up a visualization/story where your child faces and overcomes his fear. Regarding realistic fears, give assurances. For example, tell your child you have locks on the doors. Look under the bed to show your child there are no monsters if that is what he fears. If helpful, encourage your child to sleep with a favorite stuffed animal.

• Is your child a night owl, staying awake too late at night and feeling sleepy in the morning?

> Begin waking child earlier.

List any changes you plan to make:

_____
_____
_____
_____

Things That Go Bump in the Night

If you answer yes to any of the following, note the time they occurred and your response.

WEEK ONE OBSERVATION : NIGHTMARES							
	DAY 1	DAY 2	DAY 3	DAY 4	DAY 5	DAY 6	DAY 7
Nightmares:							
If yes, at what time?							

Your response:

_____
_____
_____
_____

WEEK ONE OBSERVATION : NIGHT TERRORS							
	DAY 1	DAY 2	DAY 3	DAY 4	DAY 5	DAY 6	DAY 7
Night terrors:							
If yes, at what time?							

Your response:

_____

_____

_____

_____

WEEK ONE OBSERVATION : SLEEPWALKING							
	DAY 1	DAY 2	DAY 3	DAY 4	DAY 5	DAY 6	DAY 7
Sleepwalking:							
If yes, at what time?							

Your response:

_____

_____

_____

WEEK ONE OBSERVATION : SLEEP TALKING							
	DAY 1	DAY 2	DAY 3	DAY 4	DAY 5	DAY 6	DAY 7
Sleep talking:							
If yes, at what time?							

Your response:

_____

_____

_____

_____

ANALYSIS: NIGHTMARES, NIGHT TERRORS, SLEEPWALKING, SLEEP TALKING

Sometimes, but not always, more sleep will decrease the likelihood of night terrors, sleepwalking, sleep talking, and nightmares.

PROBLEMS AND SOLUTIONS:

• **Problem: Did your child have a night terror (often in conjunction with sleepwalking)?**
  Don't try to awaken child during a night terror. (See pp. 50–51.)

• **Problem: Did your child sleepwalk (can be in conjunction with a night terror)?**
  Gently lead child back to bed. Set up an alarm (or string of bells) on the door so you are alerted if your child leaves his bedroom. Safety proof your child's room. (See p. 50.)

• **Problem: Did your child sleep talk?**
  Don't wake child. (See pp. 49–50.)

• **Problem: Did your child have a nightmare?**
  Comfort and console your child. Limit scary stories and television shows. Talk over worries and concerns earlier in the day. (See p. 47.)

List any changes you plan to make:

_____

_____

_____

_____

	DAY 1	DAY 2	DAY 3	DAY 4	DAY 5	DAY 6	DAY 7
WEEK ONE OBSERVATION : HEALTH ISSUES							
Teeth grinding:							
Snoring:							
Halted breath during sleep:							
Bedwetting:							
If yes, your response:							
Complaints of a funny feeling in legs?							
Signs of restless sleep? (tossing and turning, twisted covers)							
Allergies/stuffed-up nose?							
Note possible triggers:							
Asthma:							
Note possible triggers:							

Notes and observations (include any known triggers for allergies or asthma and the effect any medications seem to be having on sleep):

_____

_____

_____

_____

ANALYSIS: HEALTH ISSUES

PROBLEMS AND SOLUTIONS:

• **Problem: Does your child grind his teeth?**

Try stress-reducing exercises. (See the Lion, p. 52.) See your child's dentist if it doesn't improve. He may recommend a night guard.

• **Problem: Does your child have poor health, decreased immunity, frequent headaches and stomachaches?**

When a child is not getting adequate sleep, health suffers. Set an earlier bedtime and/or a later wake-up time. Reinstate a nap, if age appropriate and schedule permits.

• **Problem: Does your child snore?**

Snoring often accompanies colds and allergies. It is sometimes a sign of sleep apnea. Particularly, if your child snores, still seems tired after a full night's sleep, and/or has learning or behavior problems, see your pediatrician for a sleep apnea evaluation. (See sleep apnea, pp. 56–58.)

• **Problem: Does your child have halted breathing or gasping?**

See your pediatrician; it may be another sign of sleep apnea.

• **Problem: Does your child have allergies and/or a stuffed-up nose?**

Try to discover allergy triggers. Keep your child's room dusted. Cover mattresses, eliminate down pillows and animals in child's bedroom. Wash bedding in hot water. Use an air purifier. Close windows if the pollen count affects allergies. Use filters on forced-air vents. Consult with your child's pediatrician. (See pp. 61–63.)

- **Problem: Does your child have asthma?**

  See your physician. Asthma usually gets worse at night and it can be very serious, especially for young children. If your child is prescribed medication, administer it at the first sign of wheezing. Try to discover what triggers your child's asthma; it is often allergies. (See pp. 59-61.)

- **Problem: Does your child have restless sleep and/or twisted covers?**

  It may be a sign of restless legs syndrome. A warm bath, massage, and relaxation techniques may be helpful. If it doesn't improve, consult your pediatrician. (See pp. 55-56.)

- **Problem: Does your child wet the bed?**

  Be sure to limit consumption of liquids before bed and have child use the bathroom. If it continues past the age of four, see your physician to rule out physical issues. If it becomes emotionally troubling, work out a plan with your child's pediatrician. (See pp. 54-55.)

Notes regarding health issues:

_____

_____

_____

_____

REVIEW YOUR CHILD'S EMOTIONAL, BEHAVIORAL, AND PHYSICAL HEALTH

Physical Health: A compromised immune system and frequent illnesses often signal inadequate sleep. Headaches and stomachaches are also frequent repercussions of inadequate sleep.

Note your child's health problems and any changes you plan to make to try to solve them (be sure to take note of any medications taken and the effect they have on sleep):

_____

_____

_____

_____

Exercise: Did your child get adequate exercise during the day? Aerobic activities should not be too close to bedtime while gentle stretching and yoga may be soothing.

Notes:

_____

_____

_____

_____

Emotional: Note mood problems and any particular stressors that caused anxious or fearful behavior.

Notes:

_____

_____

_____

_____

Behavioral: Learning difficulties, hyper behavior, and inattentiveness often indicate that a child isn't getting a sufficient amount of sleep. (See ADHD, pp. 65–66.)

Notes:

_____

_____

_____

_____

PLAN OF ACTION

Look over the week's sleep journal. Review and list any changes you plan to instigate.

_____

_____

_____

_____

_____

_____

_____

_____

_____

_____

_____

_____

_____

_____

_____

PART THREE

GIVING YOUR CHILD A GOOD NIGHT'S SLEEP

CHAPTER SIX

Establishing a Healthy Bedtime Routine

Max was just eight and Andrew was eleven when their parents were seriously injured in an automobile accident. The boys' parents faced months of rehabilitation, leaving Max and Andrew with no one to care for them. Thankfully, their grandparents opened their hearts and home to their grandchildren. However, since they lived across the country, the boys had to leave behind everything that was familiar to them—their friends, their school, their home, and hardest of all, their parents.

It was a difficult time for all of them. Not surprising, due to their grief and the stress of the situation, both boys had insomnia, especially Max. Their insomnia made a hard situation all the more difficult for all of them. Debbie, the boys' grandmother, shared her troubles—including her growing concern over her grandsons' sleep problems, with her friend at church. As fate would have it, Debbie's friend was also a friend of mine, and she gave Debbie the *Floppy Sleep Game*.

Andrew and Max got some much needed sleep and were able to fall asleep with the *Floppy Sleep Game*. Several times after that, my friend told me how much Debbie appreciated the gift—and how much it had helped her grandsons. However, it wasn't until Debbie called me herself, to order a replacement CD, that her heartfelt gratitude made me realize what an impact it had made on their lives. I realized that relaxation techniques can help us to get through even the toughest of times. Somehow, even in the midst of their troubles, Max and Andrew were able to find the stillness in themselves and find enough inner peace to relax and fall asleep.

I don't want to end this story without an update on Max and Andrew. My friend reported that the boys have been reunited with their parents and that the entire family is doing well.

The Importance of a Bedtime Schedule

As parents, we need to take an introspective look at our own temperaments and decide if it is affecting our child's bedtime routine. Some of us are more scheduled and feel best when we follow a set routine, while others tend to "go with the flow" and live more spontaneously.

I definitely fall into the latter camp; I like to work when I feel the urge and play when the mood strikes me. I call my life the Magical Mystery Tour and enjoy last-minute decisions and plans. One of my dearest friends is just the opposite. She is super-organized, planning trips months in advance and making dinner reservations days or even weeks ahead of time. Her life mantra is "plan and proceed," and it suits her to a tee.

When her children were young, my organized friend zealously guarded her children's naptime and bedtime schedules, turning down any and all events that would interfere with their precious sleep. I privately thought that she was a bit rigid and prided myself with the misguided belief that my children would be more flexible. Dear reader, I would like you to learn from my mistakes. In regard to sleep, planning and proceeding is definitely the way to go. My friend's children were great sleepers while mine were not . . . until I learned the error of my ways, that is.

Even if your life is also a Magical Mystery Tour, the one area I'd like to convince you to establish a routine is with your child's sleep schedule. Having a set bedtime ritual is the most important component of a healthy sleep pattern for your child. Of course a consistent bedtime will be difficult for your child if his days and nights are completely unscheduled and helter-skelter.

Now please don't think that I'm suggesting that you shouldn't be spontaneous during the rest of your day. Unexpected, delightful events are part of the fun and wonder of both childhood and parenting. Even the smallest events can be exciting to children, and it's a wonderful gift to be able to see the world through their eyes. Take the opportunity to enjoy the surprises of the day as they arise. If you unexpectedly see a beautiful butterfly, follow it with your child. If you make a wrong turn while driving, see where it takes you. If your son or daughter wants to have a last-minute lemonade stand, go for it. However, if your children want to stay up past their bedtime, draw a line in the sand.

Children feel safe and are much more likely to be good sleepers when they have a consistent bedtime and a predictable bedtime routine. It helps ensure that they get enough sleep while giving their world a sense of order. The benefits of a consistent routine far outweigh any loss of free-dom or spontaneity that you may feel. And, a well-rested child is much more adaptable, willing and able to "go with the flow."

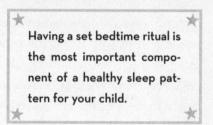

Having a set bedtime ritual is the most important component of a healthy sleep pattern for your child.

ESTABLISH A CONSISTENT BEDTIME ROUTINE

The way to set up a successful sleep schedule for your child is to create a consistent bedtime ritual—in a predictable, calming environment that serves as a bridge between the excitement of daytime and the restful quiet of nighttime. Your child should consistently go to bed at the same time every night. Even on the weekends, bedtime should not vary by more than one hour a night or a total of two hours for the entire weekend. If it does, you're setting your child up for a kind of jet lag when Monday morning rolls around. If you need to, plan activities on weekend mornings so kids have a reason to go to bed and get up at a set time.

Active play just before bed can leave children excited and can hinder their ability to fall asleep, while slow, sustained stretching and yoga is often helpful. Make sure there is a quiet period just before bed. An easing-off period is important because most children have trouble going from full throttle to sleeping peacefully. Limit television and video-game playing as well as reading an especially exciting book before bed. Tell your child five to ten minutes before their bedtime routine begins so they can finish what they're doing. A warm bath is particularly soothing for most children because it relaxes the muscles and gets their bodies ready for rest.

It doesn't matter whether you read or tell a story, sing a song, pray, or stretch, what's important is that you choose quiet activities that you and your child enjoy. As you discover the rituals that your child enjoys and finds relaxing, do them in a consistent order. For instance, you may decide to tell a story, sing a song, and then say a prayer. Of course, the stories, songs, and prayers may change, but a predictable routine will signal your child that after each of those activities, it will be time to go to sleep. When the house becomes quiet, bedtime rituals bring us together with our child for a time of intimacy and closeness. As children grow more and more independent, many parents find that their children still enjoy connecting with them, one on one, at bedtime.

Try to take care of your child's physical and emotional needs before you leave the room so there is no reason to get out of bed. Your child's pajamas or nightshirt should not restrict his movement. The room temperature should be fairly cool, around sixty-five degrees Fahrenheit (eighteen degrees Celsius). If the air is particularly dry, use a vaporizer. Make

> Tip: If older brothers or sisters are allowed to stay up later, make sure they are doing quiet activities that don't disturb their younger sibling, who will not want to miss out on any fun!

tips for a successful bedtime routine:

- Allow time for a leisurely bedtime routine.
- Have a consistent bedtime.
- Warn your children five to ten minutes before they need to get ready for bed so they can wrap up what they're doing.
- Have quiet activities before bed. (Limit television, video games, and computer time.)

sure your child has given everyone hugs and kisses. (My daughter learned early on that I could not resist when she called me back for one last kiss!) Your child may like to have a night-light on, the door slightly open, or a drink of water. Some children find it comforting to sleep with a favorite item, such as a stuffed animal or blanket. Leave your children's room while they're still awake so they learn to settle themselves. If this is a problem for your child, as it is for many children, never fear. The *Floppy Sleep Game* program in chapter 7 will systematically teach your children to relax and fall asleep on their own.

Finding Time for a Bedtime Routine

If you're a parent who works outside the home, you probably find that by the time you get off work, pick up the kids, stop at the grocery store, and then prepare and eat dinner, it's bedtime . . . and yet there are still dishes and homework to face. There may even be obligations and scheduled activities such as scout meetings or team practice to squeeze into an already jam-packed day. Some of you are probably wondering how you can possibly do all this, enjoy a leisurely, calming bedtime routine with your child, and still get him to bed at a reasonable hour. You may justify letting your child stay up too late (just this once!) in order to squeeze in some family time. Resist this urge.

You love your children very much. You probably missed them, and you may be reluctant to send them to bed shortly after you get home. But if you are allowing your child to stay up until ten or eleven (especially on school nights), it may be time to take a hard look at your life and make some changes.

In the book *The Path to Inner Peace*, Barbara Bush was quoted as having said, "At the end of your life, you will never regret not having passed one more test, not winning one more verdict or not closing one more deal. You will regret time not spent with a husband, a friend, a child or parent."

Mothers of this generation have had it drilled into their heads that they can have it all—a happy, fulfilling marriage, well-adjusted children, fulfilling hobbies, and a fast-paced, successful career. I agree—women can have it all, but perhaps we can't have it all at the same time. Try to appreciate the seasons of your life—and take delight in the period of time that is primarily devoted to raising your children. I can't imagine that you will regret it. And although you might not realize it now, take it from me: your children will be grown before you know it. If you have fallen behind on some of your goals, there will still be time to devote to them when your children are older.

When our lives are off balance, we receive little signals—a variety of problems present themselves to get our attention. If your life has become so overwhelming that it's impossible to find time to enjoy a leisurely bedtime routine with your child and have him get to bed at a reasonable hour, consider it a sign to make some changes, for your own sake as well as your child's.

QUESTIONS TO ASK YOURSELF IF BEDTIME IS CONTINUALLY PUSHED BACK

- If you and your partner work a nine-to-five job, is there a way for one of you to get off work earlier? Could one of you work from home, at least part of the time?
- Is there a way to have an earlier dinner? (Remember the Crock-Pot, freezing casseroles, and picking up food.)
- Are you able to hire help with meals and cleaning to free up some family time? (A college student is often affordable.)

- Could you do your grocery shopping and some of the cooking on the weekend, making and freezing a couple of dinners ahead of time?
- Is your child taking part in too many extracurricular activities? Are you?

Limiting Overstimulation in Your Home

Have you ever walked into someone's home and immediately felt as if you were being embraced by a feeling of warmth and peace? I remember having that feeling years ago when I walked into a friend's house— and wondered how I could emulate it in my own home. Admittedly, my friend and her husband are by nature very low key and calm, as were her children. However, for those of us who tend to be more boisterous, and have children that follow suit, it can be even more important to take steps to create a quiet and calm household, especially in the evening.

> My home . . . is my retreat and resting place from the wars. I try to keep this corner as a haven against the tempest outside, as I do another corner of my soul.
>
> Michel de Montaigne,
> French essayist (1533–1592)

- **Turn off the TV and don't have a television in your child's bedroom.**

    If you don't want to turn off the TV completely, limit television time to one or two half-hour shows that are in line with your family's values. Perhaps, you'll want to watch them together and talk about the issues that the characters face. However, don't succumb to having a television in your child's bedroom. It will take him away from the family and on average, children lose two hours of sleep a week when there is a television in their room. Also, evidence shows that childhood obesity is linked to excessive television viewing. Remember, there are only so many hours in a day and time spent watching TV is time that your child could have spent playing, stretching, reading, drawing, writing, doing home-work, listening to music . . . or interacting with you.

- **Turn on the answering machine.**

  Have you ever noticed how children are underfoot whenever you're on the phone? That's because they want to have your full attention and feel as if they are your number one priority. After dinner, you actually only have a few precious hours with your children. Make the most of it by turning on the answering ma-chine or letting your calls go to voice mail. If you feel you must take calls during the evening, don't let them interfere with your child's bedtime routine. Your child will love having your undi-vided attention during this intimate, loving time. If you'd like, you can always return the calls after your kids are tucked in.

- **Limit computer time.**

  A limited amount of computer time may be appropriate; how-ever, like the television, it takes time away from personal inter-action with you and the rest of the family. Usually younger children aren't interested in spending an excessive amount of time on the computer. Usage is on the rise, however, especially for older children, and research is showing that computer time is not replacing television time. It's a good idea to limit total "screen time," whether it's in the form of the computer or the tele-vision.

  It's also important to be selective as to which computer games you allow your kids to play because there is great variety in their content. While some may have educational value, others have no redeeming value and expose children to extreme violence— which research shows can lead to aggressive behavior.

  The Internet can be a valuable tool for older children who of-ten use it to gather information for their schoolwork. However, you must actively supervise your child when he is on the Inter-net. In addition to inappropriate, adult material, there is danger-ous material, such as hate-group sponsored sites and information on dangerous activities. There are a number of companies that sell software that is designed to block chat rooms and adult sites. However, don't rely on them completely—they aren't foolproof. Also, while adults can distinguish between sites that are designed as advertisements and those that aren't, children usually can't. Some companies are quite scandalous in their strategies to entice children into becoming their customers.

Around the age of ten or eleven, most children become very interested in instant messaging their friends. Oftentimes, children have an extensive buddy list and have a nightly chat with a fairly large group of their friends. Limit the amount of time your child can spend instant messaging, just as you would limit phone calls. While a certain amount of IM interaction may be fine, it's not an activity that kids should do all night. Also, just as we teach our children about strangers that they meet out in the world, when kids begin to use instant messaging and e-mail, they need to know that there are "bad people" who try to trick kids by pretending to be someone that they're not. Tell your children that if they ever receive an inappropriate or suspicious message that they should let you know immediately.

- **Play soothing music.**

The music that you choose to play in your house can either be stimulating or relaxing. If you play music that is angry, negative or nerve shattering, you can expect children to become irritable, fragmented, confused and sleepless. In contrast, soothing music with a slow tempo will calm the mind, lower the heartbeat and blood pressure, and slow the breathing—relieving the listener of physical tension and stress. Like relaxation techniques, soothing music can regulate stress-related hormones and boost the immune function. And, just as relaxation techniques can slow down our brain waves, taking them from the full alertness of beta waves to the slower, more meditative waves of alpha and theta waves, so can music. If things tend to be too rowdy in your house, especially at dinnertime or bedtime, play beautiful, soothing music of your choice. The entire atmosphere in your home will subtly change as your family unconsciously relaxes to the comforting sounds of music.

- **Have an early dinner.**

   When dinner is late, everything is pushed back, leaving little time for children to finish their homework and unwind before bed. You may also end up rushing through the bedtime routine— or worse yet, your children may not get to bed at a reasonable hour. If you work outside the home, an early dinner will take some planning, but it will be well worth the effort when you and your family have more time to relax and enjoy the evening.

- **Have your child complete his homework early in the evening.**

   If your child's schoolwork is done early enough, he will have time to do some stress-free activities such as playing a board game, drawing, or reading a book. It will also allow time for a leisurely bedtime routine.

Handling Homework

Limited amounts of homework in the primary grades may be beneficial; however, it should not be excessive . . . especially in the lower grades. The amount of homework assigned varies greatly from school to school and from teacher to teacher. As a rule of thumb, the National Education Association and the Parent Teacher Association recommend that children in elementary school spend approximately ten minutes on homework per grade. For instance, a first-grader would be expected to do ten minutes of homework while a fifth-grader would spend fifty minutes.

However, the time it takes to complete homework will depend on a child's ability to buckle down and concentrate, his ability to do the work, and his level of perfectionism. What one child might complete in twenty minutes could very well take another child an hour. If you feel as if your child is unduly overloaded with homework that is either too difficult or lengthy, don't try to solve the problem by doing his work. While it's difficult for parents to see their child frustrated by inappropriate homework, doing too much of your child's work is likely to lead to an overly dependent child who may be convinced that he cannot accomplish anything on his own. Most teachers are willing to individualize homework assignments if a child is truly struggling. If your child has a learning disability that is interfering with his ability to complete the homework, or is a perfectionist who spends an inordinate amount of time doing it, work closely with your child's teacher. Oftentimes, the work may be appropriate, but because your child either processes more slowly or is a perfectionist, it takes an excessive amount of time for him to complete it. If this is the case, see if your child can be assigned a shorter version of the same assignment. That way, he will still be learning the same things as the other students. If the work itself is too difficult, your child should be given a more appropriate assignment. Each child is an individual and sometimes what works for most won't work for all. One of the purposes of homework is to begin to teach responsibility and for it to serve its purpose, a child must receive appropriate homework assignments.

In the upper elementary grades, other issues may determine the amount of homework a child brings home. While some children use all their spare time at school to complete homework, others bring it home because they are not applying themselves at school. Also, teachers begin to give their students longer assignments, expecting children to budget their time and work all week toward completing it. This leads to problems for a child who procrastinates and attempts to complete a weeklong assignment in a single night. If your child has a tendency to put off his homework until the last minute, you need to be aware of his assignments. That way, you can help him to consistently chip away at a large project. Be aware that projects that require a great deal of planning and organization may be particularly difficult for a child with ADHD. Often, their problems become more noticeable in the upper grades when organization becomes more of an issue. If your child is frequently misplacing his papers and is generally unorganized, help him to set up a system to keep his papers organized.

Don't allow excessive homework to interfere with your child's sleep.

Remember, getting a good night's sleep is the most important assignment of all!

1. Have a set time and place for homework. Have your child do his homework early enough in the evening so that he will have some downtime before bed. Set up a spot for your child to complete his homework that is well lit, quiet, and away from the television.
2. Be available to help your child with his homework if he has questions, but don't do your child's work. Appropriate homework is a lesson in responsibility.

BANISH BEDTIME FEARS

Bedtime fears are very common. They often appear in the preschool years as children become more aware of things that can cause harm. Some children's fears have to do with real things and others are products of their growing imaginations. At three and four years of age, children still have some difficulty distinguishing between real and make-believe. At this age, it's very common for children to fear monsters and other scary creatures. Some "experts" advise parents to spray a bottle of pretend "monster spray" to satisfy a child that it will keep the monsters at bay. I don't think this is a good idea because you are in effect confirming your child's fear that there truly are monsters. Talk about what is real and what is make-believe. Although you might not be able to convince a preschooler that monsters don't exist, you should still begin to tell him that there is no such thing. Then, to satisfy his disbelief, follow up by showing him that there is nothing under his bed or in the closet. Eventually, children will make the distinctions themselves and the monster under the bed just won't be there anymore.

BANISHING MONSTERS, GHOSTS, AND OTHER SCARY CREATURES

- If your child thinks that there is a monster under his bed or in the closet, tell him that monsters aren't real, and then prove it by looking under the bed or in the closet together.

- Tell a story where your child is the hero, facing the monster who shrinks before his very eyes.
- Have Willy Monster become a familiar character; tell stories and sing songs about this good monster that protects children and keeps them safe from harm, all night long. By the time your child is in kindergarten, he will know that monsters aren't real. However, there is likely to be that little part of him that has a lingering doubt. I created the Willy Monster character and wrote the story, "Bedtime Fears Go Away" for children ages five and up. In the story, Willy Monster helps a child face the ever-annoying boogey monster. When the child in the story (you can individualize it by using your child's name) finally faces the boogey monster, the boogey monster ends up being the one who is frightened and runs away. Even if your child is long past the stage of being frightened by monsters, this story is beneficial because the message is clear—when you take steps toward facing your fear, you're likely to find that it was not as scary as you thought it would be.
- See "Bedtime Fears Go Away" (A Story about Willy Monster), pp. 279–285

As children move into a new stage of development, they are likely to lose their fear of imaginary creatures but may begin to worry about other types of things such as being liked, doing well in school, and so on.

Help Your Child Put Worries to Bed

While some kids have irrational nighttime fears about monsters under their beds, other children become preoccupied with worries that, though less fantastic, reflect very real and scary fears. Worrying may interfere with a child's ability to fall asleep. It's important that children feel free to confide their worries so they don't go undetected. Sometimes older children don't want to burden their parents and keep their worries to themselves. By talking over worries, you may help your child realize that they are unfounded or blown out of proportion.

In the *Floppy Sleep Game* program, we'll use visualizations as a tool to help your child fall asleep. While visualization is imagining things as you would like them, worrying is negative visualization—focusing and imagining what is not wanted. When your children are worrying about something, ask them, "What does it feel like to imagine what you don't want?" Then, have them imagine things as they want them to be and ask which thought made them feel better.

Of course, sometimes children's worries are based on realistic concerns. Reassure your children as much as possible and discuss the situation in a manner that's appropriate for their age and developmental level. If children are worried about a robbery at night, tell them that you have strong locks, a dog, and so forth. When children are worried about something in the news, such as terrorist attacks, tell them about all the safety precautions that are being taken. Be sure to limit television exposure and limit discussions about the frightening subject in front of your children, even if it's something you are worried about yourself. After giving suggestions and encouragement, tell your child that it's time to put all worries away.

Seven Ways to Put Worries to Bed

1. **Lock away worries in the worry box.** Pretend you're holding the problem or worry in your hands. Fold it like a piece of clothing. Fold it again and again until it's very small. Now pretend to put it into a box. You may wish to make the process more tangible by briefly writing down the problem on a piece of paper, continuing to fold it until it's tiny, and then placing it inside a real box. Ask your children if anything else is bothering them. If so, again have them act out folding it, or actually folding a piece of paper, putting it into the box, and attaching the lid. Now take a key and pretend to lock the box. Make a ceremony out of putting the box away. Say or sing something like:

   I put my worries away for the night.
   Out of my thoughts and out of my sight.

2. **Help worries fly away.** Have your children draw a picture or

write down what is bothering them on a piece of paper. Fold it into a paper airplane. Send the paper airplane and the worries flying as far away as possible. Your child may wish to crumple up the paper airplane afterward.

3. **Keep a journal.** Older children and teens may enjoy expressing their thoughts and listing their worries in a written journal before putting them away for the night.

4. **Keep a treasure chest of dreams.** During the day, help your child to find a box to decorate. Even better, find two boxes—one for yourself and one for your child. Each of you will be cutting out or drawing pictures to go into your box. Anything you desire can be placed into the box (the treasure chest of dreams): pictures of places you want to visit, fun activities, or things you want to do or have. Anytime, during the day or night, you and your child can drop pictures into your respective "treasure chests." If your children are old enough, they can write down things they want to be, have, or achieve. From time to time you and your child can look back through your boxes. You are likely to realize how many of your dreams have already come true. The treasure chest of dreams helps you and your child to focus on the things you want, thereby attracting and allowing them into your lives. As an added benefit, you will get to know yourselves and each other better. You can always reach into the dream box and get an idea for a story or visualization to tell your child. Remind your children that the treasure chest is filled with wonderful things to think about as they drift off to sleep.

Variation: If your child enjoys artistic activities, make a collage together and hang it on the bedroom wall. Each of you will cut out and draw pictures of places you want to go, things you want to do, achieve, or have. Best of all, you can always add to the collage as new desires arise.

5. **Tell your children stories where they face and conquer their worries and fears.** Some children like to be the "star" or main character of the stories that you tell, while others prefer to be a

step removed and hear about another character that solves a similar dilemma.

6. **Start to instill a sense of faith in a higher power.** Depending on your belief system, you may wish to suggest that your children pray or ask their inner knowledge, guardian angel, guide, universal spirit, or God to help with a problem.

7. **Instill appreciation and gratitude.** It's not possible to be upset and worried while feeling appreciative. Share good things that happened during your day and have your child do the same. The key to happiness is to notice and appreciate all the wondrous little things that make up each and every day. They don't need to be major events; it could be a hug, words of love, the sound of the birds in the morning, or a beautiful sunset. Depending on your beliefs, you may wish to encourage prayers of appreciation and thankfulness. See the following: Yoga: Gratitude Sequence One, pp. 268–270, Yoga: Gratitude Sequence Two, pp. 270–272, Quiet Blessings relaxation routine, pp. 291–293. (*This is also track 7 on the Floppy Sleep Game Book CD.*)

ESTABLISH A PERSONALIZED BEDTIME RITUAL

What separates a ritual from a mundane routine is that a ritual is done with mindfulness. The Native Americans were known for their mindfulness and consecrated everyday activities by surrounding them with ritual and prayer. Like prayer, a ritual is a habit made holy. Hopefully, you will feel that every night is a holy night as you and your child sanctify your love for each other with a nightly ritual—your child's bedtime routine. Then, as your child continues with his individual ritual, the *Floppy Sleep Game* program, he will be discovering the quiet, holy place within himself.

Your child's entire bedtime ritual consists of a personalized bedtime routine and the *Floppy Sleep Game* program, which can be thought of as an in-

> **Two basic steps:**
> 1. A shared ritual: the bedtime routine—a personalized ritual to
>   share with your child.
> 2. An individual ritual: the *Floppy Sleep Game* program—through-
>   out the program, you will be gradually giving your child less and
>   less assistance, and eventually it will become an individual rit-
>   ual that your child does completely on his own in order to relax
>   and fall asleep.

dividual ritual to relax and fall asleep. While the bedtime routine is a time for sharing, the *Floppy Sleep Game* program is a ritual that (by the end of the program) your child will do on his own to independently relax and fall asleep.

The Importance of a Personalized Bedtime Routine

As you experiment with stretches, songs, books, and storytelling, you will settle on a personalized routine that both you and your child enjoy. The predictability of the routine and the special time of closeness will bring a wonderful sense of closure to your child's day. Feeling secure in your love, your child will continue with his own individual ritual—the *Floppy Sleep Game Program*.

How to Use the *Floppy Sleep Game* Program as a Personalized Ritual

The *Floppy Sleep Game* program will become your child's personal ritual to relax and fall asleep. Each of the relaxation techniques, or steps of the program, will become part of his routine. First, he will be relaxing his body. Then, your child will begin to be mindful of his own breath. As he watches his breath flow from the outside in and from the inside out, your child will be aware of both the outside world and his quiet, inner world. His breath will provide the gateway into his inner world, carrying him to his own private sanctuary. There, he will visualize and let his imagination take flight as he falls asleep. As your child repeats his relaxing ritual night after night, he will become more and more comfortable with it. Rather than listening to a visualization from a recording or having one read to him, he will begin creating his own scenarios. Throughout the month, you will be turning more and more of the responsibility for following the steps of the program over to your child. It will become his own private ritual, which he will continue to individualize and call upon whenever he wants to turn inward, relax, and fall asleep.

The Importance of a Personalized Bedtime Ritual

Long after your child has completed the program, he will continue to use the techniques that he learned from the *Floppy Sleep Game* program. Naturally, he will modify and personalize this nightly ritual as he continually adapts it to his own changing needs and growing maturity. But one thing will not change. Your child's private sanctuary will always be available to him, even in the toughest of times. When the outside world is disturbing, harsh, or cruel, a child who knows how to quiet himself and turn inward will continue to thrive. It will open his heart and expand his consciousness as he begins to understand that there is more to life than all the "things" in the outside world. And no matter what frustrations or problems your child is facing, he will know how to leave them behind, relax, and peacefully drift off to sleep.

The gentle art of making a home involves choosing rituals that bring us together with the members of our family, sometimes one on one, and other times as a family unit. When you carefully monitor the influences from the outside world and bring a sense of calm into your home, you create a safe haven for your children. The atmosphere in your home and even the most commonplace activities and routines can have a big impact on your child, especially when you do them mindfully.

Take a few minutes to sit quietly and remember your favorite rituals from childhood. When I began to embark on this sentimental journey, memories of sultry summer nights filled my senses. Lying next to my dad on our patio and looking up at the stars, I felt both the wonder of the universe and the security of my dad's strong arms. Like spending a quiet evening looking up at the stars, many family rituals are ceremonies of the ordinary. For instance, while ordinary, family dinners are important because they bring family members together as a unit before each individual goes his separate way once again. And so it is with the bedtime ritual. It's a chance to come together with your child and share your love before you go your separate ways to sleep and dream.

Whether it's a holiday ritual or the nightly bedtime routine, rituals are memories in the making. Each memory is a pearl on a thread that connects us from generation to generation. The Christmas sugar cookies that my mom used to make are my children's favorite. And even though my father died before my children were born, his favorite songs have always been sung in our home. The string of pearls becomes an heirloom of rituals that are passed from generation to generation. Some rituals are set aside, new rituals are added, and others remain. Family rituals are a legacy of love, connecting our heartstrings.

Just as important as shared rituals are those that we do individually. Quiet moments allow us to reconnect with ourselves and our spirituality. It could involve spending time in nature, prayer, meditation, or simply consciously relaxing—as your child will be taught to do in the *Floppy Sleep Game* program.

Some of your rituals, such as rubbing a child's back or lying down with him until he falls asleep, will need to be set aside in order for your child to learn to fall asleep independently. Even if your child doesn't sleep in bed with you, many children have learned to associate falling asleep with parental assistance. If you are assisting your child to fall asleep, recognize that he has probably become accustomed to it, making it difficult for him to fall asleep without your help. Retraining your child to fall asleep independently will be a gradual process that is mapped out in the *Floppy Sleep Game* program. You will in effect be teaching your child a new ritual, a nightly routine that he can use to turn inward, relax, and fall asleep on his own.

CHAPTER SEVEN

The Four-Week *Floppy Sleep Game* Program

After Kelsey was tucked into bed, within five minutes she'd call out to her mother, complaining that she couldn't get to sleep. Wendy (Kelsey's mother) would tell her that it had only been a few minutes and she would urge Kelsey to give it some time. But five minutes seemed like an hour to Kelsey and within five or ten minutes, Kelsey would call out to her mother again—and this scenario would be repeated for up to two hours. Sometimes, Wendy and her husband, Bill, would get so frustrated that they would end up yelling at Kelsey. Sometimes Kelsey would end up crying, making the entire situation all the more difficult.

Eventually, instead of even trying to leave Kelsey's room after she tucked her in, Wendy would lightly rub her back until she fell asleep. The back rub became part of their usual routine. If Wendy got up to leave Kelsey's room before she was in a deep enough sleep, Kelsey would wake up and call her mother back to "tickle her back." Wendy became very good at discerning whether Kelsey was sleeping deeply enough for her to leave the room without Kelsey waking up and calling her back.

Even though rubbing Kelsey's back until she fell asleep made things a little easier at bedtime, it certainly didn't stop Kelsey from coming into her parent's room at least two or three times during the night. Wendy would walk her back to her bedroom and sometimes she would rub her back until she fell asleep again. The nightly sleep disruptions were taking their toll on the entire family. It was difficult for them to get up in the morning and the days often started badly. But after Wendy got the *Floppy Sleep Game* for Kelsey, it didn't take long for her to learn to relax herself to sleep. In effect, Kelsey replaced the back-rub ritual with the relaxation techniques. Once she became accustomed to falling asleep on her own, without the back rub, she would relax herself back to sleep when she briefly awakened during the night. And thankfully, Kelsey's nighttime visits to her parent's room came to an end.

Kelsey, and so many of the children I've talked about throughout the book, have the same basic problem. They don't know how to relax themselves to sleep and have grown accustomed to some sort of assistance or attention at bedtime. It is by far the most common source of sleep problems. Regardless of other issues that may have been uncovered in the sleep journal, by gradually replacing your attention at bedtime with self-soothing techniques, your child will become more capable of falling asleep independently.

You are to be congratulated for taking the time to teach your child to purposefully relax. Like everything that we teach our child, it takes some time and effort but the payoff—a self-sufficient child who takes pride in his growing independence, is well worth the effort.

During the first week of the program, you will be taking a more active role as you begin teaching your child the simple relaxation techniques that will make such a big difference in his ability to fall asleep and stay asleep. However, each week, your own responsibilities will diminish, as your child needs less and less direction and assistance. By the end of the program your child will be able to do one more thing on his own and you'll both be able to say, "Job well done!"

Every night, your child will be using the same three relaxation techniques, in the same order, to relax and fall asleep. The first step is guided relaxation: your child will be learning to purposefully relax his body. This will help him to be quiet and relaxed enough to turn inward and focus on his own breath—which is step two. In step three, he will visualize delightful images and scenes as he drifts off to sleep

---

brief overview of the
floppy sleep game program

WEEK ONE:

You will be teaching your child to consciously relax and will remain in the room as your son or daughter falls asleep, giving less direction and beginning to physically distance yourself as the week progresses.

WEEK TWO:

You will continue to physically distance yourself but will still remain in your child's room as he or she listens to track eight on the corresponding CD and follows the directions. When track eight ends, you have the choice of reading a visualization to your child or having him listen to the visualization on track nine.

WEEK THREE:

Your child will be falling asleep without you in the room; however, he will continue to use the relaxation recording as a guide.

WEEK FOUR:

Your child will be falling asleep independently and will choose for himself whether or not to listen to a relaxation recording.

WEEK ONE:
READY, SET, RELAX . . .

This week you will begin teaching your child how to relax. Remember, relaxation is a learned skill that will enable your son or daughter to fall asleep. It's important to devote a few minutes at the end of the bedtime routine to having your child practice the relaxation techniques that will be used in the program itself. Each of the first seven tracks of the *Floppy*

Sleep Game book CD is a relaxation practice session. On day one of the program, you will play track one and have your child follow the directions. Day two corresponds with track two, and so forth through track seven.

After practicing his relaxation techniques with the CD, your child is ready to begin the steps of the program. He will follow your directions

> **Tip:** Toward the end of the bedtime routine, it's very important to spend a few minutes practicing and reviewing the relaxation techniques that will be used in the *Floppy Sleep Game* program.

as you read a guided relaxation routine and focused breathing directions, followed by a visualization. This week you will be in your child's room, directing him through the steps of the program. However, it's important that you don't lie down in bed next to your child. At first, you may sit on the edge of your child's bed and guide him as he follows your directions. Little by little, as the week progresses, distance yourself by sitting in a chair and begin to give less direction.

Week One, Night One

BEDTIME ROUTINE AND RELAXATION PRACTICE

We discussed the importance of your child's bedtime routine in the last chapter but I'd like to reiterate its importance as you begin the program. Even if you have been lackadaisical about your child's bedtime routine, tonight is the night to make a fresh start. Have a set time for bed and a consistent bedtime routine. Have your child brush his teeth and put his pajamas on as you begin the bedtime routine. Bedtime activities may include: bathing, brushing teeth, discussing your child's day, reading or telling a story or visualization,

> Tell your child that bedtime is in ten minutes. Transitions can be difficult for children. The ten-minute warning will enable children to finish up whatever they're doing without feeling rushed or pressured.

singing a lullaby, stretching, and/or saying prayers. Children thrive with consistency; have your routine follow the same order each night. I have included some discussion starters that tie in with each night's visualization; it is your choice whether to use them or not.

There is some leeway as to how much time you want your bedtime routine to take. It really is a matter of personal preference. Start your routine early enough for your child to get the recommended amount of sleep for his or her age. (The National Sleep Foundation recommends that children ages three to five should have ten to thirteen hours of sleep while children ages five to twelve generally need ten to eleven hours of sleep.) I recommend allowing at least a half hour for the whole bedtime process, around fifteen minutes for your shared bedtime routine and rituals and approximately fifteen minutes for a child to soothe himself to sleep by following the program. However, during the four weeks of the *Floppy Sleep Game* program, allow a little extra time to practice and review your child's new relaxation techniques at the end of your child's bedtime routine. In addition to the importance of practicing relaxation techniques, it will help your child unwind and prepare him for the steps of the program.

> **Tip:** Meet your child's needs ahead of time: bring a glass of water for him to keep at his bedside (if there is no bed-wetting problem) and make sure the room is a comfortable temperature.

New Skills We'll Introduce in Week One

- **Tensing and relaxing muscle groups:** Children will recognize the difference between tension and relaxation. (Expect it to take one to two weeks to master the technique.)
- **Focusing on the breath:** Children will begin to calm their minds, simply by focusing on their breath.
- **Belly breathing:** Deep diaphragmatic breathing helps to still the mind and the body. With diaphragmatic breathing, the area below the navel is extended on an inhalation and retracted on an exhalation.

* **Release-only relaxation:** Just as the name implies, release-only relaxation is purposefully relaxing without first having to tense the muscles.

RELAXATION PRACTICE: TRACK ONE OF
THE *FLOPPY SLEEP GAME* BOOK CD

Track one will introduce the following week one skills: tensing and relaxing muscle groups, focusing on the breath, and visualization. Have your child stretch or move freely to the short musical introduction at the start of the track before following the subsequent directions, which will lead your child through a couple of stretches. The stretches will help children release tension as they begin unwinding and relaxing their bodies. I suggest that you and your child stretch together for several reasons: it will be fun, you'll both reap the benefits, and the easiest way for your child to learn the stretches or yoga postures is to follow your movements. Don't be overly picky about the precision of the movements. Just be sure that they are slow and sustained rather than aerobic.

Tonight, your child will practice tensing and relaxing his muscles by holding each arm and leg up tightly—before letting it loosely "flop" down on his bed. Then, your child will be directed to quietly focus on his own breath. As an aid to visualization, your child will be directed to look through the "magic window" in his own mind—where he is likely to see amazing things. Looking through the "magic window" is a theme that will be continued throughout many of the upcoming visualizations.

WHAT TO WATCH FOR Some children continue to guide their arms and legs, rather than letting them completely relax. This is more of a sustained tension, rather than true relaxation. If this is the case with your child, follow up by borrowing one of his stuffed animals and demonstrate "flopping" its limbs by lifting them up and letting them drop down limply. Remind your child to make his legs and arms as limp and floppy as the rag doll or stuffed animal that you're demonstrating with. You can also demonstrate it yourself. Relax your arms completely and let your child lightly shake them to see how floppy and relaxed they are. Have fun, but don't let this become a

> ★ Tip: If your child is continuing to guide his arms and legs, rather than letting them completely relax and "flop" down on the bed, demonstrate "flopping" and relaxing with the limbs of a rag doll or a stuffed animal. ★

wild activity or your child may have trouble calming down and falling asleep.

STEP ONE: GUIDED RELAXATION

Read the following guided relaxation exercise, the Flop Game. I call it a "sleep game" so that children will think of it as fun, yet know that its purpose is to help them fall asleep. Feel free to use it as a guide and put it into your own words, or follow it verbatim. Adapt the words to make it age appropriate. Assist your child with the movements.

> ★ Tip: To be effective, it is imperative that the relaxation routines be read in a slow, relaxed manner. Frequently pause to give your child time to slowly complete each movement and allow time to rest between each action. ★

The Flop Game is track eight on the *Floppy Sleep Game* book CD. Next week your child will be listening to it and following the directions. However, this week, rather than using the recording, read it to your child and take the time to assist him with the movements.

★ the flop game ★

(Text can be adapted for quiet time, naptime, or bedtime.
Don't forget to pause after each movement!)

Now that you're ready for bed (or ready to rest) it's time to play the Flop Game.
First, get in your bed (or find a spot where you can stretch out).
Now, lie down on your back and close your eyes.

Lift one of your legs up off your bed.

Keep it off the bed and hold your leg very straight.

Point your toes. Hold it, hold it, hold it.

Now let it flop down, as if you were a rag doll.

See how heavy your leg feels?

Now, lift up the other leg and hold it very straight.

Point your toes. Hold it, hold it, hold it.

Now let it flop.

Doesn't that feel good?

Keep your eyes closed.

Lift one of your arms up, and stretch it up high. Keep holding it up.

Stretch you fingers out as wide as you can. Keep your arm very straight.

Hold it, hold it, hold it.

Now let it flop.

Lift the other arm up and stretch it up high. Keep holding it up.

Stretch your fingers out as wide as you can. Keep your arm straight.

Hold it, hold it, hold it.

Now let it flop.

Let your whole body flop.

If you need to wiggle or move to get more comfortable, do it now.

Pull your covers up if you want to.

Let your feet fall slightly apart.

Lie very still.

You are as relaxed as a floppy rag doll.

You are safe and warm in your cozy bed.

Your body is becoming more and more relaxed.

Now, pay attention to your face.

Keep your eyes closed and lift your eyebrows.

Hold them up, hold them, hold them.

Now lower them.

Close your eyes very tightly. Keep them tightly shut.

Now, keep them closed, but relax your eyes.

Wrinkle your nose, and relax your nose.

Open your mouth widely. Hold it open. Hold it, hold it.

Now, close your mouth and relax your mouth.

> ★   ★
>
> Tip: Don't rush with any of the breathing exercises; like the guided relax-
> ation, they should be done in a slow and relaxed manner. To help pace
> yourself and resist the tendency to read too quickly, take slow breaths
> yourself as you direct your child to breathe in and out.
>
> ★   ★

STEP TWO: FOCUSING ON THE BREATH

At this point your child should be comfortably still and ready to enjoy the experience of breathing.

★ the flop game, continued ★
(Read slowly!)

Now, take a big deep breath and slowly, slowly, let all of the air out.

Now, take another breath in and let the air out very slowly.

We're going to take three more deep breaths together.

Breathe in *(pause)*, breathe out *(pause)*, breathe in *(pause)*, breathe out *(pause)*,
   breathe in *(pause)*, breathe out *(pause)*,

Now, feel how relaxed and heavy your body feels.

To help you to become even more relaxed, we're going to count from one to five
   and when I say five, you're going to be on your way to dreamland.

One, you're very, very, relaxed.

Two, you are feeling heavier and heavier.

Three, your legs are very relaxed.

Four, your arms are very relaxed.

Five, you're off to dreamland.

Let your imagination take you wherever you want to go.

Enjoy your dream flight.

> Tip: At this point, you can direct your child to quietly listen to his own breath as you prepare to read the visualization.

STEP THREE: VISUALIZATION

Unless your child is sound asleep (in which case you can quietly leave his bedroom), proceed with the following visualization. Of course you are welcome to modify this for yourself and your child. During relaxation practice, track one of the CD introduced your child to the concept of having a "magic window." In tonight's visualization your child will be looking through his magic window and "picturing" what his own special place would be like. After seeing it through his "magic window," your child will arrive in his own special place—a place where he feels comfortable, safe, and relaxed. By creating his own special place

> Tip: Read visualizations in a slow, relaxed voice. Pause to let the scene "set" in the listener's mind. The tone of voice is also very important; lowering your voice a few tones can create a more hypnotic, restful mood.

your child will be making a retreat for relaxation, a place he can visit at will, through visualization.

Read the entire visualization, or if you'd like a shorter version, you can start on p. 152, at the designated spot.

Themes for the visualization:

- You can go anywhere in your dreams.
- You can see anything in your imagination, just look through your own magic window.
- You can create your own special place where you are relaxed, happy, and safe.

Magic Window

Come look into your magic window
There's a world of wonder waiting for you
Open your window wide and step inside
The wonder of, the window of your mind
Excerpt from Magic Window (song) by Patti Teel

The Dream Maker lives far away in Dream Land. Every night, she tosses falling stars into the sky for children to wish upon. Tonight, the magic from a falling star showers down upon you. You feel warm and tingly all over and instantly, you're in Dream Land. The air is filled with sparkles in Dream Land. Each sparkle is a child's dream, darting through the sky like flying glitter. They shoot up and down, this way and that. In Dream Land, there are huge sparkling crystals in every color of the rainbow jutting out of the ground. Some of them are as tall as large trees. Several pajama-clad children have climbed to the top of a rainbow crystal. As they begin to slide down, the crystal reflects the moonlight and bathes them in soft colors. It looks like so much fun that you begin climbing to the top of the rainbow crystal so you can slide down too. As you climb, you are covered in red sparkling light, followed by orange, yellow, green, blue, and violet. Finally, you get to the top and are encircled with silver, sparkling light. You stand up tall and feel your whole body tingle as you raise your hands up toward the stars. Now sit down and enjoy sliding back down as you are bathed in colorful light: first violet, then blue, green, yellow, orange, and red. As you reach the bottom, all the crystals in Dream Land begin to vibrate and hum.

Follow the other children as they begin lining up just outside of a shimmering crystal dome. You see a ring of silver lights spelling out THE DREAM ACADEMY over the doorway. The kindly Dream Maker walks out in a swirling cloud of dream dust. She smiles directly at you and says, "I'm so glad you're here, *(child's name)*. Please join us." Before entering the Dream Academy the Dream Maker tells you and the other children to leave your worries outside with Willow. Several children hang their problems or worries on the strong, sturdy branches of a large weeping willow tree. If you have any problems or worries, give them to the willow tree now. *(Pause.)* Together, the wise tree and Mother Earth will take care of it. *(Pause.)* You follow the Dream Maker into the Dream Academy, noticing that she has golden hair and is wearing a dark blue gown that is covered with stars.

The Dream Academy is not like any school you have ever seen before. Although there are walls, there is no ceiling. Many types of musical instruments hang from the walls and from time to time they magically begin to play by themselves. In front of the classroom there is a treasure chest of dreams, where the Dream Maker keeps the falling stars. A turtle named Nomi is lying next to the chest. Small, low, sparkling clouds float near the floor. You notice that each of the other children is choosing a cloud to lie down on. You choose one too, and lie back to look up at the beautiful night sky. The cloud is softer than anything you've ever felt before and the stars in the sky are so close and bright that you feel as if you can reach up and touch them. Some of the Dream Maker's instruments begin to play a lovely song as you relax and enjoy looking up at the sky.

When the song ends, the Dream Maker says, "Tonight, you are going to learn that you can go anywhere in your dreams." Behind the Dream Maker is a very large window shade. The Dream Maker explains that her magic window is behind the shade. She opens the shade and as you look out the window you see a forest path that is lined with trees, green plants, and pink, yellow, and violet wildflowers. Birds are flying among the flowers and trees, and two bushy-tailed squirrels play a friendly game of tag, jumping from one treetop to another. *(Pause.)* A small yellow bird flies in through the open window. It flies around the classroom and then settles next to you on your cloud. He is so small that he sinks down into the soft cloud and only his little beak peeks out. He whistles happily and the frogs from the forest join in the yellow bird's cheerful song. Take a deep breath. *(Pause.)* Smell the fresh soil and the sweet wildflowers. As the Dream Maker begins to close the shade the little yellow bird quickly darts back out the magic window. The Dream Maker opens the window shade again. Now, the forest is gone and when you look through the window, you see Dream Land's large, colorful crystals.

(Continue, or if you'd like a shorter visualization, you may begin here. If starting here, set the scene by telling your child that he is lying on a comfortable cloud.) It's time for you to find your own magic window. You may find it by keeping your eyes closed and looking just above the top of your nose, between your eyes. Your window may have a shade drawn over it, but you can open it. When you look through your magic window, you will see a special place that is just for you. Before you open your window shade, imagine your special place, a beautiful place where you will be relaxed, happy, and safe. Decide whether your special place will be inside or at a beautiful spot outdoors. Remember, it can be anywhere you want it to be: in a castle, in a garden, in the woods, by the ocean, or even in Dream Land. It's totally up to you. When you're ready, open your window shade, look out your window, and see your special place. Your window is getting larger and larger. Your cloud begins to take you out through your magic window and into your special place. Step off your cloud and walk around. See the colors and smell the air. *(Pause.)* You can come here whenever you'd like. You may want to be by yourself now or you may decide to meet someone. It could be your pet, your special angel, friend, mom, dad, or even the Dream Maker. It's up to you. *(Pause.)* Your special place is a wonderful place to relax and dream.

There is a path that leads to a comfortable spot. Walk down the path and when you find the perfect place, lie down and relax. Enjoy how wonderful it feels. What do you see above you? *(Pause.)* What do you hear? *(Pause.)* Remember everything about your special place: how it looks, feels, and smells. You can come here whenever you'd like. Take a deep breath in and out. *(Pause.)* Take three more deep breaths and with each breath, find yourself getting sleepier and even more relaxed. *(Pause.)* Breathing in you are relaxed, breathing out you are relaxed. *(Pause.)* Breathing in you are happy, breathing out you are happy. *(Pause.)* Breathing in you are safe, breathing out you are safe. Back in Dream Land, the Dream Maker takes a star out of the treasure chest of dreams and tosses it into the sky. Its magic sprinkles down upon you, filling your special place with warmth and making all your dreams come true. *(Pause.)* You sleep soundly and dream peacefully all night long.

Many children will be asleep by now. However, during week one, if your child protests when you get up to leave the room, you may remain in his bedroom but be sure to sit quietly without giving him any attention. Do not engage in conversation. If your child talks to you, tell him that you will only stay in the room if he is quiet. You may find that you enjoy having a few minutes of quiet time to visualize or meditate.

Week One, Night Two

BEDTIME ROUTINE AND RELAXATION PRACTICE

In addition to your usual bedtime activities, you may wish to ask your child about the special place he created in last night's visualization. Your child may want to describe it to you in detail or may prefer not to elaborate. Tonight's visualization reminds children that everything they want to do or achieve begins by thinking about it. Encourage your child to tell you about things he or she may want to do, have, or accomplish.

RELAXATION PRACTICE: TRACK TWO ON THE *FLOPPY SLEEP GAME* BOOK CD

Track two will review and practice the following week one skills: tensing and relaxing muscle groups, focusing on the breath, and visualization. Tonight, on track two of the CD, your child will practice stretching and relaxing his neck and shoulder muscles by pretending to be a marionette. I recommend that you do the neck and shoulder stretches right along with your child. You will probably find it very relaxing. Like adults, children are prone to carry a lot of tension in their neck and shoulders. Then your child will practice tensing and relaxing his muscle groups by continuing to be a marionette. He will be holding his arms and legs up stiffly—until the puppet master releases the pretend strings that are attached to his head, arms, and legs. This causes your child to relax and loosely drop each limb down onto his bed. (The directions to The Marionette are also written out on pp. 262-265.)

WHAT TO WATCH FOR Be sure that your child's neck and shoulder movements are slow and relaxed. Also, watch to be sure that your child is truly relaxing his arms and legs, loosely dropping them onto the bed, rather than controlling the movement. And sometimes, when children start focusing on their breath, they try to alter it or control it in some way. If your child appears to be trying to control his breath, remind him that he doesn't need to try to breathe in any certain way. Tell him to just let his breath breathe for him.

> ★ Tip: Tonight's relaxation exercise (track two) begins to repeatedly use the word "relax." From now on, continue regularly using the word "relax" so your child learns to associate the feeling with the word. ★

STEPS ONE AND TWO: GUIDED RELAXATION AND FOCUSING ON THE BREATH

Repeat the Flop Game and the continued breathing portion from day one, pp. 146–149, so that your child continues to become more comfortable with it.

STEP THREE: VISUALIZATION

Feel free to read the previous visualization again, read the following one, or if you're comfortable doing so, make up your own. As always, don't hesitate to adapt the visualization to make it more interesting and appropriate for your child.

Read the following visualization in its entirety, or if you'd like a shorter version, you can start on p. 156, at the designated spot.

Themes for the visualization:

- You can do anything.
- Your thoughts and dreams are powerful and important.
- Everything that happens starts with a thought or a dream.

When You Believe

You can do anything, when you believe
Truly you hold the key, when you believe
Unlock your hearts, there are treasures within
Then journey bravely, let your dreams begin
Excerpt from *Kids World* (CD) by Patti Teel

Once you've been to Dream Land, its magic will always be with you. It is in the twinkle of your eyes, and the sparkle of your smile. You can visit Dream Land whenever you'd like. Look through your own magic window and you'll see Dream Land; the sparkling sky, the beautiful crystals, the Dream Maker Academy, and the magical, kindly Dream Maker. Walk closer to your magic window as it gets larger and larger. Step through your window and into Dream Land. Follow a path that leads toward the colorful crystals. Tonight, there is time to play and explore before your dream class begins. Looking toward the top of a tall green crystal, you recognize the small, comfortable silver cloud from your dream class. Imagine yourself sailing on it. The cloud seems to have heard your thought and it slowly, little by little, changes into the shape of a sailboat and begins to drift toward you. It stops next to you, inviting you to go for a ride. You climb aboard the cloud and sigh with pleasure because it feels so soft and comfortable. Sink down into the cloud's softness, knowing that you are perfectly safe. The cloud begins to slowly rise up into the sky, floating high above Dream Land. Looking straight down you see the large, shimmering crystals. Farther away, you see snowcapped mountains and when you look in the other direction, you see the ocean. Every single thing has a silver glow around it and sparkles like the snow when the sun shines upon it. It is very relaxing to float on your sailboat cloud and look down on all the wonders of Dream Land. You hope to see a rainbow and a unicorn in this magical land and instantly, a boy and a girl fly past you, riding on white unicorns that are being chased by a double rainbow. You all laugh with delight and wave at each other. As you float comfortably on your cloud, the sun shines down on you, warming your body and your face. Up ahead, you can see that there is a spot where the day meets the night. For a brief second you are halfway in the daylight and halfway in the night before floating into the starry, starry night sky. Looking up, you admire the bright golden moon and hope to see a moonbeam. Immediately, a moonbeam appears. You thank the cloud for the tour of Dream Land, and step onto the moonbeam, riding it like a surfboard down, down, down to the ground.

(Continue, or if you'd like a shorter visualization, you may begin here.)

The crystal prisms begin to hum, signaling that it's time for dream class to begin. You and the other children line up outside the entrance of the Dream Academy. The Dream Maker walks out of the door and greets everyone. You are happy to see the Dream Maker and you can tell that she is pleased to see you. "Welcome, *(child's name)*, I'm so glad to see you once again." Before entering the Dream Academy, put any worries or problems on Willow's strong branches so that he and Mother Earth can take care of them. *(Pause.)* You follow the Dream Maker into the classroom and discover that your little silver cloud is already back in class waiting for you. Lie back on the "comfy" cloud and look up at the beautiful night sky. The Dream Maker says, "I enjoyed watching you through my magic window. In Dream Land, whatever you think about happens instantly. Thoughts work the same way on Earth but they may take a little longer." Think of something that you want to do. *(Pause. Individualize the following sentence according to your child's interests.)* You may want to be good at a sport, play a musical instrument well, make a new friend, or go somewhere special. In your imagination, see it happening. *(Pause.)* Enjoy the good feeling it brings.

Now, it's time to rest. You may wish to return to your own comfortable bed or you can rest in your own special place. *(Pause.)* Go there now. Every part of your body is comfortable and relaxed. You are ready to sleep and dream. Breathing in you are happy, breathing out you are happy. *(Pause.)* Breathing in you are safe, breathing out you are safe. Breathing in . . . breathing out . . . breathing in . . . breathing out. As you drift off to sleep the Dream Maker reaches into the treasure chest of dreams and chooses a star. She tosses it into the sky and its magic sprinkles down upon you, filling you with warmth and making all your dreams come true. You sleep soundly and dream peacefully all night long.

Week One, Night Three

BEDTIME ROUTINE AND RELAXATION PRACTICE

In addition to your normal bedtime activities, you may wish to follow up on the previous night's visualization by asking your child what he dreamed of doing. If you'd like, share a dream or goal of your own. Show your child that you are interested, but respect his preference in regard to sharing his dreams and visualizations. In tonight's visualization children will be discovering that in Dream Land, they can fly. Ask you child if he has ever wanted to fly or dreamt of flying.

RELAXATION PRACTICE: TRACK THREE OF
THE *FLOPPY SLEEP GAME* BOOK CD

Track three will review and practice the following week one skills: tensing and relaxing muscle groups and focusing on the breath. Then belly breathing will be introduced.

Have your child stretch or dance to the short introduction at the beginning of track two. Then, stretch with your child as he follows the directions on the recording. Your child will practice tensing and relaxing his muscle groups by curling himself up tightly in a little cocoon, squeezing tightly, and then relaxing. He will also hold his legs up straight, pointing and flexing his toes, before relaxing his legs and his entire body.

Tonight, "belly breathing" (diaphragmatic breathing) is introduced. Deep, diaphragmatic breathing helps children to relax their muscles, focus attention, and quiet their minds. It's important for children to practice and learn diaphragmatic breathing while they are awake and alert. Soon, your child will be using diaphragmatic breathing to relax and induce sleep. If your child tries the new guided relaxation routine Let Go, he will be directed to watch his belly rise and fall as he breathes in and out.

WHAT TO WATCH FOR The belly should be extended on an inhalation and retracted on an exhalation. Watch to see if your child is breathing slowly and smoothly. If your child seems to be having difficulty with belly breathing, take a few minutes to practice it when track three ends.

★ belly breathing ★
(A variation of diaphragmatic breathing)

Lay on your back.

Put one hand on your belly.

Take a deep breath in.

Does your belly rise?

Take slow deep breaths and let your belly rise and fall.

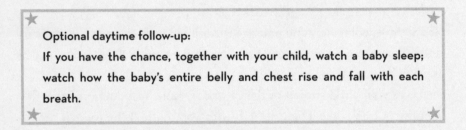

Optional daytime follow-up:

If you have the chance, together with your child, watch a baby sleep; watch how the baby's entire belly and chest rise and fall with each breath.

STEP ONE: GUIDED RELAXATION

The following guided relaxation usually works best for children ages eight or nine and up. If your child is younger, you may wish to stick with the Flop Game on pp. 146–149. Before beginning the following guided relaxation routine, be sure to review the following body parts: palms, shoulders, hips, knees, shoulder blades, elbows, chin, neck, forehead, eyelids, cheeks, jaw, and chin. As you read the directions, help your child with any movements that he doesn't understand.

★ let go ★

(Adapted from *Yoga Therapeutics* by Dr. Gloria Kaye)

DIRECTIONS:

Lie down on your back. Spread you legs apart so they are comfortable.

Have your arms loosely at your sides, *palms up . . . shoulders loose and free,*

Hips loose and free . . .

Now with your mouth closed, take a deep breath in, hold your breath. *(Pause.)*

And breathe out very slowly. Breathe in . . . hold . . . and breathe out all the air.
   Feel yourself relaxing.

And now, point your toes away from your face . . . hold it, hold it . . . Now let
   them go, let them go. Point your toes toward your face . . . hold it, hold it, now
   let go. Good.

And now, tighten your bottom really tight, pull it in . . . tighter . . . and let go,
   let go.

And now pull your belly way in, way in, all the way, all the way . . . Good, now
   let go.

And now *open your chest by trying to have your shoulder blades touch each other
   in the back,* but they won't really touch each other. Just stick your chest way
   out . . . way, way out. All the way, come on . . . Good, and relax.

And now, keeping your arms straight, make a fist; do not bend your elbows, and
   lifting your whole arm, raise your whole arm. And as you do this I want you to
   make such a tight fist that you actually begin to shake. Really tight. Tight, tight,
   tighter . . . and now just let go, just drop your arms. Good. Very good.

And now, keeping your head on the floor just *press your chin into your neck.*
   (Pause.) Good, relax.

Now focus your attention on your face. Wrinkle your forehead. Relax. And now lift your eyebrows, way up, way up. *(Pause.)* And relax. And now close your eyes very tightly, very tightly, tighter, tighter . . . good, and relax. Good. And now wrinkle your nose, wrinkle your nose . . . relax your nose. Now open your mouth very widely, very widely, wide, wide, wide. *Move your mouth to the right and to the left and back to the middle* . . . and now relax your mouth.

Feel your whole body relaxing. Just let your body go.

Now once again, I want you to breathe in through your nose with your mouth closed, breathe in deeply and fully, hold your breath, hold, and as you breathe out, breathe out any problems or worries, just let them go. *(Pause.)* And again, breathe in deeply, hold your breath, hold . . . and breathe out any problems or worries. And breathe in . . . hold . . . and breathe out. Allow yourself to relax fully and completely.

And now let your hands float up to your face . . . just float slowly up to your face. Let them move by themselves as they wander up to your face, just let them float up . . . floating up to your face . . . very slowly . . . let your hands float to your face . . . and now, place your fingertips on your forehead and just begin to gently have your fingertips walk across your forehead, so slowly, and now *let your fingertips touch the sides of your forehead, your eyelids, your cheeks and jaw and chin* . . . and ears . . . now *place your hands on the back of your neck and gently press.* And now slowly allow your hands to float down to your sides, just floating . . . let them move slowly by themselves. Relax. Allow yourself to feel as if you're floating. *(Pause for at least five seconds.)*

STEP TWO: FOCUSING ON THE BREATH

★ let go (breathing portion) ★
(Read slowly!)

Feel every part of your body, lightly floating.

Try to feel every part of your body at the same time.

Now pay attention to your breath.

The quiet breath.

Soft breaths in and long, soft breaths out.

Breathing in, I feel my whole body.

Breathing out, I feel my whole body.

Breathe in, one, two, Hold, one, two, Breathe out, one, two, three, four.

Breathe in, one, two, Hold, one, two, Breathe out, one, two, three, four.

Feel your body lightly floating, and feel your breath.

Body and breath. *(Pause.)*

Now feel the breath in your belly.

The rising and falling of the breath in your belly.

Breathing in, I feel my belly rise.

Breathing out, I feel my belly fall.

Rising as you breathe in and falling as your breathe out,

Rising as your breathe in, falling as you breathe out.

Watch your breath. *(Pause.)*

Now bring your attention up into your chest and feel the breath in your chest.

Breathing in, I feel my chest rise.

Breathing out, I feel my chest fall.

Rising as you breathe in and falling as you breathe out,

Rising as your breathe in, falling as you breathe out. *(Pause.)*

And now, from the belly, breathe in and draw the breath up to the throat

and breathe out, from the throat down to the belly.

Breathing in, I feel my breath float from my belly to my throat.

Breathing out, I feel my breath float from my throat to my belly.

Again, breathe in from the belly and bring the breath up to the throat;
breathe out from the throat down to the belly.

And now, don't try to do anything at all
Just let go.
Breathing in, I let my thoughts go.
Breathing out, I let my thoughts go.

Letting go, letting go.
Letting go, letting go.

Step Three: Visualization

Read the following visualization in its entirety, or if you'd like a shorter version, you can start at the designated spot on p. 163.

Themes for the visualization:

* Creativity, imagination.
* Anything is possible.
* A feeling of freedom.

You Can Fly

It's a beautiful world,
See the moon and stars in the sky,
It's a beautiful world,
Oh, how I love to fly!

Excerpt from *The Christmas Dream* (CD) by Patti Teel

Close your eyes and look through your magic window. You'll see that something very special is happening in Dream Land tonight. There are hundreds of butterflies and birds flying through its sparkling skies. Step through your magic window and into Dream Land.

The Dream Maker has used her magic to provide trees and flowers for her flying guests. They make the air smell fresh and sweet. Hummingbirds flit from one brightly colored flower to another, small birds flap their wings for short flights from tree to tree, and large hawks flap their wings and then soar through the air with outstretched wings. Several dreaming children are flying on colorful kites and others are riding in hot-air balloons.

The crystals begin to hum and several of the birds and butterflies join you and the other children as you line up outside the Dream Academy. You feel something tickling your shoulder and when you turn your head, you notice that there is a beautiful butterfly sitting on your shoulder. When you look more closely, you are surprised to see that it is really a tiny little person with butterfly wings. He is wearing a hat made from an upside-down white flower. The petals hang down on his forehead and the stem is sticking straight up. The little guy says, "Come on, let's go." He flutters his orange-and-black wings and begins flying toward the Dream Academy. Tonight, instead of walking, the Dream Maker floats out of the crystal dome doorway and welcomes you, "Good evening, *(child's name)*, it's so nice to see you tonight." The Dream Maker also says hello to the birds and the butterfly people; she says they are dreamoids.

Walk over to your favorite cloud, lie back, and make yourself comfortable. The little dreamoid that was sitting on your shoulder earlier joins you on your cloud. He lies back next to you, crosses his legs and smiles contentedly. He tells you that his name is Ozzie.

(Continue, or if you'd like a shorter visualization, you may begin here. If starting here, direct your child to close his eyes and lie on a floating cloud in Dream Land)

The Dream Maker begins the dream lesson. She says, "Tonight, you are going to fly. Although you cannot fly on Earth without a plane, in Dream Land, you can fly whenever you'd like. Ozzie, would you demonstrate?" Ozzie has butterfly wings and is an excellent flyer. The cheery little dreamoid smoothly circles the classroom and then lands back on your cloud. Then, the Dream Maker begins to slowly float higher and higher above the ground, stopping high above the classroom. "Now it's your turn," she tells you and the other dreamers in the class. The butterflies, birds, and dreamoids begin to fly, but you and the other children do not. The Dream Maker sees that you are having trouble believing that you can fly. She tells you that although wings come in handy for birds; dreamers don't need them to fly. Nomi the turtle has been sitting by the treasure chest of dreams, quietly watching and listening. He begins to rise up into the air. When you see that a turtle can fly you know that you can too. The Dream Maker says, "Remember, the dream dust is all around you. Breathe in its magic." Ozzie flutters above you encouragingly. "Come on, you can do it," he whispers. You feel your body becoming lighter and lighter with less weight on the ground under your feet. Then, without even trying, you begin to float higher and higher. The Dream Maker's musical instruments begin to play a flying song as you, the other children, the birds, Nomi, and the Dream Maker begin to fly in a circle around the large classroom. "Follow me," says the Dream Maker as she flies up and out of the classroom, into the moonlit night. You and the other children follow the Dream Maker as she flies around the large crystal rocks. You break away from the others and fly on your own for a while. The soft evening breeze feels wonderful on your face and you have never felt so free. You keep your arms spread and pretend you are an eagle, soaring through the sky. Then, you follow the Dream Maker as she flies to the top of a large green crystal. There is a large flat space on the top of the crystal; you and the other children sit in a circle around the Dream Maker. Everyone is quiet as they breathe in the beauty of the night. The full moon glows, the sparkling stars glimmer, and the colorful crystals gleam in the moonlight. (Pause.) The Dream Maker breaks the silence with a soft voice. "You have done very well. Continue to practice flying in your dreams. Tonight, I know that you truly understand the magic of dreams. From now on, each of you are on the Dream Team. Right now, it's time for you to return to your cozy bed, or rest in your own special place."

You are totally relaxed, ready to sleep and dream. As you fall asleep, listen to your breath. Breathing in, I am relaxed. Breathing out, I am relaxed. Breathing in, I am relaxed. Breathing out, I am relaxed. Breathing in, breathing out. Back in Dream Land, the Dream Maker reaches into the treasure chest of dreams, chooses a star, and tosses it into the sky. Its magic showers down upon you and you know that you will have wonderful dreams all night long.

Week One, Night Four

BEDTIME ROUTINE AND RELAXATION PRACTICE

In addition to your usual routine, ask your children if they enjoyed flying in last night's visualization. In tonight's visualization, children become part of the Dream Team; they help plants and animals by sprinkling dream dust on them. Ask your child where he would sprinkle the magical dream dust, if he had the chance.

RELAXATION PRACTICE: TRACK FOUR OF THE *FLOPPY SLEEP GAME* BOOK CD

Track four will review and practice the following week one skills: tensing and relaxing muscle groups, focusing on the breath, visualization, and belly breathing.

Encourage your child to move and stretch to the music at the beginning of track four and then stretch together, following the directions. Your child will practice tensing and relaxing by pretending his hands are blinking stars, making fists and then opening his hands with outstretched fingers—and finally individually dropping them down onto the bed as if they are falling stars. Then your child will practice belly breathing by imagining that there is a balloon in his belly; it fills up and deflates with each breath. He will visualize the color and size of his balloon as he continues breathing on his own at the end of the track.

WHAT TO WATCH FOR If your child is guiding his arm, rather than letting it drop down onto the bed, take a few minutes to have him practice holding up each arm, completely relaxing it, and letting it drop loosely. When he is pretending that there is a balloon in his belly, watch to be sure that his belly rises with each inhalation and falls on each exhalation. Also, watch to see if the breathing is slow and rhythmical. If your child needs additional practice, take a minute to review belly breathing. Counting may help him to keep his breath slow and rhythmical and it may also help him to remain focused on his breath.

★ balloon breathing ★

Have your child place a hand on his belly and imagine that there is a balloon
inside.

Breathing in, two, three, four—your balloon fills up. Breathing out, two, three,
four—letting out the air.

Breathing in, two, three, four—your balloon fills up. Breathing out, two, three,
four—letting out the air.

STEPS ONE AND TWO: GUIDED RELAXATION AND FOCUSING ON THE BREATH

Repeat the Flop Game and the corresponding breathing portion from day
one, pp. 146–149, or choose Let Go on pp. 159–160 and the breathing
portion that follows it on pp. 161–162.

STEP THREE: VISUALIZATION

Read the following visualization in its entirety, or if you'd like a shorter
version, you can start at the designated spot on p. 168.

Themes for the visualization:

* Reverence for all living things on Earth.
* Imagination and fantasy.
* Friendship, cooperation, and working together toward a common
  goal.
* Giving: the more you give, the more you get.

The Dream Team

You can join the dream team,

All you have to do is dream a dream.

Feel the rhythm of the world's heartbeat.

Have you ever heard a song so sweet?

Excerpt from "The Dream Team" (Song) by Patti Teel

Now that you are nice and relaxed, it's time to visit Dream Land. Look through your magic window and you'll see that Ozzie is already there waiting for you, just outside the Dream Academy. As you step through your magic window and greet your little friend, he flutters his little butterfly wings with happiness. Dream Land's crystals are already humming and dream class is about to start. Leave any worries or troubles you may have in Willow's sturdy branches before entering the Dream Academy. The wise willow tree and Mother Earth will take care of any worries you may have. The Dream Maker greets you and the other dreamers. As you walk through the doorway, she puts a hand on your shoulder and says, "Welcome, *(child's name)*."

When you enter your classroom the Dream Maker says, "Now that you understand the magic of dreams, you will be able to help others. That's what being on the Dream Team is all about." The Dream Maker hands each of you a pouch filled with dream dust. "Tonight, you will be sprinkling dream dust where it is needed. When your pouches become full, return to your homes and go to bed. A dreamoid will be going with each of you. Because the dreamoids have spent a lot of time among the plants on Earth, they will be able to show you the places that need our help. *(Child's name)*, Ozzie will be going with you." You look down at the little dreamoid that has been by your side since you arrived and you both smile at each other. The Dream Maker takes her finger and draws a circle in the air, around both you and Ozzie. You and Ozzie find yourselves inside a beautiful rainbow bubble. Each of the other children is paired up with a dreamoid and the Dream Maker continues to encircle each of them inside a bubble. She blows softly; you and the other children and dreamoids begin floating down toward the Earth, each bubble drifting off in a different direction. When you are only a few feet above the ground, your bubble dissolves. You fly behind Ozzie and follow him toward a meadow that is filled with snow-white moonflowers; they are the same kind of flower that he wears as his hat. Ozzie tells you that moonflowers only bloom at night but none of these moonflowers are blossoming; their stems are drooping down toward the ground and their petals are closed.

(Continue, or if you'd like a shorter visualization, you may begin here. If starting at this point and your child is not familiar with the character Ozzie, explain that he is a tiny little person with butterfly wings [a dreamoid])

You and Ozzie begin flying back and forth over the meadow, sprinkling the fields of flowers with dream dust. When the dream dust showers down upon the flowers, they spring back to life, the stems become straight and tall, the white flowers blossom, and the grass becomes healthy. Ozzie gives you a high five with his tiny hand and you both smile happily. You follow Ozzie and fly over a quiet stream, sprinkling dream dust on the still water. When the sparkling dream dust touches the water, the quiet stream suddenly becomes lively. It begins to flow and babble happily. Several of the fish leap out of the water as if to say thanks and then they dive back down under the water. The frogs begin to sing and the turtles swim happily. When the nearby animals and plants drink the stream's water they immediately become healthier and stronger. Little Ozzie is getting tired so you let him rest in your pocket. You continue flying over the stream, following it toward the ocean. When you reach the ocean, Ozzie gets out of your pocket and you both begin flying over the ocean, sprinkling dream dust on the dark blue sea. Down below the water, the plants on the ocean floor begin to sway back and forth while schools of fish start swimming happily. The dolphins jump up and flip their tails at you to show their appreciation and a whale blows water out of his spout. The warm water from his spout sprays you and Ozzie and you both laugh joyously. Your pouch of dream dust is overflowing and you realize that the more dream dust you give away, the more you have in your pouch. Remember, the Dream Maker told you to return home when it was full.

You and Ozzie are both getting sleepy. You fly back to your own bed and get under your warm, cozy covers. The Dream Maker is watching you and Ozzie through her magic window. She uses her magic to put a bubble around Ozzie; he waves as he begins floating back to Dream Land. You know you'll be seeing your little friend again soon. You can invite him back anytime you'd like and you can always visit him in Dream Land. You are happy as you think of how you and Ozzie helped the moonflowers and the plants and animals that live in the rivers and oceans. Keep the happy feeling with you as you fall asleep. Feel the warmth in your heart. Breathing in, you feel happy, breathing out, you feel happy. Breathing in, two, three, four. Breathing out, two, three, four. Breathing in, two, three, four. Breathing out, two, three, four. Back in Dream Land, the Dream Maker reaches into the treasure chest of dreams and chooses a star. She tosses it into the sky and as its magic showers down upon you, all your dreams for the world come true.

Week One, Night Five

BEDTIME ROUTINE AND RELAXATION PRACTICE

Last night's visualization, as well as tonight's, emphasizes the beauty of plants and animals. You may wish to discuss simple things that we can do to make the Earth a healthier place for them.

RELAXATION PRACTICE: TRACK FIVE OF THE *FLOPPY SLEEP GAME* BOOK CD

Track five will review and practice the following week one skills: tensing and relaxing muscle groups, focusing on the breath, belly breathing, and visualization.

Encourage your child to freely stretch to the music at the beginning of track five. Then together with your child, follow the directions to the yoga postures and stretch with him. Tonight, your child will be tensing every part of his body at the same time, holding the tension for several seconds before relaxing. Then, he will practice belly breathing and watch as his own belly rises and falls with each breath.

WHAT TO WATCH FOR Watch to see if your child is able to relax his entire body, after tensing all of his muscle groups simultaneously. With continued practice, he will be able to relax his whole body in a matter of seconds.

STEPS ONE AND TWO: GUIDED RELAXATION AND FOCUSING ON THE BREATH

Repeat the Flop Game on pp. 146–148, or Let Go on pp. 159–160, along with the breathing portions that follow them.

STEP THREE: VISUALIZATION

Themes for the visualization:

- Imagination.
- Appreciation.
- Reverence for all living things.

The Sound of Dreams

(This visualization is also track 9 on the Floppy Sleep Game Book CD)

The sunlit sea and sand, form Mother Earth's grandstand,
a spinning wonderland for all its living things.
Excerpt from *Kids World* (CD) by Patti Teel

The animals and plants that were sprinkled with dream dust are happy and healthy and they want you to visit them. You happily accept the invitation. The Dream Maker tosses a falling star into the sky. As it streaks down through the sky, its dream dust showers down upon you and you find yourself in a meadow, lying on a soft blanket. The meadow has thick green grass and is filled with sleeping flowers. Breathe in the fresh scent of the grass and the flowers. The meadow is a gentle place and you know you are safe. The moon is shining very brightly and thousands of stars are dancing in the sky. One of the stars is winking and twinkling especially for you. You can feel the light from your special star shining down upon you. Like a hug from your mom, its light fills you with warmth, from the tips of your toes to the top of your head. Enjoy how this feels. *(Pause.)* The meadow is very quiet and peaceful but when you listen closely, you hear the sound of running water. A mother and baby deer walk across the meadow and down a path toward the sound of the water. You quietly pick up your blanket and follow them down toward the sound of a stream. Some friendly frogs are talking to each other and they say hello to you too. When the path ends you find a beautiful running stream. You sit on a rock at the edge of the stream. Listen . . . the frogs and the running water are singing a song. A very large but gentle turtle swims over to the edge of the water and invites you to ride down the stream on his back. You place your cozy blanket on the turtle's back and climb aboard. Off you go, floating gently down the stream. He carefully floats on top of the water so that you won't get wet. If you want to, you can put your hands in the cool clean water. The water is so clear that you can see the rocks on the bottom and the rainbow fish that are swimming by. Two of the fish are playing and take turns leaping out of the water. When the moon shines on them they glisten. Deer, raccoons, and rabbits have come to the edge of the stream and they nod a friendly good-night to you as you drift by. It's bedtime for the baby animals and they are curling up in their grassy beds on the edge of the stream. You are feeling very sleepy too but you can't resist one last look at the beautiful round moon. It follows you as you float down the stream. You tell the moon good-night and close your eyes. You enjoy the soothing sound of the stream and the wonderful feeling of floating. You hear the sound of the ocean and know that this is where the turtle is taking you. You hear the sound of the tide going in and out. *(Pause.)* In and out. *(Pause.)* In and out. *(Pause.)* In and out *(Pause.)* You feel as if you are a wave on the sea. You find yourself breathing to the rhythm of the ocean's tide, in and out. *(Pause.)* In and out. *(Pause.)* In and out. *(Pause.)* You're drifting toward dreamland. Enjoy your dreams! *(Whisper).* Good night.

Week One, Night Six

Bedtime Routine and Relaxation Practice
In tonight's visualization, children will be visiting the moon. Ask your child if he thinks it would be fun to visit the moon. Point out that we share the moon with children from all around the world.

RELAXATION PRACTICE: TRACK SIX OF THE
FLOPPY SLEEP GAME BOOK CD

Track six will review and practice the following week one skills: tensing and relaxing muscle groups, focusing on the breath, belly breathing, and visualization. Track six will introduce release-only-relaxation.

Have your child stretch freely or dance to the opening music at the beginning of track six before following the directions to the stretches that follow. Your child will be tensing and relaxing many muscle groups simultaneously by curling himself up into a tiny ball—holding himself in that position before stretching out and relaxing. Then, he will focus on his breath by breathing to the sound of the ocean's tide. Tonight, your child will be introduced to the concept of release-only relaxation, which is relaxing without first tensing the muscle groups. Your child is directed to breathe in and say, "I am," and as he breathes out say, "relaxing."

WHAT TO WATCH FOR Watch to see if your child is able to relax after tensing many muscle groups by curling himself up into a tight little ball. This is more difficult than simply tensing and relaxing one muscle group at a time. Also, some children will have a difficult time relaxing without first tensing their muscle groups. This is not a great concern; however, it's a useful skill to have because it can enable a child to relax very quickly. If your child is not ready to relax without first tensing, don't worry about it. Periodically, you can reintroduce it until your child can simply relax his muscle groups without first tensing them.

STEP ONE: GUIDED RELAXATION

If your child is able to relax without first tensing the muscle groups, you may wish to try the following release-only relaxation routine, Heavy and Relaxed. Some children will be ready for this step and others will not. It's not a problem if your child needs to tense his muscles before he can relax them. If this is the case, repeat the Flop Game on pp. 146–148 or Let Go on pp. 159–162. Remember, children like repetition and it will help them to become more comfortable and secure with the movements if you repeat a routine that is effective and that they find enjoyable.

> ★ Tip: Sometimes, even younger children can do well with the relax-only technique; however, if your child is in the three-to-eight-year-old age range, be sure to review, skip, or reword the body parts that he may be unfamiliar with, such as the palm, sole, nostril, buttock, groin, and collarbone.

★ heavy and relaxed ★

This relaxation routine is less whimsical than the others; however, some children may appreciate a straightforward approach.

DIRECTIONS:

Lie down on your back. Wiggle or move your body to make it comfortable. Now be still and close your eyes. Allow your feet to fall slightly apart and turn your palms upward.

Feel your right hand. It is heavy and relaxed. Relax your thumb, first finger, second finger, third finger, fourth finger, the palm, and the back of your hand. Take a deep breath in and as you breathe out, relax your whole right hand.
(*With younger children add,* Good night, hand.)

Feel your right arm. It is heavy and relaxed. Relax your wrist, lower arm, elbow, upper arm, and shoulder. Take a deep breath in and as your breathe out, relax your whole right arm.
(*With younger children add,* Good night, arm.)

Feel your left hand. It is heavy and relaxed. Relax your thumb, first finger, second finger, third finger, fourth finger, the palm, and the back of your hand. Take a deep breath in and as your breathe out, relax your whole left hand.
(*With younger children add,* Good night, hand.)

Feel your left arm. It is heavy and relaxed. Relax your wrist, lower arm, elbow, upper arm, and shoulder. Take a deep breath in and as your breathe out, relax
your whole left arm.
(*With younger children add,* Good night, arm.)

Feel your right foot. It is heavy and relaxed. Relax the big toe, second toe, third
toe, fourth toe, fifth toe, bottom of your foot, top of the foot, and heel. Take a
deep breath in and as you breathe out, relax your whole right foot.
(*With younger children add,* Good night, foot.)

Feel your right leg. It is heavy and relaxed. Relax your ankle, calf, shin, knee,
thigh, and hip. Take a deep breath in and as you breathe out, relax your whole
right leg.
(*With younger children add,* Good night, leg.)

Feel your left foot. It is heavy and relaxed. Relax your big toe, second toe, third
toe, forth toe, fifth toe, bottom of your foot, top of the foot, and heel. Take a
deep breath in and as you breathe out, relax your whole left foot.
(*With younger children add,* Good night, foot.)

Feel your left leg. It is heavy and relaxed. Relax your ankle, calf, shin, knee, thigh,
and hip. Take a deep breath in and as you breathe out, relax your whole left leg.
(*With younger children add,* Good night, leg.)

Take another breath in and as you breathe out, relax your right buttock and your
left buttock. Feel your lower back. It is heavy and relaxed. Take a deep breath
in and as your breathe out, relax your whole lower back.
(*With younger children add,* Good night back.)

Feel your shoulders. They are heavy and relaxed. Take a deep breath in and as
you breathe out, relax your shoulders.
(*With younger children add,* Good night, shoulders.)

Feel your neck. It is heavy and relaxed. Take a deep breath in and as you breathe out, relax your neck.

(*With younger children add,* Good night, neck.)

Feel your head. It is heavy and relaxed. Relax the back of your head, the top of your head, your forehead, right eyebrow, left eyebrow, right eye, left eye, right ear, left ear, right cheek, left cheek, right nostril, left nostril, upper lip, lower lip, and chin. Take a deep breath in and as you breathe out, relax your whole head.

(*With younger children add,* Good night, head.)

Feel the front of your body. It is heavy and relaxed. Relax your throat, right collarbone, left collarbone, right side of chest, left side of chest, the belly, the right groin, left groin. Breathe in and as your breathe out, relax the front of your whole body.

(*With younger children add,* Good night, body.)

Feel your arms and legs. Your arms and legs are heavy and relaxed. Relax your whole right leg, your whole left leg, your whole right arm, your whole left arm. Breathe in and as you breathe out, relax your arms and legs completely.

(*With younger children add,* Good night, arms and legs.)

Step Two: Focusing on Your Breath

Feel your whole body. Your whole body is heavy and relaxed. Breathe in and as you breathe out, relax your whole body, your whole body, your whole body.

Pay attention to your breathing. Feel your breath as it flows in and out, in and out. Softly breathing in and slowly, softly breathing out. Softly breathing in and slowly, softly breathing out.

STEP THREE: VISUALIZATION
Themes for the visualization:

- Imagination.
- Gratitude.
- Reverence for all living things.

Moonstones

Thanks for the moon when day is done,
shining round the world on everyone
Thank you for your guiding light,
shining down on the world tonight
excerpt from the *Christmas Dream* (CD) by Patti Teel

The Dream Academy is closed tonight because the Dream Maker has gone on a vacation to visit her good friend, the moon. Still, she is thinking of you and has crafted a dream for you to enjoy. From the moon, she tosses a falling star into the sky. As it streaks down through the sky, its magic showers down upon you and you find yourself at the edge of a tree-lined path. You hear the sound of waves and know that the ocean is nearby. You follow the moonlit path toward the sound of the waves. It takes you to the top of a tall cliff. You look down over the railing and see the beautiful ocean below, shimmering and sparkling in the moonlight. You see that there are steps leading down to the beach. Step by step, you begin to make your way down toward the beach. Coming to the first landing, you pause and breathe in the fresh ocean air. You feel very small as you gaze out at the ocean. It looks as though it goes on forever. As you continue walking down the stairs, you notice that there are small silver circles scattered along the beach. You step onto the sandy beach and walk over to one of the glowing circles. Picking it up, you see that it is a beautiful silver stone. Your hand tingles as you hold it. You look at the glowing stone in your hand and then up at the glowing moon. "That's right," you hear the Dream Maker's voice say. "It's a moonstone." The

Dream Maker has let you know that she is thinking of you. You walk along the beach picking up the beautiful silver stones. The moon seems to be watching and it shows its approval by glowing even brighter. You're getting sleepy so you lie down in the sand and rest, carefully placing the moonstones beside you. Close your eyes and enjoy the sound of the ocean's song. Although you're not watching the waves, you listen to each one as it rolls in. Just as one wave finishes its ride to shore, the next wave begins its roll. Over and over . . . rolling in, rolling and rolling and rolling in. It's like a beautiful song that never ends. It gets louder and softer, stronger and then more gentle. You find yourself breathing to the sound of the waves as they wash in and out, in and out, in and out. While you rest, the Dream Maker and the moon are planning a surprise for you. The moonstones that you collected begin to make a staircase up into the sky. All the other moonstones from near and far become part of the staircase, until it reaches all the way up to the moon. You know that the staircase is a special invitation from the Dream Maker and the moon herself. You begin to walk up the stairs toward the glowing moon. Along the way, you stop and look down at the beach below. As you walk farther up the steps, you can see more and more of the land and ocean below. When you've almost reached the moon you can look down and see the entire Earth. You are awestruck and amazed by its beauty. When you get to the moon, the Dream Maker is waiting for you. She takes your hand as you step onto the moon. The moon is excited that you've come to pay her a visit and glows even brighter. The Dream Maker walks with you and enjoys watching you explore the giant rocks and craters. When you take a step or jump, you float a long way before coming down. Enjoy floating slowly from rock to rock and crater to crater. You are moving slower and slower as you become sleepier and sleepier.

It's time to go back to your own cozy bed. You look down at the moonstone staircase but feel too tired to climb all the way down. The Dream Maker picks up a moonstone and gives it some of her magic. She puts it in your hand and has you close your eyes while you think of being in your comfortable bed. A warm tingly feeling starts in your hand and spreads throughout your entire body. Before you know it, you're under your own warm covers. You take one last look out your window, thank the moon, and then fall asleep. In your mind, you still hear the music of the waves lulling you to sleep. Breathe to the rhythm of the waves as they roll in and out, in and out, in and out.

Week One, Night Seven

Bedtime Routine and Relaxation Practice

Tonight's visualization focuses on thankfulness and gratitude; it also encourages children to look into their own hearts. Take turns looking back over your day, sharing the things that warmed your heart or made you laugh.

Relaxation Practice: Track Seven of the *Floppy Sleep Game* Book CD

Track seven will review and practice the following week one skills: tensing and relaxing muscle groups, focusing on the breath, belly breathing, and visualization.

Track seven is a whimsical relaxation routine that is written in rhyme. Your child will be stretching and then thanking each part of his body, starting with his toes. It is a good review of relaxation skills that were introduced in week one because it is a combination of stretches, tensing and relaxing muscle groups, guided relaxation, imagery, focusing on the breath, and even diaphragmatic breathing. If you would like to read this to your child in the weeks to come, it's also written out in the appendix on pp. 291–293.

WHAT TO WATCH FOR There are a lot of instructions directing your child to stretch and tense and relax muscle groups in a variety of ways. The first time your child does track seven, be sure he understands the directions and assist him with the movements. Be a keen observer and watch to see if your child uses belly breathing, even when he is not specifically directed to do so.

STEPS ONE AND TWO: GUIDED RELAXATION
AND FOCUSING ON THE BREATH

If your child is doing well with release-only relaxation, repeat Heavy and Relaxed on pp. 173–175 along with the corresponding breathing portion. If your child prefers or does better with a progressive relaxation routine (one where he is directed to tense and then release muscle groups), repeat the Flop Game on pp. 146–148 or Let Go on pp. 159–160.

STEP THREE: VISUALIZATION

Read the entire visualization, or if you'd like a shorter version, you can start on p. 181, at the designated spot.

Themes for the visualization:

- Quietly finding the answer within your own heart.
- Gratitude.
- Love.

The Hidden Treasure

(Adapted from the Inside-Out Blessing Game *CD)*

A voice whispers, "Come inside"
That's where all the answers hide
We played a game of hide-and-seek
It was my heart, I heard it speak
Inside out, outside in,
Send love out and bring it in

The Dream Maker is calling. She has a wonderful dream adventure planned for you tonight. Close your eyes, be very still, and find your magic window. *(Pause.)* Look through the window and you will see your dream class. The Dream Maker is taking stars out of the treasure chest of dreams and polishing them one by one. She is sitting cross-legged while floating in the air, surrounded by swirls of magical dream dust. She sees you through her own magic window and invites you to come to class. Step through your magic window and into the classroom. Lie back on your favorite cloud and look up at the moon and stars. The other dreaming children magically appear on the other clouds. When each cloud has a child, your dream class is ready to begin.

The Dream Maker is holding Nomi the turtle. She says, "Tonight, each of you is going to explore on your own, looking for things that you are thankful for. Along the way, I want you to search for your hidden treasure. The answers are inside." Nomi pops his head out of his shell and says, "I'll see you in your dreams." Then he tucks his little head back in his shell.

The Dream Maker has everyone close their eyes. She reaches into her pouch and sprinkles a little dream dust on the other children. As soon as they're touched by the dream dust they are off on their own dream adventure. When she sprinkles dream dust on you, it magically takes you to the top of a mountain. The view is beautiful. You look down and see trees and houses. Even further away, it's hard to tell where the blue sky ends and the ocean begins.

The Dream Maker left a huge heart on the ground, made out of rocks and twigs. It must be a clue to help you find your hidden treasure. You walk around the heart and then sit quietly on the ground inside the heart. You pick up a colorful rock that is in the center of the heart and are very surprised when it speaks to you. It says, "I told you we'd meet in our dreams." You look closely and discover that it's your friend, Nomi the turtle. You are happy that Nomi has come to be with you in your dream. You ask Nomi if he is the hidden treasure. "No," replies Nomi, "but I'll help you look for it." Carefully, you set Nomi down and the two of you walk down the mountain path. You take slow steps so that Nomi can keep up. You don't mind. You're in no hurry. You come to a beautiful tree that has a branch hanging over the path. You lay your ear against the beautiful tree and stretch your arms around its thick trunk. You can almost feel the tree breathing. You feel as if you are a part of the tree and you are thankful. You send love to the tree and rub its solid rough trunk with your hand. The tree carries the love down through its roots, and all the plants drink it in. The growing plants send the love to all the animals and people and the love comes back to you even stronger and your heart is even warmer. You walk farther down the path; it crosses a very small trickling stream. "I am always thankful for water," says Nomi. He happily crawls into the water and begins to swim down the stream. "Meet you later, alligator," he calls out merrily. "After a while, crocodile," you answer. *(Continue, or if you'd like a shorter visualization, you may begin here. If starting at this point, tell your child that he is on a beautiful mountain path, looking for his own hidden treasure.)*

You step on rocks to cross over the small stream and continue walking down the path, keeping an eye out for the hidden treasure. Up ahead you see a light and it keeps getting brighter and brighter. The path ends and you step out of the woods and into the bright sunshine. You're on a beautiful sandy beach next to the beautiful blue sea. Feel the warm sand between your toes as you walk on the beach. You see a beautiful shell and bend down to pick it up. Holding it up to your ear you hear the sound of the ocean's waves. *(Pause.)* You feel like you are a part of the sea and you are thankful. You send your love out to the sea and the sea sends it through the water, to all the streams and rivers, to the dolphins, the fish, and all the sea creatures. As the waves wash over the rocks and shells, the rocks and the shells feel the love and the love comes back to you and it is even stronger and your heart is even warmer. You gently and lovingly lay the seashell back down and look toward the clear, clean blue water. You laugh out loud as warm water splashes on your legs. A wave splashes your face and you get a taste of the warm, salty water. You look down and see that Nomi the turtle has joined you again. He swims next to you and then happily dives under a wave, thankful for the warm, salty water. You get out of the water and find a smooth sandy spot to lie down. A warm wind blows on your face. It feels like a gentle breath. You feel as if you are a part of the wind and you are thankful. You join the wind and blow white fluffy clouds across the sky. Breathe in, and softly blow the clouds. Breathe in, and softly blow the clouds. Breathe in, and softly blow. You and the wind send love to the sky and the breeze of the wind's breath carries it to all the clouds, the birds, and the sun. The sun sends the love back to you and the love is even stronger and your heart is even warmer. You feel the love from the sun as it warms your face, your arms, and your legs. The golden sun sinks slowly, slowly, ever so slowly. The sky is putting on a colorful show. Just before the sun disappears the sky turns violet and pink, then yellow and orange. As the sun sets it asks the moon and stars to shine on you and watch over you as you sleep and dream. You look up at the moon and laugh to yourself. Nomi the turtle is lying upside down and inside out on the moon. He is sound asleep. You are getting sleepy too. You are so comfortable that you begin to fall asleep. You hear a beautiful, soft voice calling you. "Come inside, come inside." You listen. Is it Nomi? No, but the voice sounds familiar, like someone you know. You listen even more closely. "Come inside." You know what it is. It's your hidden treasure. You found the hidden treasure inside your own heart. From far away, the Dream Maker smiles happily and sends her love. It circles the universe spreading love faster than any spaceship. You know that you are part of the love and you are thankful. Breathing in, you are thankful. Breathing out, you are thankful. Breathing in. (Pause.) Breathing out, breathing in. (Pause.) Breathing out.

This has been a very important week. Your child has been introduced to the relaxation techniques that will be used throughout the program. Here are some questions to help you discern which skills your child is acquiring nicely as well as those that may require extra attention:

- **Is my child beginning to associate the word "relax" with the corresponding feeling?**

    Most young children don't have an understanding of the word "relax." Begin to use the word "relax" more and more by pointing out how relaxed your child's arms and legs are after they are "flopped" down on the bed.
- **Is my child able to tense a muscle group and then release the tension suddenly?**

    You want your child to be able to release the tension in a muscle group suddenly, causing it to become relaxed and limp. Watch for a tendency to guide a muscle group, instead of letting it relax completely. Remember, this is more of a sustained tension, rather than true relaxation. Work on this by having your child practice "flopping" his own arms and legs on a soft surface such as a bed. Also, practice with tracks one and two of the *Floppy Sleep Game* book CD.

• **Can my child quiet himself and focus on his own breathing?**

Most children enjoy listening to their own breath. But to do so, they must get very quiet. If it's hard for your child to get still, try asking him to be quiet enough to hear his own heartbeat—and then have him listen to his breathing. Also, quietly listen to your own breath as your child does the same. Practice with the *Floppy Sleep Game* book CD. Each track contains focused breathing instructions that are paired with the sounds of the ocean's tide or music. The cadence of these soothing sounds may help your child enjoy the rhythm of his own breath.

• **Is visualization becoming easier for my child?**

If visualization is difficult for your child, try to include more storytelling in your bedtime routine. Storytelling requires your child to use his imagination because the illustrations are provided by his own imagination. Also, take turns telling a part of a story. You may start the story and turn it over to your child at an exciting point so that he can use his own imagination to determine what will happen next.

Recognize the progress that your child is making and be sure to point it out to him. Each child is a unique individual who will learn and become comfortable with the relaxation techniques at his own pace. Consistency will be your key to success. Various research shows that it takes from three to four weeks to develop a habit and that's exactly what your child is doing. If possible, take a few minutes to have your child practice his new relaxation techniques during the day. Just pop in the CD and spend a few quiet moments relaxing together. If you do it in the morning, it can change the tone of the entire day as well as reinforce your child's new relaxation skills.

This week your child was introduced to three very important relaxation techniques. As your child continues with the *Floppy Sleep Game* program, those skills will become more and more ingrained. We want them to almost feel like second nature. At that point, your child will be able to effortlessly use these techniques whenever he wants to relax or fall asleep.

WEEK TWO: TRANSITIONING TO A RECORDING

This week, rather than reading the guided relaxation exercise and focused breathing instructions, your son or daughter will be listening to them on track eight, the Flop Game. Then, you have your choice of having your child listen to the visualization on track nine or reading a visualization.

During and After the Bedtime Routine

You've heard it before but it bears repeating:

- Tell your child that bedtime is in ten minutes.
- Follow your routine. Have a set bedtime and a consistent bedtime routine.
- Be sure to set aside a few minutes devoted to having your child practice his relaxation techniques (relaxation practice)

Toward the end of the bedtime routine, it is still very important to take a few minutes to review and practice the relaxation techniques that were introduced in week one. We will not be introducing any new techniques this week because it's very important that your child continues to become more comfortable and adept at the techniques that were already introduced. Oftentimes, your child will not specifically be practicing visualization during relaxation practice. However, imagery is interspersed throughout the relaxation practice. For example, children will curl up in a tiny ball while pretending to be a tiny seed, and they will imagine that they are squeezing the juice out of a lemon. If your child finds it difficult to visualize, try to include storytelling in your bedtime routine. Books are wonderful; however, with storytelling your child has to "see" the pictures in his own mind, rather than relying on illustrations.

Remember, just because relaxation is important, it doesn't mean it can't be fun. Relaxation exercises can be a delightful form of play that your children will enjoy during their bedtime routine. You can continue to practice with tracks one through seven or you will find some activities listed. Use your imagination; you'll probably come up with your own fun ways to practice.

Acknowledge the progress your child is making toward sleeping independently. Help him to recognize and feel excited about his own improvement. Although you are still in the room this week, you are beginning to take a less active role, giving your child less attention as he relaxes and falls asleep. As your child listens to the Flop Game on track eight, sit on a chair, placing it farther and farther from him as the week progresses. When the Flop Game ends, either let the visualization on track nine continue to run or softly read the visualization from the program. Afterward, get up to leave your child's bedroom. If your child protests, stay in his room, sitting in a chair that's away from his bed. Don't engage in conversation. Continue to use tracks eight and nine each evening, or play track eight and read the night's visualization. Of course you always have the option of making up your own visualization. You child will be getting very comfortable with the Flop Game, and unlike adults, children don't seem to tire of hearing the same thing over and over. (I've had parents buy a new tape from me after an old one finally wears out. They admit that while they are a bit tired of hearing my voice, their children are not.)

Week Two, Night One

BEDTIME ROUTINE AND RELAXATION PRACTICE

Contine with your usual bedtime routine and be sure to allow time for your child to practice his relaxation techniques. You may wish to start with a couple of stretches to help your child to relax. See Stretching with Yoga (pp. 262–276) Be sure that when your child is tensing and relaxing his musle groups that you have him hold the tension for at least five seconds before releasing it. Tonight's visualization is about planting seeds. Your child will also be pretending to be a seed during relaxation practice. You can teach children to respect the Earth through learning about growing things. If you'd like, take a minute to talk about seeds. You could mention that they are found in many of the foods you eat, and that they come in all shapes and sizes.

> ★ Tip: When tensing and relaxing muscle groups, be sure that your child holds the tension for at least five seconds before releasing it. ★

Relaxation Practice

Choose from tracks one through seven or practice with the activities below. Note: This week, you are reinforcing the skills that have already been introduced. At this point, tracks one through seven do not need to correspond with a particular day of the program. On day one you may choose to listen to track four, and so forth.

Practice tensing and relaxing muscle groups:

Directions:
Clench your fists. Hold it while you count to five . . . and relax your fists.
Suck in your tummy and hold it for the count of five . . . and relax.
Shrug your shoulders. Hold them up and count to five . . . and relax your shoulders.
Wrinkle your forehead, and keep it wrinkled while you count to five . . . and relax your face.

★ a growing seed ★

Directions:
Curl your knees up to your head.
Close you whole body as tight as a flower bud. (Hold.)
Now very slowly, unfold like a flower and relax. (Repeat.)

Practice focusing on the breath:

★ feeling the air as you breathe ★

DIRECTIONS:

Feel the air as your breathe in and out through your nose.

Breathe in, feel the cool air.

Breathe out, feel how it's warmer.

Breathe in, feel the cool air.

Breathe out the warm air.

Breathe in, two, three, four.

Breathe out, two, three, four.

Breathe in, two, three, four.

Breathe out, two, three, four.

Once again, feel the air as you breathe in and out through your nose. (Repeat.)

STEPS ONE AND TWO: GUIDED RELAXATION AND FOCUSING ON THE BREATH

Have your child listen to and follow the directions of the Flop Game on track eight.

STEP THREE: VISUALIZATION

Continue having your child listen to track nine on the CD, or read the following visualization.

Themes for the visualization:

- Take steps to make your dreams come true.
- Be patient.
- Plant seeds and watch what grows.
- Respect and reverence for Mother Earth.

Planting Seeds

I plant my seeds in the early spring

Water each morning and start to sing

Little seeds of mine

Time to rise and shine

And greet the morning sun

Excerpt from "Grow Garden Grow" (song) by Patti Teel

It's time to go to Dream Land. The Dream Maker wants to plant seeds in celebration of the springtime. In fact, she wants you to help her plant a forest of dreams. When Willow hears her plan, his leaves begin to sway back and forth. The Dream Maker understands what Willow is saying. She answers, "You're right, Willow. It would be the perfect place for a forest of dreams." A secret door on Willow's tree trunk opens up and the Dream Maker ducks inside. She beckons you and the other children to follow her. As you step into Willow's trunk you see that you are at the top of a long slide and that far away—at the bottom of the slide—there is a glowing light. The Dream Maker is already sliding down and you and the other dreamers follow her. You continue to slide down toward the light below. You keep sliding down—farther and farther and farther down. Finally, you reach the bottom and step outside. You see that the light was coming from a gigantic tree that is covered with thousands of twinkling lights. The entire tree is aglow. You walk over to take a closer look at the amazing tree. What you thought were lights are really glowing seeds. The Dream Maker tells you that this is the mother of all trees and that her nickname is Memaw. Memaw's seeds are magical. The Dream Maker asks Memaw if she would share her seeds in order to plant a forest of dreams; Memaw answers by showering seeds onto the ground. You and the other dreaming children gather them. There is plenty of space to plant the seeds. Except for Memaw, there are no other plants, trees, or animals. There are just miles and miles and miles of rich brown dirt. With the help of the Dream Maker and the other children, you plant the seeds.

Then the Dream Maker gives you a blanket and you find your own private space to lie down. Now that the magic seeds have been planted, it's time to imagine the forest of dreams. Your eyes are closed and you are very, very relaxed. Your body sinks down into the Earth. You imagine all of the beautiful plants, trees, and flowers that will fill the forest of dreams. Of course, there could also be fairies, dreamoids, and unicorns. It's up to you. You planted the seeds and now your dreams will make them grow. What sorts of animals do you see in the forest of dreams? Is there a special, secret spot for you to play? Sleep and dream now. Tomorrow night you can come back and check on your seeds.

Week Two, Night Two

BEDTIME ROUTINE AND RELAXATION PRACTICE

Continue to have a predictable bedtime routine and take time to have your child practice his relaxation skills. In tonight's visualization, the seeds that were planted (in last night's visualization) will become a forest of dreams. You may wish to discuss that "in real life," it takes time for seeds to grow. Perhaps, you'll want to make plans to plant some seeds with your child.

RELAXATION PRACTICE

Choose from tracks one through seven or practice with the activities below.

Practice tensing and relaxing muscle groups:

★ a growing seed ★

DIRECTIONS:

Curl your knees up to your head.

Close you whole body as tight as a flower bud. (Hold.)

Now very slowly, unfold like a flower and relax. (Repeat.)

★ an elephant steps on your stomach ★

DIRECTIONS:

An elephant isn't watching where he is going and you don't have time to get out of the way. Lie down and make your stomach and other muscles very tight because an elephant is about to step on you. You did it! Now, relax. (Repeat.)

Focusing on the breath: it's calming for children to simply be quiet and focus on their breath. Have your child spend a couple of quiet minutes watching his own breathing.

Practice release-only relaxation: sigh breathing is an especially effective way to practice release-only relaxation and to help your child relax quickly.

★ sigh breathing ★

DIRECTIONS:

Breathe in through your nose.

Hold it, hold it. (Pause.)

Now sigh and relax, letting out all of your air.

(Repeat several times.)

Children often enjoy exaggerating the sound of the sigh.

★ belly breathing ★

DIRECTIONS:

Lie on your back and place your hand on your belly.

Breathe in through your nose and feel your belly rise.

Breathe out through your nose and feel your belly fall.

Breathing in, breathing out, breathing in, breathing out. (Repeat for several rounds.)

STEPS ONE AND TWO: GUIDED RELAXATION
AND FOCUSING ON THE BREATH

Have your child follow the directions on track eight, the Flop Game.

STEP THREE: VISUALIZATION

Have your child continue with track nine, or read the following visualization.

Themes for the visualization:

* Imagination.
* Dreams really do come true.

The Forest of Dreams

My seeds have sprouted, I think I know
How my parents feel as they watch me grow
Little seeds of mine, time to rise and shine
And greet the morning sun
Excerpt from "Grow Garden Grow" (song) by Patti Teel

You are ready to go to Dream Land. Tonight when you arrive, the Dream Maker has already gone down to check on the seeds that you planted the night before. You and the other dreamers gather around Willow's wide trunk. You see a bluebird in an open cage, hanging down from one of Willow's branches.

You wait for Willow's secret door to open. But first, if you have any problems or worries, hang them on his branches. He'll work on them while you dream. *(Pause.)* Willow opens his secret door for you and you step inside his trunk. Then, you begin sliding down the long slide, toward the light below. When you get to the bottom and step out of Willow's trunk, you cannot believe your eyes. Overnight, the seeds have grown into a forest. Memaw (the mother tree), is glowing with pride because her seeds have grown so beautifully. You see pine trees, oak trees, willow trees, and every kind of wildflower imaginable. Take a minute to just look at how beautiful they are. *(Pause.)* Breathe in the wonderful scent of the trees and flowers.

It's so quiet in the forest of dreams that you can hear your own breath. *(Pause.)* You can even hear your own heartbeat. *(Pause.)* You realize that the reason it's so quiet is that there are no birds or animals. You miss them. The Dream Maker throws some dream dust into the air and says, "Close your eyes and think of them, and they will appear." You close your eyes and invite all kinds of animals to make their home in the forest of dreams. The breeze carries the sparkling dream dust to creatures near and far. A second later, a single robin appears. He flies away and returns with the rest of his family. Then when you look up, you see that hundreds of birds are flying toward the forest of dreams. You see crows, owls, robins, blackbirds, ducks, geese, and hummingbirds. Groups of butterflies arrive next. Then there is a procession of squirrels, deer, chipmunks, and rabbits. In the distance, you see a beautiful white unicorn galloping through the woods. Soon, every type of creature imaginable has come to make his home in this magical place. Whatever you dreamed of is here, in the forest of dreams.

You are perfectly safe in the forest of dreams and decide to explore. You begin walking around the path than encircles the forest. Rabbits dart across your path and there is a friendly squirrel following you.

Because you are so quiet, you don't disturb the forest creatures and they continue to chatter as you walk by. The frogs and crickets are singing their lovely songs and an owl is hooting. You come to a field of beautiful wildflowers. They cover the ground with a blanket of red, yellow, blue, and purple. You hear a rustling among the flowers and catch a glimpse of a tiny flower fairy. Listen—you'll hear her tinkling laughter. You want to find the flower fairy but you don't want to step on the beautiful wildflowers. You wonder what it would be like to be the size of a flower fairy. You have some dream dust in your pocket and you sprinkle a little on yourself. As you continue walking you start to get smaller and smaller and smaller. Soon, you are only four inches tall. You're smaller than most of the flowers. Now you can walk through the flowers without hurting them. You begin to look for the fairy. The flower blossoms loom above your head like giant, colorful umbrellas. You see that there are many flower fairies, but each time that you get close to one it flutters its wings and flies over to another flower. You and the fairies laugh as you play a game of hide-and-seek among the flowers. When it's your turn to hide, you climb up the stem of a flower and nestle in the petals of a beautiful yellow buttercup. You are so comfortable that you close your eyes and rest. The soft petals make a comfortable bed. Close your eyes and breathe in the sweet scent of the flowers. You have never felt so comfortable. You are falling asleep. The flower fairies cover you in a blanket of petals. You sleep and dream. *(Pause.)* The Dream Maker finds you but doesn't want to wake you because you are sleeping so peacefully. You are perfectly safe. Nothing can hurt you in the forest of dreams. You can stay and sleep with the flowers for as long as you'd like.

Week Two, Night Three

BEDTIME ROUTINE AND RELAXATION PRACTICE

Follow your usual routine and include time to have your child practice his relaxation skills. In tonight's visualization your child will become a flower, a bumblebee, and a fish. When a child puts himself into the situation of another living thing, be it a plant or an animal, it helps him to develop empathy and understand the idea of living in harmony with Mother Earth.

RELAXATION PRACTICE

Choose from tracks 1-7 or practice with the activities below.

Practice tensing and relaxing muscle groups:

★ s q u e e z e   a   l e m o n   ★

DIRECTIONS:
Have your child pretend to get as much juice out of a lemon as he can, one hand at a time. Repeat and relax.

★ sour lemonade ★

DIRECTIONS:
Have your child pretend that the lemonade is very, very sour. Have him scrunch up his entire face (holding it for approximately five to seven seconds) before relaxing his face. Repeat.

Practice focusing on the breath:

★ breathe with the ocean ★

DIRECTIONS:
Tell your child to pretend that each time he breathes in, the waves of the ocean splash on the shore. With each breath out, the waves pull away.
Coming in . . . and going out . . . coming in . . . and going out.
Coming in . . . and going out . . . coming in . . . and going out.

STEPS ONE AND TWO: GUIDED RELAXATION AND ATTENTION TO THE BREATH
Have your child follow the directions to the Flop Game on track eight.

STEP THREE: VISUALIZATION
Continue with track nine or read the following visualization.
Themes for the visualization:

* Empathy.
* Reverence for all living things.

Wondering

When we feel what others feel
Our understanding will be real
Differences will disappear
Loving kindness will be here
Excerpt from *The Christmas Dream* (CD) Patti Teel

It's time to dream now. You arrive in Dream Land and walk over to Willow's large, sturdy trunk. The bird cage that has been hanging from Willow's trunk is still there with the cage door open. But tonight, the bluebird is singing happily and he is perched on top of his cage, instead of in it. Willow's leaves are rustling with happiness. You put your arms around Willow and feel his strength, kindness, and wisdom. Then, you enter the secret door in Willow's trunk and begin sliding down toward the forest of dreams. When you step out of Willow's trunk, the Dream Maker is there waiting for you. She has a very special dream planned just for you. She sprinkles you with dream dust and tells you that in tonight's dream, anytime you wonder how it would feel to be another living creature, you will become that creature for as long as you'd like. You don't really know what she means, but you'll soon find out.

You hear the sound of a running stream, and decide to try to find it. You begin walking down a path, following the sound of the stream. You come to a meadow that is filled with lavender, blue, and yellow wildflowers. They are so beautiful. You begin to wonder what it would be like to be a flower. As soon as you have the thought, you become a beautiful lavender flower. *(Pause.)* Your legs become a flower stem and you have roots that are reaching below the ground, down into the cool, moist soil. The sun shines down upon you and fills you with warmth. Your blossoms begin to turn toward the warmth of the sun. They move slowly, slowly, ever so slowly. It feels nice to be a flower. There is nothing you have to do except soak up the beautiful sunshine. *(Pause.)* A honeybee comes to visit and his tiny legs and fluttery wings tickle your petals. As he turns to leave, he brushes off some of the pollen that he collected from other flowers. You don't mind at all. You are perfectly happy to blossom in the sunshine and share your pollen with the bees. Another honeybee lands on your petals and you find yourself wondering what it would be like to be a honeybee. Suddenly, you find yourself sipping nectar from a flower. You have become a honeybee. You buzz over to another flower and suck in the sweet nectar. Buzzing and flying from flower to flower. After a while you feel full and decide it's time to be yourself again. *(Pause.)* You continue walking toward the sound of the stream. The running water is louder now. Just as you walk around a bend in the path, you find the lovely little stream. Its water is as clear as crystal glass and it looks very inviting. Since it's not deep, you wade in. A few feet away, where the water is a little deeper, you see a green fish slowly swimming by. You wonder what it would like to be a fish and swim all day long. As soon as you have the thought, you find yourself swishing your tail and swimming through the clear, clean water. You almost feel as if you are part of the water and you barely make a ripple as you effortlessly swim past rocks and plants. You find that you can breathe underwater, because you have gills. You have a wonderful time exploring the hidden delights of the stream and from time to time you chase a school of speedy minnows. But after a while, you think about how nice it would feel to dry off and feel the warm sun on your body. Suddenly, you are yourself again. You lie down on a soft blanket and let the sun warm your feet, your legs, your arms, and your face. Mmm . . . it feels best of all to be yourself. You remember how the flower felt, with nothing to do but be himself and soak up the sunshine. Right now, that's all you have to do. Your eyes are closed and just like the flower, you turn toward the sun to soak up its warmth. There is nowhere you have to go and nothing that you have to do. Just relax and dream in the warm sunshine. The Dream Maker watches you from her own magic window and smiles. Sleep and dream in the warm sunshine for as long as you'd like.

Week Two, Night Four

BEDTIME ROUTINE AND RELAXATION PRACTICE

People have been telling stories about unicorns for more than five thousand years. In tonight's visualization, your child will meet the elusive unicorn. If you'd like, tell your child that unicorns are usually described as being white and horselike. The horn that comes out from the unicorn's forehead is thought to give him his magical powers.

RELAXATION PRACTICE

Choose from tracks one through seven or practice with the activities below.

Practice tensing and relaxing muscle groups:

★ show me how small you can be ★

DIRECTIONS:

Curl up in a tiny ball, hold your head up to your knees, and squeeze. Squeeze, squeeze, squeeze; now rest. I think you can be even smaller. One more time, curl up in a tiny ball. Press your head against your knees. Hold it, hold it, hold it; now rest. Let your arms and legs fall back down by your side.

★ simon says ★

DIRECTIONS:

Simon says clench your right fist tightly. Simon says relax your fist.
Simon says clench your left fist tightly. Simon says relax your fist.
Simon says show me your strong arm muscles. Simon says relax your arms.
Simon says wrinkle your forehead tightly. Simon says relax your forehead.
Simons says close your eyes tightly. Now relax your eyes and open your eyes.
Simon says clench your jaw and put your teeth together. Relax your jaw.
Simon says relax your whole body.

Practice focusing on the breath:

★ basic diaphragmatic breathing ★

DIRECTIONS:

Lie on your back and place your hand on your belly.

Breathe in through your nose and feel your belly rise.

Breathe out through your nose and feel your belly fall.

Breathing in, breathing out.

Breathing in, breathing out. (Repeat for several rounds of breathing.)

★ counting with diaphragmatic breathing ★

DIRECTIONS:

Counting may help to keep diaphragmatic breathing slow and smooth. Ideally, you want to have the exhalations longer than the inhalations. For example; breathe in, one, two, breathe out, one, two, three, four. (Each count is approximately one second.)

STEPS ONE AND TWO: GUIDED RELAXATION AND ATTENTION TO THE BREATH

Follow the direction to the Flop Game on track eight.

VISUALIZATION

Have your child continue with track nine, or read the following visualization.

Themes for the visualization:

- Fantasy.
- Don't give up on your dreams.

In Search of the Unicorn

**Maybe you will dream a dream—of flowers in fields with rainbow streams
With unicorns and elves at play—a magic world in which you stay**
Excerpt from *Kids World* (CD) by Patti Teel

It's time to go to Dream Land. And tonight, you go directly to the forest of dreams. When you arrive, you see Memaw, the gigantic mother tree. Her seeds continually twinkle like the lights on a Christmas tree. The Dream Maker is sitting quietly in front of Memaw. She is happy to see you and beckons you to come sit down beside her. She asks you what you'd like to do tonight in the forest of dreams. You tell her that you've seen a unicorn from a distance, but you haven't been able to meet him. The Dream Maker encourages you to keep watching for signs that he may be nearby. You begin walking down the path in search of the unicorn. Before you've gone too far you discover his prints in the dirt. You begin to follow them. They lead you down to the crystal-clear stream that you visited last night. The unicorn might come back here for a drink of water so you decide to wait for him. The sound of the water and the warmth of the sunshine are so soothing that you lie down and close your eyes. You dream of riding through the forest on the back of the beautiful, white unicorn. A shadow crosses over you and you think that a cloud is passing in front of the sun. Then, you are softly nudged by something that makes your whole body feel warm and tingly. You open your eyes and realize that the unicorn has softly nudged you with his magical horn. You gently reach up and touch him on the side of his head. The unicorn softly touches your forehead with his horn and when he does, you can hear his thoughts. He tells you that he would love to take you for a ride but he wants to be sure that you "hold on tight." Then, he bows down, inviting you to climb onto his back. Climb on and put your arms around the unicorn's strong neck. First, he walks along the path. Once he feels sure that you are secure and safe, he begins to run like the wind. The breeze feels wonderful on your face. Suddenly, you realize that you are no longer on the ground. The unicorn is flying. You see your forest friends down below and you wave to the Dream Maker and the other dreaming children. The Dream Maker waves and smiles happily. She knows that you are enjoying one of your favorite dreams. There is a rainbow up ahead and the unicorn jumps over it. Enjoy flying through the sky on the magnificent unicorn. *(Pause.)* Finally, the unicorn begins to slow down and he gracefully lands on the ground. You and the unicorn walk over to a thicket where you will be hidden from view. He lies down to rest. You sit next to his head and gently touch his horn. When you do, you hear his thoughts telling you that he'll meet you later in your dreams and take you flying again. You feel wonderfully tired. You lie down and close your eyes. Soon you will be sleeping and dreaming about the unicorn. You begin to listen to your own breath as you get sleepier and sleepier. You hear the unicorn's slow, steady breathing and know that he is already asleep. He's ready for you to join him so you can continue riding in your dreams.

Week Two, Night Five

BEDTIME ROUTINE AND RELAXATION PRACTICE

As usual, follow your routine and be sure to include time for your child to practice his relaxation skills. In the following visualization, the children and forest creatures pay homage to the mother tree who shared her magic seeds in order for a forest of dreams to grow. If you'd like, you may wish to explain how different our lives would be without trees. Remind your child that trees are the home of many animals and discuss ways we can protect and care for them.

RELAXATION PRACTICE

Choose from tracks one through seven or practice with the activities below.

Practice tensing and relaxing muscle groups:

★ give yourself a bear hug ★

DIRECTIONS:

Give yourself a great big bear hug. Squeeze, squeeze, squeeze; now lay your hands back down by your side and relax. I think you can give yourself an even bigger bear hug. (*Repeat.*)

Practice focusing on the breath:

★ the tree ★

DIRECTIONS:

Be as still and strong as a tree.

Feel as if you are a part of the tree.

Together you and the tree,

Breathe in, hold the breath, softly blow the leaves.

Breathe in, hold the breath, softly blow the leaves.

Breathe in, hold the breath, softly blow the leaves.

(Remind your child to breathe in and out of his nose.)

STEPS ONE AND TWO: GUIDED RELAXATION AND FOCUSING ON THE BREATH

Follow the directions to the Flop Game on track eight.

VISUALIZATION

Continue with track nine or read the following visualization.

Themes for the visualization:

- Thankfulness, appreciation.
- Reverence for all living things.
- World unity and love.

A Celebration

Faster than you can blink an eye
Love circles the planet and fills the sky
Your light grows brighter with each heart you meet
It starts when you're still and feel your heart beat
Excerpt from the *Inside-Out Blessing Game* (CD) by Patti Teel

It's time to dream. As you're drifting off to sleep, let your thoughts take you to Dream Land. You walk over to Willow and stand in front of his trunk. The bluebird is holding a note in his beak. It's from the Dream Maker. He flies over to you and you take it from his beak. Then, he flies back to perch on top of his cage. In the note, the Dream Maker asks you to meet her in the forest of dreams. Willow happily opens his door for you. If you have any worries, leave them behind with Willow before you go. *(Pause.)* Then step into his familiar trunk and begin sliding down toward the forest of dreams. Stepping out into the forest of dreams, you see that the Dream Maker is waiting for you. Welcome, *(child's name).* The Dream Maker is planning a party for Memaw. If the mother tree hadn't shared her magical seeds, there would be no forest of dreams. The seeds on Memaw's leaves are twinkling merrily as she watches the preparations for her party. All the forest animals begin making their way toward the mother tree. Together, you, the other dreaming children, and all the living creatures in Dream Land form a very large circle around her gigantic trunk. Birds flutter in her branches and there are nests filled with baby birds and eggs that will soon be hatching. Butterflies and flower fairies fill Memaw's branches. The wings of the butterflies and flower fairies glimmer in soft shades of orange, pink, lavender, and yellow. Sparkling dream dust swirls around all of you. Then, together everyone sings a beautiful song to Memaw. It is a choir that is made up of birds, frogs, crickets, and dreaming children. Memaw's seeds light up and blink to the sounds of the beautiful music. The Dream Maker gives you a blanket and you lie down, gazing up at the amazing tree. Then Memaw has a surprise for you. For a split second her seeds' lights go out and the only light in the forest of dreams comes from the sparkling dream dust and the stars in the sky. Then, her magic seeds put on a beautiful light show and begin to rapidly turn on one at a time. The seed's lights form the outline of each of the forest creatures. Watch as the lights form a bird, a butterfly, a child, and a frog. In her own special way, Memaw is telling you that she is glad you are here. As a parting gift, a shower of sparkling seeds slowly floats toward the ground. A wonderful feeling of relaxation spreads throughout your entire body. You feel as if you are one of the seeds, slowly floating down to the ground. With every breath, you are becoming more and more relaxed. The stars in the sky and Memaw's seeds are very beautiful and you discover that even with your eyes closed, you can still see them. Several of Memaw's seeds have landed on your blanket and you wonder what your dreams will grow. Sleep now, and find out. Sleep, sleep, sleep.

Week Two, Night Six

BEDTIME ROUTINE AND RELAXATION PRACTICE
Follow your usual routine, including relaxation practice. Throughout the visualizations this week, there has been mention of a little bird who is afraid to leave his cage. Even though his cage door is open, because he's used to being in a cage, he is afraid to fly freely. However, little by little throughout the week, he's been gaining confidence. In tonight's visualization, he finally leaves his cage and flies freely. If you'd like, discuss the limitations that we put on ourselves when we don't believe we can do something.

RELAXATION PRACTICE
Choose from tracks one through seven or practice with the activities below.

Practice tensing and relaxing muscle groups:

★ mother earth says (a variation of Simon says) ★

DIRECTIONS:

Mother Earth says clench your right fist tightly. Mother Earth says relax your fist. Mother Earth says clinch your left fist tightly. Mother Earth says relax your fist. Mother Earth says show me your strong arm muscles. Mother Earth says relax your arms.

Mother Earth says wrinkle your forehead tightly. Mother Earth says relax your forehead.

Mother Earth says close your eyes tightly. Now relax your eyes and open your eyes. Mother Earth says clench your jaw and put your teeth together. Relax your jaw. Mother Earth says relax your whole body.

★ muddy toes ★

DIRECTIONS:

Wouldn't it be fun to squish your toes in a mud puddle? Pretend you are standing barefoot in a very big mud puddle. Squish your toes deep, deep into the mud. Try to get your toes all the way to the bottom of the mud puddle. Spread your toes apart and feel the mud squish between your toes as you push down. Now step out of the mud puddle and relax your feet. I'll bet your toes feel nice and relaxed.

★ keeping the rain out of your eyes ★

DIRECTIONS:

You are outside and it is raining. Squeeze your eyes tightly shut. Squeeze, squeeze, squeeze. Now gently and softly close your eyes. Keep your eyes shut and open your mouth wide to catch some raindrops. Hold your mouth open wide. Hold it open. Hold it, hold it, hold it, hold it. Mmmmmm. Now, gently close your mouth and your eyes.

Practice focusing on the breath:

★ ball breathing ★

DIRECTIONS:

Pretend your belly is a ball.

Breathe in and slowly fill your ball with air.

Now breathe out and slowly let out the air.

Breathe in and fill your ball with air.

Breathe out and let the air out. (Repeat for several rounds of breathing.)

STEPS ONE AND TWO: GUIDED RELAXATION AND ATTENTION TO THE BREATH

Follow the directions to track eight, the Flop Game.

VISUALIZATION

Continue with track nine or read the following visualization.

Themes for the visualization:

- Kindness and helping others.
- Growing independence.
- Overcoming limiting beliefs.
- Universal love.

Free to Fly

When you dream you are free

To be the things you want to be

When you dream you are free

To see the things you want to see

Sometimes in my dreams I fly

Through the starry, starry sky

When I see the moon I laugh

It's a great big bed for the tall giraffe

You're ready to sleep and dream. You arrive in Dream Land and walk over to Willow. The sparkling dream dust is swirling around his trunk. The bluebird's open cage is still hanging from Willow's branch. The bluebird is perched on top of the cage but he leaves it and flies over to you. He wants to visit the forest of dreams with you. For the first time, the bluebird is leaving his cage behind. You step into Willow's secret door with the little bird and carry him on your lap as you slide all the way down to the forest of dreams. Then, the bluebird perches on your shoulder as you step out of Willow's trunk. You and the bluebird sit down on the ground in front of Memaw, the mother tree. Memaw is huge and she is the home for many, many animals. Memaw notices every creature in the forest and she is watching the bluebird. She knows that he has been living in a cage. But once he gets a taste of his freedom, Memaw knows that he will love it. Her sparkling seeds are tempting the little bird. He sees the other animals hungrily eating Memaw's seeds and he wants one too. He has heard that they are magic. The little bird takes a few little hops toward Memaw's giant trunk. Then he flies back to the safety of your shoulder. Suddenly, he flies all the way over to Memaw's branch and picks up a seed with his little beak. He starts singing and flying from branch to branch. You can feel his happiness. Memaw is happy too. She is truly like a mother to all the living things in the forest of dreams. A hammock is hanging from one of Memaw's strong branches. You sink down into the hammock, feeling content to be a part of this happy forest family. You are so happy for the little bluebird. It feels good to do something nice for someone else. Your heart feels warm. *(Pause.)* Think of all the animals and plants, those in Dream Land and those on Earth. You fall asleep knowing that the whole universe is a gigantic family and you are a part of it.

Week Two, Night Seven

Bedtime Routine and Relaxation Practice

Follow your usual bedtime routine and allow some time for your child to practice his relaxation skills. In tonight's visualization, your child will be remembering all the visualizations that he has done throughout the week. Its purpose is to help a child realize that he can visualize at will. And that he can imagine scenes from the visualizations you've read, or things that he enjoys doing in real life. Ask your child to think of activities that make him happy. Then remind him that he can always imagine himself doing those things just before he falls asleep at night.

RELAXATION PRACTICE
Choose from tracks one through seven or practice with the activities below.
   Practice tensing and relaxing muscle groups:

★ show me how strong you are ★

DIRECTIONS:
Show me your strong arm muscles. Make a muscle. Hold the muscle with your fists clenched. Hold it, hold it, hold it. Now, relax. Open your hands and rest your arms back down by your side. (*It will probably make your child happy when you feign surprise at his strength.*)

★ i'm taking your picture ★

DIRECTIONS:
I'm taking your picture to hang on the refrigerator. Smile, smile, smile; now rest. Let's take another picture. Just for fun, wrinkle up your face while I take your picture. Wrinkle your face. Hold it, hold it, hold it. I got the picture! You can relax.

   Release-only relaxation:

★ the jellyfish ★

DIRECTIONS:
See if your child can pretend to be a jellyfish, with all his muscle groups as loose and limp as jelly.

   Practice focusing on the breath:

★ balloon breathing ★

DIRECTIONS:

Imagine there is a balloon in your belly.

Place one of your hands on your belly.

Breathe in slowly and feel your balloon fill with air as it raises your hand.

Now breathe out slowly and gently let the air out of your balloon.

(Repeat several times.)

STEPS ONE AND TWO

Have your child listen to track eight, the Flop Game, and follow the directions.

STEP THREE: VISUALIZATION

Continue with track nine or read the following visualization.

Themes for the visualization:

- Self-worth and value.
- Imagination.

Remembering

When I go to sleep at night
I dream of rainbows and colors bright
Ice cream castles in the sky
Or riding on a big balloon a-way up high
Excerpt from *Kids World* (CD) by Patti Teel

As you begin to dream, you hear the Dream Maker softly calling. You look through your magic window and see that the Dream Academy is in session. Step through your magic window and into the class for dreamers. When you find your favorite little cloud, you lie down and sink into its softness. You realize how much you've missed the wonderful feeling of floating on your soft, little cloud. Lie back and relax. Look up at the stars. Try to draw lines to connect the stars in your imagination. See what pictures they make.

The Dream Maker begins tonight's lesson. "We had many wonderful adventures in the forest of dreams. I want you to know that you can remember them anytime you'd like and it will be just as if you are there again. Remember lying on a blanket, surrounded by beautiful flowers . . . how it felt, and how it smelled. *(Pause.)* There was nothing to do but soak up the sunshine. Do you know that in your own way, you are just as beautiful as a flower? Remember feeling the softness of the flower's petals. *(Pause.)* Do you know that your face is just as soft?"

Remember how it felt to ride the magical unicorn? See yourself flying through the sky on this magical creature, your hair blowing in the breeze. The unicorn is truly magical. *(Pause.)*

And remember when you were only four inches tall and you played hide-and-seek with the flower fairies? Then, you slept in a flower. *(Pause.)* What color was the flower? The fairies covered you with petals and you were relaxed and comfortable. *(Pause.)* Fairies are very kind, and so are you. You were a good friend to the bluebird and helped him to realize that he could leave his cage and be free.

You can remember these things anytime you'd like, perhaps when you're relaxing and getting ready to fall asleep. The memories are always in your mind. Right now, think of your favorite adventure in the forest of dreams. Was it riding on the unicorn, or playing hide-and-seek with the fairies? *(Pause.)* Or was it swimming through the cool, clean stream in the body of a fish? Think of your own favorite dreams as you drift off to sleep.

Week Three: Introduce the Rules and Make Your Personalized Tape

This week, you will be leaving your children's room after the bedtime routine and they will be relaxing themselves to sleep on their own by listening to a recording. You can either have your child listen to tracks eight and nine, or he can listen to the tape that you prepare. There are several advantages to making your own tape:

1. You can personalize a tape that will emphasize your child's unique interests and abilities, choosing positive thoughts and affirmations that will be especially meaningful and helpful. Affirmations can include suggestions for healing, positive behavior, self-esteem, specific achievements, improved attitude, and assertions that specific things will work out for the best. Remember to focus on what you want for your child, rather than the lack of it.
2. Your child will drift off to sleep listening to the voice he loves best.
3. You can have fun and be creative.
4. You can choose the approach that works best for your child—a progressive relaxation routine, (ie the Flop Game or Let Go) or a release-only relaxation routine, (ie Heavy and Relaxed).

At this point, your child should be able to relax and follow the directions of the Flop Game (track eight) independently. This is important because you're going to begin leaving the room with the expectation that your child will listen to the recording, follow its directions, and fall asleep. If your child has been vying for you attention and asking you to watch him as he flops his arms and legs, stay in his room for a couple more evenings. Tell your child that you need some quiet time or meditation time and don't wish to be disturbed. Encourage your child to follow the directions on his own. If he is still not relaxing on his own, instigate a reward system in the form of a sticker or star chart. (You can download a star chart on my website at dreamflt.com.) When your child follows the directions on the recording and goes to sleep by himself, he will receive a star in the morning. You'll have to personalize this according to your child's age. For instance, just the joy of getting a star may be enough for a three-year-old. However, for a ten-year-old, the stars might go toward a night at the movies, bowling, or some other fun activity. Gradually, your child will need more and more stars to earn the reward, until it's no longer needed.

How to Create Your Own Bedtime Tape

Arrange some quiet time of your own to make a tape for your son or daughter. The tape should follow the same steps that you introduced in week one: first a guided relaxation, then focusing on the breath, and ending with a visualization. For the guided relaxation and focusing on the breath, you can choose from: the Flop Game on pp. 146–148, Let Go on pp. 159–160, or Heavy and Relaxed on pp. 173–175. These guided relaxation routines were given as an option in week one. The Flop Game and Let Go are similar in that they both use progressive relaxation; children are directed to tense their muscles and then relax. The language and directions that are used in Let Go are a bit more adult—it may be a good choice if your child is eight years of age or older. Heavy and Relaxed uses release-only relaxation; children are directed to relax without first tensing their muscle groups. Sometimes young children do well with this approach; however, be sure that they are truly capable of relaxing, without first tensing, if you plan to use this routine. You may record any of the visualizations from the program or create your own. In addition, you can sign up to receive monthly dream starters (i.e. visualizations) at dreamflt.com.)

Tips for Making Your Own Relaxation Tape

1. Find some uninterrupted time when you won't be rushed. (It may take a few tries before you're satisfied.)
2. Have fun and don't be afraid to experiment and be creative.
3. Speak slowly, in a relaxed voice. Pause between movements, giving your child time to do them in a relaxed fashion.
4. When you want to place special emphasis on a thought or instruction, say the words slower, drawing out the vowel sounds. For example, You are sooooooo sleepy.
5. Although some children enjoy music in the background, unless you have professional recording equipment it can be difficult to get the correct balance with the voice. Also, depending on the

background music, stopping and starting may be a problem. That being said, I don't want to squelch your creativity. Give it a try, if you so desire!

> ★ When making up your own visualization, keep in mind that it often works best if all of the senses are involved; seeing, hearing, feeling, tasting, and smelling. ★

This week, you will be leaving your children's room after the bedtime routine and they will be relaxing themselves to sleep on their own. If you plan to make your own tape but haven't had a chance to do so yet, play tracks eight and nine for now.

Bedtime Routine and Relaxation Practice

As you have been doing over the last two weeks, continue to give your child a ten-minute warning before bedtime, and have a set bedtime as well as a consistent bedtime routine. Continue to include relaxation practice toward the end of your child's bedtime routine.

Week Three, Night One

RELAXATION PRACTICE
Choose from tracks one through seven or practice with the activities below:
   Tensing and relaxing muscle groups:

★ squeeze through the fence ★

DIRECTIONS:
Pretend that you want to squeeze through a very narrow fence. Let's practice first so we're sure you won't get stuck. Suck your belly in and try to squeeze it

all the way against your backbone. Hold it, hold it. Now let your belly relax. You did well so I think you can really squeeze through the fence now. Squeeze your belly all the way against your backbone. Make it really small and tight. Hold it and try to squeeze throught the fence. You made it! You can relax now.

Focusing on the breath:

★ the waves ★

DIRECTIONS:
Waves sound like breathing.
Breathe with the sea as if you are part of it.
Together you and the sea.
Breathe in, hold the breath, slowly breathe out the sound of the ocean.
Breathe in, hold the breath, slowly breathe out the sound of the ocean.
Breathe in, hold the breath, slowly blow out the sound of the ocean.

STEPS ONE, TWO, AND THREE
Tell your child good night and leave the room. Have him listen to tracks eight and nine on the *Floppy Sleep Game* book CD, or a tape that you made for him consisting of a guided relaxation routine, instructions for focusing on the breath, and a visualization.

Week Three, Night Two

RELAXATION PRACTICE
Choose from tracks one through seven or practice with the activities below.

Tensing and relaxing musle groups:

★ simon says ★

DIRECTIONS:

Simon says make a fist with your right hand.

Simon says make a fist with your left hand.

Simon says show me your strong arm muscles. Hold it . . . and relax.

Simon says wrinkle up your face like a raisin. Hold it . . . and relax.

Simon says stretch your shoulders back. Hold them . . . and relax.

Simon says relax your whole body.

Focusing on the breath:

★ review belly breathing ★

DIRECTIONS:

Lie on your back and place your hand on your belly.

Breathe in through your nose and feel your belly rise.

Breathe out through your nose and feel your belly fall.

Breathing in, breathing out, breathing in, breathing out. *(Repeat for several rounds.)*

STEPS ONE, TWO, AND THREE

Tell your child good night and leave the room. Have him listen to tracks eight and nine on the *Floppy Sleep Game* book CD, *or* a tape that you made for him.

Week Three, Night Three

RELAXATION PRACTICE

Choose from tracks one through seven or practice with the activities below.

Tensing and relaxing muscle groups:

★ there's a fly on my nose! ★

DIRECTIONS:

A fly has landed on your nose. Can you get him off without using your hands? Wrinkle your nose. Try to wrinkle it a little more so the fly will get off your nose. Good. He went away so you can relax your nose. Oh no! He's back on your nose again. *(Repeat.)* Now the fly has landed on your forehead. Make lots of wrinkles. Try to catch him between the wrinkles you're making. Hold it tighter and tighter and tighter. Now close your eyes tightly. Oh good. He's gone now. You can open yours eyes. Relax and let your face be smooth and relaxed.

Release-only relaxation:

★ be a noodle ★

Try to make each arm as limp as a cooked spaghetti noodle.
Make each leg as limp as a long cooked spaghetti noodle.
Make your whole body feel like a limp, loose spaghetti noodle.

Focusing on the breath:

★ review belly breathing ★

DIRECTIONS:

Lie on your back and place your hand on your belly.
Breathe in through your nose and feel your belly rise.
Breathe out through your nose and feel your belly fall.
Breathing in, breathing out, breathing in, breathing out.
(Repeat for several rounds.)

STEPS ONE, TWO, AND THREE
Tell your child good night and leave the room. Have him listen to tracks eight and nine on the *Floppy Sleep Game* book CD, *or* a tape that you made for him consisting of a guided relaxation routine, directions for focusing on the breath, and a visualization.

Week Three, Night Four

RELAXATION PRACTICE
Choose from tracks one through seven or practice with the activities below.

Tensing and relaxing muscle groups:

★ toe tensing ★

DIRECTIONS:
Lie on your back.
Pull all of your toes back toward your face and count to ten.
Now, relax your toes. *(Repeat several times.)*
(Ask your child if he can spread out his toes so that none of them are touching.)

Tensing and relaxing musle groups:

DIRECTIONS:
Clench your fists. Hold it while you count to five . . . and relax your fists.
Suck in your tummy and hold it for the count of five . . . and relax.
Shrug your shoulders. Hold them up and count to five . . . and relax your shoulders.
Wrinkle your forehead, and keep it wrinkled while you count to five . . . and relax your face.

Focusing on the breath:

⋆ i relax my whole body ⋆

DIRECTIONS:

Breathing in, I feel my whole body.

Breathing out, I feel my whole body.

Breathing in, I relax my whole body.

Breathing out, I relax my whole body.

STEPS ONE, TWO, AND THREE

Tell your child good night and leave the room. Have him listen to tracks eight and nine on the *Floppy Sleep Game* book CD, *or* a tape that you made for him consisting of a guided relaxation routine, directions for focusing on the breath, and a visualization.

Week Three, Night Five

RELAXATION PRACTICE

Choose from tracks one through seven or practice with the activities below.

Tensing and relaxing musle groups:

⋆ stretch and relax ⋆

DIRECTIONS:

Point your fingers and toes while stretching all the muscles in your arms and legs.

Really stretch and hold. (Hold for at least five seconds.)

Take a big breath in and as you breathe out, let your whole body soften and relax.

(Repeat.)

Focusing on the breath:

★ review belly breathing ★

DIRECTIONS:

Lie on your back and place your hand on your belly.

Breathe in through your nose and feel your belly rise.

Breathe out through your nose and feel your belly fall.

Breathing in, breathing out, breathing in, breathing out. *(Repeat for several rounds.)*

The following exercise is often difficult for children under the age of six or seven. Children will be learning to isolate three areas: the head, the chest, and the abdomen. Don't introduce it unless your child is proficient at diaphragmatic breathing. Daytime follow-up: blow up a real balloon. Show children how it fills up, from the bottom, the middle, and finally the top. Let out some air. Watch the balloon deflate from the top, the middle, and the bottom. Explain that they can inflate and deflate the air of their imaginary balloon (in their bellies and chest) in the same way.

★ elevator breathing ★

DIRECTIONS:

Your breath is an elevator taking a ride through your body.

Breathe in through your nose and start the elevator ride.

Breathe out and feel your breath go all the way to the basement, down to your toes.

Breathe in and take your elevator breath up to your belly.

Hold it. Now, breathe out all your air. *(Pause.)*

This time, breathe in and take your elevator breath up to your chest.

Hold it. Now breathe out all your air. *(Pause.)*

Now breathe in and take your elevator breath up to the top floor,

up through your throat and into your face and forehead.

Feel your head fill with breath. Hold it.

Now breathe out and feel your elevator breath take all your troubles away,

and worries down through your chest, your belly, your legs,
and out through the elevator doors in your feet.
(Repeat.)

Steps One, Two, and Three

Tell your child good night and leave the room. Have him listen to tracks eight and nine on the *Floppy Sleep Game* book CD, *or* a tape that you made for him consisting of a guided relaxation routine, directions for focusing on the breath, and a visualization.

Week Three, Night Six

Relaxation Practice

Choose from tracks one through seven or practice with the activities below.

Tensing and relaxing musle groups:

★   s i m o n   s a y s   ★

Directions:

Simon says clench your right fist tightly. Simon says relax your fist.

Simon says clinch your left fist tightly. Simon says relax your fist.

Simon says show me your strong arm muscles. Simon says relax your arms.

Simon says wrinkle your forehead tightly. Simon says relax your forehead.

Simons says close your eyes tightly. Now relax your eyes and open your eyes.

Simon says clench your jaw and put your teeth together. Relax your jaw.

Simon says relax your whole body.

Focusing on the breath:

★ the wind ★

DIRECTIONS:

The wind sings if you really listen.

It sounds like a gentle breath.

Feel as if you are a part of the wind.

Join the wind and together you softly blow white fluffly clouds across the sky.

Breathe in, hold the breath, softly blow the clouds,

Breathe in, hold the breath, softly blow the clouds,

Breathe in, hold the breath, softly blow.

Repeat Elevator Breathing from night five.

STEPS ONE, TWO, AND THREE

Tell your child good night and leave the room. Have him listen to tracks eight and nine on the *Floppy Sleep Game* book CD, *or* a tape that you made for him.

Week Three, Night Seven

RELAXATION PRACTICE

Choose from tracks one through seven or practice with the activities below.

★ tighten the whole body at once ★

DIRECTIONS:

Take a deep breath . . . wrinkle your face . . . push up your shoulders into your neck . . . belly pulled in . . . fists clenched. Hold for a count of five. Let go and relax.

(Repeat several times.)

Focusing on the breath: repeat Elevator Breathing from night five. Have your child spend a few quiet minutes simply focusing on his breath.

STEPS ONE, TWO, AND THREE

Tell your child good night and leave the room. Have him listen to tracks eight and nine on the *Floppy Sleep Game* book CD, *or* a tape that you made for him.

WEEK THREE: THE RULES

After the Bedtime Routine

This week when the bedtime routine is coming to an end, matter-of-factly introduce two simple "rules."

1. Go to sleep on your own.
2. Stay in your bed all night.

The exception to staying in bed all night would be a nightmare, night terror, sleepwalking, or illness. Don't tell your children about the exceptions ahead of time or they may be tempted to tell you that they are sick or had a bad dream if they get out of bed in the middle of the night. I say this from personal experience; I'll never forget the sound of my daughter's little feet running lickety-split down the hallway and into my room. She learned that I would be considerably more pleasant if she told me she had a bad dream.

Once you have explained these two rules to your child, you will proceed with the following steps:

- Tell your child good night and give them a hug and kiss.
- Turn on the tape.
- Leave the room.

At this point most kids will obligingly listen to the tape, do the relaxation exercises, and independently fall asleep; however, it's best to be prepared in case you are tested. For some children, at every stage of reduction of parental attention, problems get worse before improvement begins. If your child protests about you leaving the room, don't turn it into a power struggle. Agree to sit in a chair away from your child; you can meditate or read if there is enough light. The next night, reiterate the two rules with the promise of a reward for going to sleep on his own and staying in bed until morning. The reward could be a sticker or star to put on a chart, or a trip to the park upon awakening. Parents usually know best what excites their child. If your child is very young, make sure he receives the "reward" first thing in the morning after staying in bed all night. Little by little, as your child becomes more successful at falling asleep independently and staying in bed all night you can lengthen the time it takes to earn the reward. For instance, make a star chart; at first your young child needs only one star, and then three stars, to earn his reward. Gradually, your child will be able to go longer and longer without the reward until it's no longer an issue. Each day, reinforce your child's progress, telling him that it is wonderful that he is learning to go to sleep by herself. (Star charts can be downloaded from my website at dreamflt.com.)

Week Four: Sleeping Solo

Preparation

Try out different relaxation and breathing exercises as well as visualizations that you create during your child's bedtime routine. If you discover ideas or themes that your child loves and finds restful, put them on a tape. Again, don't be afraid to be creative and record your own visualization ideas, custom-made with love, especially for your child. Before long, your son or daughter will be able to choose from a small library of recordings, selecting the one that suits his mood. Now that your child can relax on his own, give him the choice of listening to a recording, or relaxing and falling asleep without it.

Bedtime Routine and Relaxation Practice

As always, continue to tell your child that bedtime is in ten minutes, and have a set bedtime and a consistent bedtime routine.

PRACTICE CREATING VISUALIZATIONS

Remember, this week your child will choose whether or not to listen to a recording. When children have the ability to relax and visualize delightful stories at will, bedtime becomes enjoyable. A fun way to develop the ability to visualize is to have a partner visualization with your child, taking turns telling portions of a visualization.

1. Take turns picking the opening setting of the story. If one of you is stuck, give ideas to your partner. (Your visualization could take place anywhere: on an island, a mountaintop, the beach, or a fantasyland that you make up.)

2. Start the visualization with each of you contributing. For instance, a visualization might start something like this.

> PARENT: You are swimming in the warm ocean and see some mermaids down below. What are the mermaids doing?
>
> CHILD: The mermaids are talking to each other and getting ready to go to a party.
>
> PARENT: Dive down into the warm, salty water and ask the mermaids if you can go to the party with them. What did they say?
>
> CHILD: They said that I can go with them and they are going to help me dress up like a mermaid.

Gradually, encourage your child to take a more active role in the shared visualization. Soon your child will take the lead and you will be the one who simply fills in some details.

Here are a few ideas to get you started:

- Riding on a hot-air balloon
- Riding on a magic carpet
- Shrinking to the size of a frog or a bug on a floating leaf
- Talking flowers
- Meeting fairies in the woods
- Meeting the tooth fairy
- Making friends with an animal who talks

Your children will have the best ideas. There is nothing that compares to a child's imagination!

If your child has enjoyed the visualization in the Floopy Sleep Game program, you may wish to continue having them start in Dream Land. Or, they can begin in your child's own special place.

RELAXATION PRACTICE

Although progressive relaxation is not a new skill, this week your child will learn an abbreviated routine. It may be a very useful exercise for him to do independently as he falls asleep; however, it's important to practice it so that it becomes effortless.

Your child will also be practicing an abbreviated release-only relaxation routine. By trying both approaches, your child will be able to decide which he finds the most relaxing.

Week Four, Night One

★ abbreviated progressive relaxation routine ★

DIRECTIONS:

Make a muscle with both arms and show me how strong you are.

Hold your fists tight. Keep showing me your strong muscles.

Hold it, hold it, and relax.

Now wrinkle up your face so that it looks like a raisin.

Wrinkle your forehead as you tightly close your eyes. Hold, hold, hold; now relax.

Open your mouth as wide as you can. Wider, wider wider; now relax.

Bring your shoulders all the way up to your ears

Hold it, hold it, hold it. Relax.

As you take in a deep breath,

pull your shoulders so far back that they try to touch each other.

Hold it, hold it, hold it. Relax.

Take a deep breath in and push your belly out. Hold it, hold it. Relax.

Straighten both of your legs and point your toes back toward your face.

Keep your legs as straight as you can. Hold it, hold it. Relax.

Straighten both of your legs, point your toes away from you and tighten your bottom.

Hold it, hold it, hold it. Relax.

Take a deep breath in and as you breathe out, relax your whole body.

After the abbreviated progressive relaxation routine, have your child quietly focus on his breath for a minute or two.

Week Four, Night Two

RELAXATION PRACTICE

Repeat the abbreviated progressive relaxation routine from night one. After the abbreviated progressive relaxation routine, have your child quietly focus on his breath for a minute or two.

Week Four, Night Three

RELAXATION PRACTICE

★ abbreviated release-only routine ★

DIRECTIONS:
Both of my arms are heavy.
I am calm and relaxed.
My right leg is heavy.
My left leg is heavy.
I am calm and relaxed.
Both of my arms are heavy.
I am calm and relaxed.
My entire body is heavy. I am calm and relaxed.

After the abbreviated release-only routine have your child practice belly breathing for a minute or two.

Week Four, Night Four

RELAXATION PRACTICE
Repeat the abbreviated release-only routine from night three. After the abbreviated release-only routine have your child practice belly breathing for a minute or two.

Week Four, Night Five

RELAXATION PRACTICE
Let your child choose between the abbreviated progressive relaxation routine and the abbreviated release-only routine.

★ elevator breathing ★

DIRECTIONS:

Your breath is an elevator taking a ride through your body.

Breathe in through your nose and start the elevator ride.

Breathe out and feel your breath go all the way to the basement, down to your toes.

Breathe in and take your elevator breath up to your belly.

Hold it. Now, breathe out all your air. *(Pause.)*

This time, breathe in and take your elevator breath up to your chest.

Hold it. Now breathe out all your air. *(Pause.)*

Now breathe in and take your elevator breath up to the top floor,

up through your throat and into your face and forehead.

Feel your head fill with breath. Hold it.

Now breathe out and feel your elevator breath take all your troubles

and worries down through your chest, your belly, your legs,

and out through the elevator doors in your feet.

(Repeat.)

Week Four, Night Six

Let your child choose between the abbreviated progressive relaxation routine and the abbreviated release-only routine. Repeat elevator breathing from night five or review belly breathing.

Week Four, Night Seven

Let your child choose between the abbreviated progressive relaxation routine and the abbreviated release-only routine. Have your child practice belly breathing.

After the Bedtime Routine

As you wind up the bedtime routine, reinforce your two rules, acknowledging your child for his or her previous success.

- Say good night and give your child a good-night kiss and hug.
- Turn on the recording or have your child relax on his own.
- Leave the room.

Many children will choose to continue using a recording to help guide them through the relaxation exercises. Others will be ready to relax themselves to sleep without it. At this point, I would advise you to let your child make the choice. Younger children are more likely to continue listening to the recording for a period of time. There is nothing wrong with a child choosing to use a recording some evenings and not others. Although the ultimate goal is for children to learn to relax and fall asleep effortlessly, with or without the recordings, if your child continues to want to listen to the recording every night as he falls asleep, don't worry. Periodically, remind him that he knows the recording by heart and encourage him to do the relaxation routine at bedtime without listening to it. Like relinquishing a teddy bear or a favorite blanket, your child will give up the recording when the time is right. In the meantime, your child is continuing to practice relaxation techniques that will help him throughout his life.

PROBLEMS AND SETBACKS

There will be times when you will be unable to enforce a set bedtime and consistent bedtime routine. Moving, vacations, or illnesses can throw off the schedule of even the most diligent parents. Remind your children to use the relaxation skills they have learned, even when their routines are thrown off. As your child becomes more skilled at relaxing, he will gain the ability to relax in any setting. This can be a lifesaver during family vacations!

Stressful Interludes

Throughout childhood, there may be occasional periods when stresses cause your child to once again have trouble sleeping. While it may be best to talk about serious problems earlier in the day, children often like to discuss their problems during the bedtime routine because they have you all to themselves and it's a time of closeness. It's not a good idea to turn your child away when he comes to you with a problem, so from time to time you may end up having a serious discussion during the bedtime routine. End the discussion with a focus on the positive. Make a ceremony out of putting the troubles or worries away for the night. (See Ways to Put Worries to Bed, pp. 134–136.)

If your child is struggling with something specific, you may wish to make up a story where he solves a similar problem. (While some children love for stories to be about them, others would prefer to be one step removed and have it be about someone else.)

If your child ever tells you that he can't get to sleep, respond by saying, "That's okay. Think of something wonderful." If your child asks you what to think about, feel free to give him an idea that may jump-start the visualization. Encourage your child to visualize his dreams coming true. Tell your child to be the director and star of his own movie; choosing and picturing things just the way he wants them to be.

During stressful times, keep the bedtime routine very consistent. Reintroduce a relaxation recording for a period of time, even if your child was previously able to relax and fall asleep without it. If necessary, sit in your child's room and over a period of days, gradually ease yourself back out. Remind your child of the two rules: (1) going to sleep on his own, and (2) staying in bed all night.

If necessary, reinstigate a reward system. At first, reward your child in the morning for every successful night that he followed the rules. Gradually, reward your child for longer periods of compliance, until the reward is no longer needed. If your child is very young and has trouble giving up the reward, it's okay. Eventually, as your child grows up, the external reward will become less important.

- Talk to your child during the bedtime routine. End the discussion with a focus on the positive.
- If your child is struggling with something specific, make up a story where your child (or another child) solves a similar problem.
- Tell your child to be the director and star of his own movie, picturing things the way he wants them to be.
- Give your child an idea to jump-start his visualization.
- Take turns thinking of things you're thankful for. Make it a game and see who can come up with the most.
- Keep the bedtime routine consistent.
- Practice relaxation techniques during the bedtime routine.
- Reintroduce a relaxation tape for a period of time, if needed. If necessary, sit in your child's room and ease yourself back out over a period of days.
- If necessary, reinstigate a reward system for complying with the two bedtime rules: (1) going to sleep on his own, and (2) staying in bed all night. (Star charts can be downloaded at dreamflt.com.)

Night Waking

Once children are falling asleep independently, getting up in the middle of the night usually becomes a thing of the past. But if your child still wakes up and gets out of bed in the middle of the night, it is important that you *not* respond by lying down in bed with him or by allowing him to lie down in bed with you. It is difficult for parents to hold their ground in the middle of the night because they are tired and vulnerable. Don't let your child get into bed with you. No matter how tired you are, walk him back to bed, with as little interaction as possible. Keep the conversation to a bare minimum. Hopefully, this will not happen more than one time in a night. If it does, repeat the process. Set up a reward system for your child before the next evening. Remind your son or daughter of the two rules. Don't give up! It will soon be worth the effort when the whole family is getting a good night's sleep. Night waking is normal; children need to learn to fall back asleep without assistance.

A LOVELY MORNING RITUAL

Make the first moments of the day special by spending some time with your child just after he wakes up. Rather than chaotically rushing about, get in the habit of taking just a few minutes for your child to tell you about his dreams. Don't worry if your child is telling you about a dream and it turns into storytelling. Young children have a hard time understanding exactly where their dream memories end and the imagination frequently takes over. Listen carefully to your child's deams and share your own as well. Don't try too hard to analyze your child's dreams. Just enjoy a delightful time of sharing and laughter; it may set the mood for the entire day. In addition, it will give you a greater understanding of your child while giving your child a greater understanding of himself. By teaching children to try to remember their dreams you are encouraging them to develop their intuition and pay attention to subtle messages.

Parents share the dream of raising happy children who grow up to be capable adults. With that goal in mind, we teach our children many things

---

Tip: Don't worry if your child is telling you about a dream and it turns into storytelling. Young children have a hard time understanding exactly where their dream memories end and the imagination frequently takes over.

Tip: Listen carefully to your child's dreams and share your own dreams as well.

Tip: Don't try too hard to analyze your child's dreams.

and one of them is to relax and fall asleep independently. You are to be congratulated for helping your child to take this important step toward self-reliance. Sleeping independently is a tremendous accomplishment.

However, the benefits of conscious relaxation far outweigh even this worthwhile achievement. By learning how to purposefully and intentionally relax and calm themselves, children will be better equipped to deal with life's inevitable ups and downs. When you teach your children these valuable exercises, you give them tools that they will be able to use throughout their lives.

In the next chapter we'll explore some of the special challenges that children face when they are fearful, stressed, or anxious, and we'll discuss some of the ways your child can use relaxation techniques to effectively deal with stress in everyday situations, not just at bedtime. Take a moment to reflect on the importance of relaxation and, in addition to falling asleep, think of situations in which you and your child could benefit from relaxing and quieting your bodies and minds.

CHAPTER EIGHT

Overcoming Anxiety and Maintaining Sleep Success

The *Floppy Sleep Game* program had worked like a charm for Cassie. For more than a year, she was able to fall asleep by herself and she slept well all night long. Then a series of events disrupted Cassie's life and, accordingly, her bedtime routine. Her mother, Geneva, had to go out of town and Cassie went to stay with her aunt and uncle and her cousin, Stacy. Stacy and Cassie were only a year apart in age; Cassie was seven and Stacy was eight. Since it was summer and the girls were having so much fun, Cassie and Stacy were allowed to stay up long past Cassie's usual bedtime. Stacy shared her bed with Cassie and they'd stay up for hours, giggling and telling stories.

After ten days apart, Cassie and her mother were reunited. The first night that they were back home, Cassie didn't want her mother to leave after being tucked in. Geneva thought she'd give Cassie a little extra attention after having been gone for so long and she decided to lay down with her for a few minutes. Cassie didn't want her to leave until after she fell asleep. The next night, the same scenario was starting up. Geneva realized that she was going down a slippery slope. The following night,

Cassie's mother was prepared. She used the *Floppy Sleep Game* book CD to have Cassie practice the relaxation techniques. Then, she stayed in Cassie's room and had her relax and fall asleep with tracks eight and nine. Within a few days, she had completely phased herself back out of Cassie's room. Once again, Cassie was able to fall asleep on her own.

It's easy to become complacent about our child's sleep habits when things are going well. Try to keep in mind that things have gone well due to healthy sleep habits and the self-soothing techniques that your child has acquired. Of course, there will be times when your child's bedtime routine is disrupted. Vacations, moving, illnesses, and an assortment of problems will all throw off your child's bedtime routine. But even when your child's bedtime routine is disrupted, self-soothing techniques will help him to sleep. They will help him relax and fall asleep when he's on vacation far from home, or when he has to deal with the stress of an illness or moving. But as soon as it's feasible, after things settle down, it's important to have your child resume his healthy sleep habits.

Whether it's something relatively trivial like a lost library book or a life-altering event such as a divorce, it's guaranteed that all children will have to deal with stress. And if it's not dealt with well, sleep will be one of the first things to be affected. To sleep well, a child needs to be at ease . . . both physically and emotionally. If a child learns to soothe himself and is able to calm his body and mind, he will be able to thrive in the toughest of times.

A child is unlikely to know when there is too much stress in his life. It's up to you as his parent, to watch for those telltale signs. Even in the same family, each child is unique. The number of activities that could be overwhelming for one child might be quite comfortable for another. Although the advice shared earlier in the book referred to sleep, the suggestions regarding the importance of quiet time, exercise, and reducing sugar intake also apply to relieving anxiety and related stress.

While all children have to learn to effectively deal with fear and anxiety, children with special challenges are likely to be in a continual state of stress and self-calming skills become a necessity. In particular, children with ADHD, mood disorders, sensory integration difficulties, autism, and

Asperger's may have sleep-related difficulties as well as a harder time coping with anxiety-provoking situations. It's imperative for them to learn self-soothing skills, which will bring their bodies back to a balanced, unstressful state.

How to Combat Fears and Phobias

By nature, some children seem to have more fears than others. When the word "fear" is used correctly, it refers to the feeling experienced in response to a tangible danger, such as a speeding car or an angry dog. "Phobias" are excessive or exaggerated fears of specific objects or situations. Common childhood fears (or phobias) include a fear of the dark, dogs, heights, spiders, and storms.

Jean Piaget is well known for his research regarding children's cognitive development. He calls ages two to four the "preoperational period" of development. It is characterized by reason being dominated by perception. This explains why preschoolers are often afraid of the dark and imaginary creatures such as monsters.

Piaget's research revealed that at around the age of six or seven, children's thinking begins to become more logical. Not surprisingly, around this age, children usually lose their fear of imaginary creatures but may become worried about other types of things such as school performance and social relationships. Encourage your children to tell you about their fears. If your child's fear is having a negative impact on his life, there are steps you can take to help your child overcome it early on.

Many adult fears begin in childhood. Completely avoiding feared objects and activities tends to increase rather than diminish the level of fear associated with them. We can see many examples of this—a fear of drowning is not likely to lessen by avoiding water; a fear of flying is not going to go away by avoiding airplanes; and a fear of school is not going to go away by allowing a child to stay home.

Children often generalize their fears. For example, a child is likely to think that all dogs are mean and unfriendly after a frightening experience with just one dog. A friendly golden retriever may happily approach a child with his tail wagging, but the child with a fear of dogs is likely to perceive the dog as a mean animal that is coming to attack. If a fear is not overcome, a child may begin to generalize it further and develop phobias about other types of animals in addition to dogs.

Some fears must be confronted and dealt with because they will interfere with a child's daily life. Other phobias and fears may not have to be confronted very often. Even when that is the case, beware that you can unwittingly teach your children to have the same phobias that you have. My husband and I both have a rat phobia. I have generalized my fear to include opossums, hamsters, gerbils, and other rodents. Years ago, when we had a pet rabbit, he could even give me the creeps! While it seemed to me that I was only being a conscientious mother by passing along the dangers of rats to my daughter, when she screamed and came running out of her first-grade classroom in a panic because the teacher had a pet rat, I realized that I had probably overdone it.

Much more so than the actual events themselves, children's reactions to fear and anxiety will affect the quality of their lives, both emotionally and physically. Their response can lead to personal growth, or it can impair that emotional growth. When children respond to the emotions of fear and anxiety by becoming stressed, it can affect their ability to be happy and experience pleasure. Because we cannot control all of the things that will happen in our children's lives, it's important for us to help them learn healthy ways to cope.

Reactions to fear can include:

- Shortness of breath, fast breathing
- A racing heart
- A tightness in the chest
- A lump in the throat
- Butterflies in the stomach

- Light-headedness, dizziness
- Shaking, trembling, tingling feelings
- A surreal feeling that things seem strange
- Tightening muscles

Steps to Overcoming Fears and Phobias

1. **Learn relaxation and self-calming skills.** We learned a lot about different relaxation exercises in chapter 7 during the *Floppy Sleep Game* program. Use those techniques, such as progressive relaxation and belly breathing, during the daytime, too. Also, see the simple anytime relaxation tip below.
2. **Desensitize your child.** By gradually exposing your children to their fears, you will be helping them to take progressive steps toward overcoming them.
3. **Clear up misconceptions.** Many fears are based on misconceptions. For instance, many children are afraid of thunder, but if you explain what it is, the fear will begin to give way to curiosity.

LEARN RELAXATION AND SELF-CALMING SKILLS

When children are continually unable to control their response to fear and anxiety, unhealthy reactions to this fear will become automatic. One

---

simple anytime relaxation tip:

Sigh breathing is an especially effective way to practice release-only relaxation and to help your child relax quickly. Simply have you child breathe in through his nose, hold it, and then sigh and relax, letting out all of his air. Children often enjoy exaggerating the sound of the sigh. (Repeat several times.)

common side effect of anxiety is sleeplessness (as many parents can attest to!). Although it is important to reduce the number of stressors in children's lives, especially when they're chronically anxious, we will never be able to completely eliminate them. But parents can help their children become more resilient to fear-inducing situations by teaching them how to purposefully quiet and relax themselves and thereby interrupt the fight-or-flight response.

It's very important to practice relaxation in a fun, imaginative way. The last thing you want your child to think is that relaxation is "just one more thing to do." After all, relaxation is not so much doing as it is an *undoing*, or a letting go. If you imagine that you are relaxed, your tension is likely to abate and your muscles will relax. In contrast, if you try to *will* youself to become relaxed, you are likely to become tense. Still, the ability to let go and relax will improve with practice. A daily routine of self-calming exercises is important in order that children learn to relax and quiet themselves whenever they feel the need to do so. At first, have children practice relaxation exercises when they are not frightened or overly anxious. It's best to practice them at least once, and preferably twice, a day. In order for children to relax when they encounter stressful situations, the relaxation response needs to become second nature. Progressive relaxation, breathing exercises, and visualizations not only facilitate sleep, they assuage stress. Stress cannot coexist with the state of relaxation. Children who can voluntarily relax will also have greater motor control as well as more poise, self-control, and an overall comfort with their bodies.

The more fearful and anxious the child, the more he needs to learn to relax. In addition to helping kids sleep, the techniques that are described in the *Floppy Sleep Game* program, and in the appendix, can effectively help frightened or anxious children to calm and relax themselves.

WHEN TO INCORPORATE RELAXATION EXERCISES

- **During transitions.** Before falling asleep, before and after an exciting event, after lunch, after an outing.
- **To decompress.** Use relaxation exercises to calm and focus after an energetic activity or frustrating event.

Children's fear can escalate into panic in a heartbeat and their behavior is likely to become irrational and unorganized. You see this most often when children have a specific phobia. For instance, if a child has a fear of spiders and one is approaching him, his fear can intensify quickly. At that point, he will probably be too upset to calm himself. After removing your child from the perceived fear, help him to use his relaxation skills to gain composure and calm down.

Have a cue that quickly and privately signals your child to use his relaxation skills to become calm or to focus. It can be a word, or a physical cue. Whether your child is prone to panic, aggression, meltdowns, or tantrums, try to give him the cue to relax before all control is lost. If possible, remove your child from the stressful situation and provide some quiet time to become calm. Anticipate problems that are likely to occur and give your children a chance to use their self-calming skills. This will take some keen observation on your part; however, most parents have developed a sixth sense regarding what is likely to upset their child.

The ultimate goal is to be able to relax quickly when faced with stressful situations. Have your child begin to practice relaxing directly after active activities when his heart rate is up. Then, have him practice when he seems a little annoyed or frustrated. While it often helps to practice relaxation with the eyes closed, if you are around other people and this makes your child self-conscious, it's not necessary. Associating a certain hand position with the state of relaxation can help to induce the relaxation response, as your child's unconscious mind begins to connect this cue with being calm and relaxed. For example, a cue could be holding a wrist with the other hand, putting a hand on the belly, or putting the thumbs and pointer fingers together. This could also be the same cue which you use as a signal to remind your child to relax.

Once your child becomes adept at "letting go," or relaxing, this calm state can be achieved quite quickly. In fact, with practice, children can learn to relax and bring their bodies back to a balanced, un-stressful state, just by purposefully relaxing in a few short moments. At first, count out loud for your child and give him the following directions. Later, he can do it on his own.

DIRECTIONS:

Close your eyes. Take two or three slow deep breaths,

breathing in and out through your nose.

Breathe in, one, two,

Hold, one, two,

Breathing out, one, two, three, four,

Breathing in, I am relaxed. (*Pause.*)

Breathing out, I am relaxed.

DESENSITIZE YOUR CHILD TO A PERCEIVED FEAR

Most fears can be successfully dealt with, simply by exposing your child to the object that he fears. However, this must be done very gradually. It's very effective to plan a series of small steps that will help your child get closer and closer to the thing he fears. It's important to be patient and let your child set the pace. As he gradually faces and overcomes his fear, a child will gain a feeling of confidence and self-mastery.

- Sing songs about the object of your child's fear.
- Read books and look at pictures. Begin with books that have cartoonlike pictures, gradually leading up to realistic photos.
- Watch TV, videos, and movies that put the feared object or creature in a positive light.
- Play act.
- Tell stories to help a child visualize positive interactions with the feared object or creature.

CLEAR UP MISCONCEPTIONS

It's best to talk with your children about fears and phobias at a time when they're not frightened. Unless it's a specific bedtime fear that needs to be dealt with at that time, try not to talk about your child's fears at bedtime. Earlier in the day, discuss the reality of the fear in a manner that's appropriate for your child's age and developmental level. Continuing with the example of a fear of dogs, you might help your child to understand a dog's behavior by telling him that while you shouldn't pet dogs that you don't know, most dogs are friendly and loving. Let your child know that a wagging tail usually indicates that a dog is friendly and that dogs bark to protect their home and family.

LEARN TO OVERCOME ANXIETY

Fear and anxiety are related. Primal anxiety always precedes fear, even if it's just for a split second. While fear is the feeling experienced in response to a clear and present danger, anxiety is the feeling experienced in response to a less tangible threat. When people say they are stressed out, they are generally referring to anxiety.

We have all experienced anxiety and it is, in fact, a normal part of life. Anxiety is not always negative. Healthy levels of anxiety can be a call to action and adventure; motivating students to complete assignments, performers to rehearse, and athletes to train. Anxiety can warn children of real problems and help prevent them from making poor decisions. For example, "street smarts" can be a beneficial state of anxiety; when children activate their nervous systems to a higher level of attentiveness it can help keep them alert and safe from harm. In some ways our society has a love-hate relationship with anxiety. If our anxiety level is too low, we may call it boredom and try to raise it in acceptable ways—for example, watching scary movies or taking part in competitive sports.

Anxiety can also be extremely destructive if it escalates into intense terror and panic. Anxiety triggers the fight-or-flight response, causing hormones and adrenaline (epinephrine) levels to increase and activate the alarm state. There is often a genetic predisposition to be overly anxious. Some kids are biologically wired to have an exaggerated fight-or-flight response. Their stress response can kick in over seemingly minor events such as a forgotten library book or lunch. Other children "roll with the punches" and are much more resilient to life's ups and downs.

When children don't have a handle on anxiety, it's likely to escalate when they become teenagers. Children who struggle with anxiety are more susceptible to developing depression and mood disorders. Anxious teens are at risk of becoming involved with drugs and alcohol in a desper-ate attempt to relieve their discomfort.

Anxiety is a much greater problem for children than society has recog-nized. Anxiety disorders are a reflection of children's distress and have be-come the number one psychological problem of both children and teens. Today, children are anxious and stressed for a lot of the same reasons that they are sleep deprived. Anxiousness often leads to sleeplessness and the resulting sleep deprivation leads to anxiousness, perpetuating a vicious cy-cle that wreaks havoc in millions of families. When children are at ease, there is less chance for their bodies to be at unease, or ill. Chronic stress and anxiety can lead to disease, which is aptly named because it is often preceded by dis-ease, a lack of relaxation and tranquillity. As parents, it's important to recognize the symptoms of childhood stress and to help our children pay attention to the signals that they get from their own bodies.

Watch for Anxiety Red Flags

Both of my daughters have suffered from anxiety, which resulted in stress. While my oldest daughter showed signs of anxiety from a very young age, my youngest daughter first began experiencing it as a teenager. In the midst of her suffering she asked me, "Why did this happen to me?"

Oftentimes, it takes some detective work on the part of a parent to fig-ure out what is causing their child's anxiety. For instance, your child may suddenly not want to go to school and it's up to you to figure out why. While some children are forthcoming with their feelings, others are not. Spend one-on-one time with your child and see if he will open up. When children are only three or four years old one of the best ways to reach them is through play. When young children are anxious about something, they may not even realize themselves that it is the source of their emotional and physical symptoms. Teach your kids that feeling upset and/or sick can be a red flag, signaling them that something is wrong.

PHYSICAL SYMPTOMS OF STRESS OR ANXIETY IN CHILDREN
- Recurring headaches
- Stomach pain and nausea
- Sleep disturbances, nightmares, bedwetting
- Decreased appetite
- Stuttering

EMOTIONAL SYMPTOMS OF STRESS OR ANXIETY IN CHILDREN
- Moodiness
- Difficulty with concentration (spaciness)
- Being easily upset, crying, whining, excessive anger
- Scary thoughts
- A tendency to worry a lot
- Low self-esteem
- Restlessness
- Clinging
- Aggression
- Stubbornness
- Not wanting to participate in family or school activities

THE MOST COMMON ANXIETY DISORDERS THAT AFFECT CHILDREN

SPECIFIC PHOBIAS Fear of a specific object, creature, or situation. Examples: fear of water, certain animals, storms.

SEPARATION ANXIETY Fear of being away from the main caregiver, typically the mother. Often, children with this disorder fear sleeping alone.

SELECTIVE MUTISM An inability to speak in certain social situations, such as school, but no trouble talking at home when they are more comfortable. (Ninety percent of children with selective mutism also have social phobia.)

SOCIAL PHOBIA Characterized by uncomfortable shyness and fear of being judged negatively by others.

GENERALIZED ANXIETY DISORDER Often described as worrywarts, children with generalized anxiety disorder frequently worry about a number of things in their lives. They are often particularly worried when they encounter a new situation.

POST-TRAUMATIC STRESS DISORDER This disorder can develop after a traumatic event. The child may have bad dreams, flashbacks, and vivid memories that keep replaying in his mind. It may cause sleep difficulties and an overactive startle response. It could occur after a robbery, a car accident, a natural disaster, or abuse.

OBSESSIVE-COMPULSIVE DISORDER The child repeats certain thoughts or actions. Sometimes, this disorder can be combined with other unusual behaviors, tics, and neurological problems. If you suspect your child has this disorder, be sure to seek the advice of a professional.

PANIC DISORDER Panic attacks occur unexpectedly and are accompanied by uncomfortable physical sensations such as dizziness, a racing heart, nausea, and trouble breathing. Typically, it affects teenagers, rather than children.

When children or adults feel anxious, naturally they want to relieve the uncomfortable feelings that come with it. If we face our anxiety and deal with it by quieting and calming ourselves and paying attention to our feelings, we grow from the experience. Because many children don't have the tools to do so, they often try to relieve themselves of their anxiety in unhealthy ways; by denying it exists, distracting themselves from it, or dumping it on others. When older children feel that they have no control over the anxious feelings that overwhelm them, they sometimes try to exert control in unhealthy ways such as binge eating or bulimic or anorexic behavior.

Unhealthy Ways That Children Respond to Anxiety

Denying

This involves stuffing anxiety and suppressing anxious feelings deep inside in the hope that they will disappear. Children who deny anxiety disown their own feelings and create inner walls in order to keep themselves from facing it. They may also put on a "happy face" because they think that's what the important people in their lives want to see.

Distracting

Distracting involves trying to keep as busy as possible in order to be distracted from anxiety. This is a common reaction of older children and teens who feel the need to be constantly busy or entertained so they won't have time to face their feelings. Behaviors could include overeating, over-doing, over-shopping, and watching too much TV. Teens could get involved in alcohol and drug use.

Dumping

Dumping anxiety involves trying to get rid of anxious feelings by putting them on others. Criticizing, blaming, manipulating, and being angry at others are examples of dumping. Children learn to blame at a very young age. "He made me do it" is a common childhood response to misbehavior. Begin to teach your child that while someone else may have done something that made him upset, he is still responsible for his reaction. This is a lesson that will need to be repeated many times throughout childhood.

Children often direct their hurtful, angry words toward their parents, because it's safest. Afterward, they can be filled with regret and may redirect the anger inward, toward themselves. Remind your child that it's important to learn from his mistake and that you forgive him. Encourage your son or daughter to count to ten or to take a few deep breaths before speaking while angry. If your child's verbal attack caused you to retort with your own angry and unkind words, you may wish to apologize as well. It's important that your child doesn't think that you no longer love him. This may sound obvious, but it's easy for parents to get their feelings hurt and withdraw or give their child the silent treatment after having hurtful comments hurled at them.

How to Model Positive Behavior for Your Child

Our children are deeply affected by our emotional states. Because there is a stong genetic component for anxiety, if you are a parent of a sensitive or anxious child, you may suffer from high anxiety yourself. If so, be sure that you are able to face and handle your own anxiety, not only to feel better yourself but also to model healthy behavior for your child. Your child is likely to follow your example. Kids have an uncanny ability to see through "do as I say" and go straight to "do as I do."

Our emotions are a built-in monitor that lets us know when all is well or if something is awry. Even if young children cannot name the emotion they are feeling, they can tell if they feel good or bad.

Teach your child to try to feel better by thinking about or remembering things that make him feel happy. This shows your child that he has control over a situation and that he can deliberately improve the way he feels. Children's stress response often improves when they feel they have more control over their life situations.

Get in the habit of telling your child how you feel. Empathize with his feelings, even if you don't agree with his actions. He will know that you love him unconditionally and it will help him to become more aware and better able to describe how he's feeling.

When children are emotionally upset, it rarely works to try to have a conversation about what is upsetting them at that time. Often, the best thing that parents can do is just give their full attention and listen. This type of silent, attentive listening is a vote of confidence and shows our children that we care and that we accept them without judgment. Sometimes it's best not to intervene with words of wisdom or help. When your child is done venting, simply validate the feelings that were expressed. This type of trust and support can give children the power to gain their own insight.

While most children don't like to be lectured to, almost all kids love to hear a story. Tell you child a story about someone else who was similarly upset by a comparable situation. Encourage your child to come up with solutions that will make the character feel better.

ANGER

Anger can be a common reaction to anxiety. Sometimes parents give children the message that it's never okay to express anger. Teaching children to deny how they feel is not the answer. Usually, anger feels bad to children; however, when they are shut down and depressed, it can actually provide some relief and move them in a positive direction.

It's not fun to be around children who are angry, and it's important not to stay angry. We certainly don't want anger to become our child's knee-jerk reaction to life's frustrations. However, if a child is angry, it is important that he learns how to express it in appropriate ways. Remind children to stop and try to calm themselves. Sigh breathing, diaphragmatic breathing, or counting to ten can help them to become calm enough to express their anger appropriately. Let children know that it's normal to feel angry, but that expressing anger by hurting others or breaking things is not acceptable.

Anger often comes from a feeling of impotence or powerlessness, a belief that there is nothing that can be done to change or improve an unfair or uncomfortable situation. Even if there is no tangible action taken to resolve the problem, a change in attitude may be helpful. When children's angry and hateful feelings are expressed and listened to, they can usually move through the emotion and feel better afterward. While it's commonly believed that blowing off steam by punching a pillow or a punching bag releases anger, research suggests that such activities can actually increase anger and aggression. Slow, sustained exercise such as tai chi and yoga may be a more beneficial way to help children dissipate their anger and become more aware of their feelings.

Always be aware of your child's developmental level. Conversation may not be as useful as imaginary play when you're trying to help your three- or four-year-old express and work through anger. For older children, journal writing can be a particularly effective way to express their anger and other feelings. Writing an uncensored letter to the person a child is angry with and then ripping it up also can help a child to release anger.

WORRY

Most children seem to be born optimists. They have a wonderful feeling of expectation and anticipation and have absolute faith that their desires will be attained. However, some children seem to be born worriers. They may be worried about speaking in front of the class, that they are stupid, that no one will like them, and so forth. The list of worries can go on and on. Children who worry a lot are great candidates for visualization and imagery. The truth is, worry is negative visualization and it takes a vivid imagination to imagine such horrible scenarios!

Worrying is one of the most disregarded forms of stress. It is wanting or desiring things to go your own way, but focusing on what will happen if it doesn't. For example a child may be convinced that he is going to fail a test. If that is all that he can think of as he takes the test, it's likely to become a self-fulfilling prophecy. When your child is worried about something specific, help him to come up with some affirmations to repeat to himself. They can be particularly effective when they're used in conjunction with slow, relaxed, deep breathing.

Many parents, myself included, have a tendency to worry about their children. Worrying projects negative energy and it doesn't do you or your child a bit of good. In fact, when children are aware that you are worried about them it projects a lack of faith and they tend to feel more anxious.

Of course, there are times when our worries may be well-founded. Even then, try to focus on the positive outcome that you desire and on actions that can help to bring it about.

While many children are outspoken about their thoughts and worries, others are more likely to keep them to themselves. If you suspect that your child has unspoken worries or fears, some gentle probing may be in order. Sometimes, you just have to be available when they're ready to talk. My son kept a lot of his thoughts to himself; however, he would be more likely to open up and talk when we were riding in the car together.

If a child has not learned to relax his body and turn off the negative thoughts and worries that fill his mind, the stillness of bedtime can be particularly difficult. The uncomfortable sensations associated with anxiety are likely to make a child avoid going to bed. He won't want to lie in bed with nothing to distract himself from a head full of worries and a body that reacts to them with discomfort.

I feel that it would have been remiss to write a book about children and sleep without having discussed stress and anxiety. It's an important sleep issue because you can be almost certain that an anxious, stressed child will have trouble sleeping. Could there be anything less condusive to sleep than worrying? The worried mind is like a runaway train that keeps gathering momentum. However, children can learn to stop the runaway train. And when a child's thoughts turn toward their hopes, dreams, and desires, rather than their worries and fears, they will be able to relax and consequently sleep. And you can rest assured that a carefree, relaxed, and tranquil child will be able to "sleep like a baby."

MAINTAINING SLEEP SUCCESS

When a child is anxious, his thoughts are focused on some sort of danger, or an uncomfortable situation. His imagination has kicked into high gear but it's keeping him from sleeping, rather than helping him to sleep. It's in direct contrast to using the imagination to visualize wonderful images that make drifting off to sleep enjoyable. Teach your child that he has the power to lose those fearful thoughts and choose positive thoughts, delightful visualizations and affirmations instead.

Often, a parent may be unaware that troubling thoughts are keeping their child awake at night. It's important to talk with your child about his worries and fears so that he doesn't keep them stuffed inside. When you are aware of your child's fears and anxieties, you can take steps to help him overcome them. Often, by talking to your child about his worries or fears, you can help him to realize that he has blown them out of proportion. You can also give him suggestions on how to deal with a difficult situation. Don't bring up troubling issues at bedtime unless it's something your child wants to discuss. And have your child get in the habit of putting his worries out of his mind before he goes to sleep. (See Seven Ways to Put Worries to Bed, pp. 134–136)

An anxious child will feel physically uncomfortable and will have a difficult time falling asleep. However, relaxation techniques can help your child to calm his body and relieve the uncomfortable sensations. And when a child's body becomes calm, his mind will follow suit.

Overcoming Anxiety for a Healthy Life

You may recall that toward the beginning of this chapter, my daughter asked the profound question regarding her anxiety, "Why did this happen to me?" Today, her anxiety has lessened considerably. She recently told me that she doesn't regret a single thing that has ever happened to her because she has learned from every problem and mistake. Believe me, this was music to my ears! My daughter believes that if she had not experienced anxiety and bouts of depression that stemmed from her reaction to it that she would not have the same understanding of other people's pain. I agree. Although no parent wants their child's life to be difficult, there is no doubt that the pain of anxiety has helped my daughter to become more compassionate, empathetic, and nonjudgmental. She has already been able to help one of her friends release the tight grips of anxiety.

I believe that many, if not most of our children's problems come from their inability to deal with anxiety in a healthy way. I mentioned earlier that our emotions are a built-in monitor that let us know if all is well. Our monitor comes with a warning device, which is anxiety. When we refuse to pay attention to its warning, we become out of touch with our true selves, our true nature and wholeness. Children who can't be themselves develop tension and/or self-suppression. Of course, children will not be aware that this is the source of their anxiety and parents need to begin teaching their children to be aware of their feelings, to identify them and face them.

In our society, it's certainly understandable how children can become overly focused on their superficial aspects, rather than their innermost feelings. When a child's sense of self-worth doesn't come from within, it's likely to come from the feedback of the outside world. This attitude is likely to become intensified when your child becomes a teenager and it's important to begin planting the seeds of inner knowing at an early age.

Children who have anxiety suffer needlessly. We cannot protect our children (or ourselves) from every painful experience; however, by teaching our children to be aware and accepting of how they feel and giving them the tools to courageously face their emotions and anxious feelings, we can prevent it from becoming suffering. Anxiety can lead to inner peace and can actually be an opportunity to learn and grow.

Anxiety does not have to be a lifelong problem. I remember being so afraid to speak in front of my class in junior high that my whole body shook. Now, I speak at educational seminars across the country and also enjoy performing at concerts. I remember being so upset if someone was rude to me that I dwelled on it for hours. Now, I can't remember the last time anyone was rude; I'm sure it's because I'm no longer overly sensitive to what other people say. When children are relaxed and tranquil, they will no longer be fearful or anxious. Ease of being comes from a letting go, getting our personalities and egos out of the way, and having an awareness of spirit. When children become quiet, their bodies and minds reveal a lot of healing wisdom. Relaxation techniques provide a framework and the fertile ground for something wonderful to grow. That something wonderful is your child's inner self, or soul. I've often heard the analogy of the ocean, which has waves on the surface, while its inner depths are calm. We live in a world that is filled with waves. Don't let your children get carried away by the current. Start teaching them to explore their own inner depths and help them to discover the peace and goodness of who they are. Eventually, even if the outside world is "making waves," your children will still be able to have peace within their own hearts.

Conclusion

We have covered a lot of ground: healthy sleep habits, diet, sleep disturbances, the *Floppy Sleep Game* program, and ways to maintain sleep success throughout the ups and downs of childhood. Establishing healthy sleep habits and teaching your child to fall asleep independently are wonderful accomplishments. But you may not realize that in addition to helping your child to sleep well, you have also helped him to feel safe, loved, and valued.

Parents do many things to ensure their children's safety. For instance, they teach their children not to ever get into a car with a stranger. But it's also important for parents to be aware of and identify the less obvious enemies such as overstimulation, overscheduling, and extensive television exposure. Once the opponents to a child's well-being have been identified, a parent can take steps to minimize their influence.

If parents had the power to do so, they would make the world 100 percent safe for their children—and completely free of anything that could possibly harm them. But as children become older and more independent, parents will not be able to control everything that their kids are exposed to. However, by making your home a haven from the outside world, your child will feel safe and secure and he will be also be more likely to be able to relax and fall asleep in the evening. And the relaxation techniques that he has learned will also help him to feel safe, by helping him to gain control of his body and mind by purposefully relaxing them.

Your child will also feel safe, secure and loved when you consistently take the time to share loving, familiar bedtime rituals. This is a time to come together and share your love at the end of the day, before being separated during the night.

And while it's very important for a child to feel loved, it's also important for him to feel valued, accepted, and appreciated. Be aware of destructive attitudes that may be impacting your children. Our society has very narrow parameters regarding the traits that are deemed to be desirable. At an early age, these attitudes begin to affect children, who begin to base their self-worth on whether they're good at school, popular, athletic, or good-looking.

By attending our children's events and celebrating their accomplishments we show them that we value what they do. And accepting their individual nature shows them that we value who they are. But most important, a child needs to value himself, not only for what he does but for who he is. A child who bases his self-worth solely on his accomplishments is likely to fall apart when things inevitably go wrong. He is also likely to lie in bed, replaying his mistakes, rather than sleeping. A child who has an understanding of his true value will be able to weather the storms and learn from his mistakes, rather than becoming overly distressed by them. Taking a few minutes each night to focus inward, rather than outward, will help children to discover their own value and self-worth and it will help them to peacefully fall asleep.

I'd like to extend my heartfelt wish that each and every one of your children feels safe, loved, and valued. And may that knowledge enable him to sleep peacefully. In closing, I'd like to encourage you to slow down and enjoy this wonderful season in your life by sharing a poem that was published several years ago in my daughter's school newsletter. (It was written by an anonymous young girl who was terminally ill.)

SLOW DOWN, DON'T DANCE SO FAST

Have you ever watched kids on a merry-go-round?

Or listened to the rain slapping on the ground?

Ever followed a butterfly's erratic flight?

Ever gazed at the sun in the fading light?

You'd better slow down, don't dance so fast.

Time is short, the music won't last.

Do you run through each day on the fly?

When you ask, "How are you?" do you hear the reply?

When the day is done do you lie in your bed,

with the next hundred chores running through your head?

You'd better slow down, don't dance so fast.

Time is short, the music won't last.

Ever told your child, "We'll do it tomorrow," and in your haste not see his
    sorrow?

Ever lost touch, let a good friendship die,

'cuz you didn't have time to call and say "Hi."

You'd better slow down, don't dance so fast.

Time is short, the music won't last.

When you run so fast to get somewhere,

you miss the fun of getting there.

When you worry and hurry through your day,

it's like an unopened gift . . . thrown away.

Life is not a race, do take it slower. Hear the music before the song is over.

bedtime activities and rituals

MOVEMENT 256

MASSAGE 261

STRETCHING WITH YOGA 262

READING AND STORYTELLING 275

PRAYER 287

MOVEMENT

Music and Movement

For adults as well as children, it can be very relaxing to listen to soothing music while stretching. Young children love to combine music, or chants with their movements. Be sure to sing or chant the rhymes in a soothing voice and encourage slow sustained movements so your child doesn't become too excited or energized just before bed.

Grow Garden Grow

Excerpt from "Grow Garden Grow" (song) by Patti Teel

MUSIC	MOVEMENTS
I plant my seeds in the early spring,	Crouch down on the floor.
water each morning and start to sing,	
little seeds of mine, time to rise and shine,	Slowly begin to rise, stand on tiptoes and stretch both arms up.
and greet the morning sun.	
Grow garden grow, grow garden grow,	Slowly stretch higher and higher.
	Stretch hands down to the ground.
your strong roots below grow and grow,	Slowly begin to rise, stand on tiptoes, and stretch both arms up.
Grow garden grow.	

(Repeat.)

If your child has trouble separating from you, during the day or at bedtime, "Tick Tock" may be particularly reassuring.

Tick Tock

Excerpt from *Kids World* (CD) by Patti Teel

WORDS

My mommy (daddy) loves me
higher than the highest tree,
deeper than the deepest sea.
She'll (he'll) always come back
   to me,
(Repeat.)

MOVEMENT

Child stretches on tiptoes,
   reaching arms up.
Reach down to the ground.
Parent and child hug.

Sky so Blue

(Tune: "Twinkle, Twinkle, Little Star")

WORDS

Way up high in the sky so blue
Two little clouds said "hi" to you
The wind blew the clouds as
   hard as it could
Down came the raindrops,
They felt good
The wind blew the clouds
As hard as it could
Down came the raindrops
And they felt good!

MOVEMENTS

Reach on tiptoes, arms up to
   the sky.
Stretch up, close and open fingers.
Stretch arms from side to side.
Flutter fingers down to the ground.

Stretch up, arms swaying.

Flutter fingers down the body, legs,
   and down to the ground.

Row, Row, Row Your Boat

WORDS	MOVEMENTS
Row, row, row your boat gently down the stream Merrily, merrily, merrily, merrily life is but a dream	Parent and child sit on the floor facing each other, hands clasped and legs extended. Gently rock backward and forward with a rowing motion.

Variation: Do the same movement with legs wide open. Depending on the parent's flexibility, feel free to make adjustments.

Great Big Elephant
(Tune: "The Itsy Bitsy Spider")

WORDS	MOVEMENTS
The great BIG elephant went out one day to play. Down came the rain and then he couldn't stay.	Clasp hands, bend over, and swing trunk.

Hands flutter toward the ground. |
| Out came the sun and dried up all the rain. The great BIG elephant came out to play again. | Arms outstretched, make an arc toward the sun. Clasp hands, bend over, and swing trunk. |

Motor Boat

WORDS	MOVEMENTS
Tiptoe up, tiptoe down	Stretch up on toes, down on heels,
Start your motor	deep knee bend, arm motion
And turn around	mimics starting a motor.
(Repeat.)	Turn slowly, keeping the knees
	deeply bent.

The Great Big Cat

WORDS	MOVEMENTS
A great big cat	Stand on tiptoes, arms outstretched.
saw a wee little mouse.	Get down on all fours.
He looked all around	While on all fours, twist your head
the high, high house.	around to see your feet. Twist
The wee little mouse	the other way.
got caught at last.	Sit back on heels, arms outstretched.
Now the great big cat	Spread knees apart, sit on heels,
is asleep on his mat.	head on the floor, put hands
	over head.
	Stay on heels, put head on the
	floor, arms outstretched in front
	on the floor.
	(Pretend to sleep.)

Drive Down the Freeway

WORDS	MOVEMENT
Drive down the freeway, drive down the freeway, drive down the freeway, stop.	Sit on the floor, legs straight out in front. Hands are pretend cars, driving down each leg. When they get to the toes, stop and hold the stretch.
Down goes the traffic gate.	Stretch arms straight up, then place hands by hips, arms straight.
Up goes the drawbridge.	Bend knees.
Under go the little boats, all in a row.	Have fingers be pretend boats, floating under the bent knees.

MASSAGE

Loving touch in the form of a massage can be very soothing and relaxing for children. You may wish to tell a story as you give the massage or your child may want to listen to relaxing music or a story on tape.

Begin with a light touch and gradually add more pressure as you experiment to find out what feels best to your child as you massage his hands and feet, back, shoulders, neck, and legs. If your child has sore points, find them and gently return to work on them, kneading with thumb pressure.

When you massage your child's hands, use an allover firm thumb pressure. Rub both sides of your child's hands and massage their fingers, starting at the base and working toward the fingertips, pressing on their nailbeds with your thumb and forefinger. Massage your child's whole foot, again watching for and returning several times to any tender areas. *If you're trying to teach your children to go to sleep independently, don't continue to massage them as they drift off to sleep or they are likely to have trouble falling asleep without it.*

After the massage you may wish to try to remove blockages and get energy flowing in the following way: have your child lie on his back with closed eyes. Rub your hands together until they feel nice and warm. Keep one of your hands about 1½ to 2 inches above your child's body and make long sweeping *upward* passes from the sternum or from the bottom of the feet, all the way up the midline of the body and over the crown of the head. Your children may enjoy closing their eyes and telling you where your hands are as they feel the energy moving throughout their bodies.

STRETCHING WITH YOGA

Many parents may want to incorporate gentle stretches into their child's bedtime routine. Stretching is a wonderful way to de-stress; it reduces muscle tension and improves circulation by increasing the blood flow.

Neck Stretches

Neck and shoulder stretches can remove tension and help children to relax or fall asleep. It's a good idea to do a few neck stretches before continuing with more intense stretches or yoga asanas.

The Marionette
(track 2 on the *Floppy Sleep Game* book CD)

SETTING THE STAGE:
Have you ever seen a marionette? It's a puppet that has strings attached to it. The puppet master moves the marionette's strings to make it move. Pretend that you are a marionette. Sit cross-legged. Because you are made of wood, your back is very straight. Your hands are on your knees. You have

a string attached to each of your arms, your legs, and the top of your head. The puppet master is getting ready to put on a puppet show with you.

Head Up, Head Down

DIRECTIONS:

The string from your head releases and you drop your head forward so that you're looking down at your belly. Then the string moves your head back up straight. The string releases and your head drops back so that you are looking up at the ceiling. The puppet master practices having you move your head slowly and smoothly; forward and back and forward and back, again forward and back . . . and once again forward and again back. And now, your head is upright and you're looking straight ahead.

Head Left, Head right

DIRECTIONS:

Without moving your shoulders the puppet master slowly turns your head as far to the right as it can go. And now your head comes back to the front. Now your head turns as far to the left as it can. Now your head comes back to the front. Again to the right, back to the front, to the left and front again, to the right, back to the front, the left, back to the front.

Ear to Shoulder

DIRECTIONS:

The puppet master puts your right ear toward your right shoulder, but it doesn't actually touch your shoulder. And now he brings your head up. To the left. And the head comes up. The puppet master does not lift your shoulders, only your head. To the right and up. To the left and again up. To the right and up, to the left and up.

Chin Out, Chin In

DIRECTIONS:

The puppet master has you drop your chin slightly. Then he extends your neck as far out in front of you as it can go. Then he brings your chin in, forming a double chin. You don't drop your head but your chin comes in as you form a double chin. And repeat. All the way out and back in, all the way out and in. Again, all the way out and back in.

Slow Head Circles
DIRECTIONS:
The puppet master drops your hands onto your knees. You begin moving your head in a slow circle over your right shoulder and back and over your left shoulder and forward in slow, slow, circles. Make three more slow circles with your head. Now circle to the left by moving your head slowly over your left shoulder and back and over your right shoulder and forward. Slowly circle your head around three more times.

The Shoulder Drop
DIRECTIONS:
The puppet master lifts up your shoulders as you take in a deep breath. As you breathe out, he drops your shoulders suddenly. And again up and down and up and down and up and down.

The No, No, No Movement
DIRECTIONS:
Now the puppet master has you turn your head from side to side as if you're saying no, no, no, no, no, no, no.

Shoulder Circles
DIRECTIONS:
The puppet master rotates your shoulders in full, slow circles. Now, he circles your shoulders the other way.

Relaxed and Ready
DIRECTIONS:
It's almost time for the puppet show to begin. The puppet master wants to be sure that you are relaxed and ready for the show. He has you shake your

hands. Then, he has you rub your left shoulder with your right hand. Now with your left hand, massage your right shoulder.

Yoga

Yoga postures and deep breathing before bedtime can help kids to relax and sleep. Yoga works muscles and organs that most other forms of exercise don't touch. Its greatest gift may be that it puts children in touch with their own bodies, locating and quieting the sources of physical and emotional tension.

Don't expect yoga for children to be the same as yoga for adults. If you overzealously try to correct your child's positioning, it is likely to take the enjoyment out of it. Longtime yoga instructor Dr. Kaye says that for children, the movements are "very imprecise." Rather than concentrating on the technical aspects of the asanas, consider the practice with children as an introduction to the joy of yoga. Children love to assume the role of flowers, animals, and trees and they will be entranced when you incorporate postures into imaginative stories.

Enjoy doing yoga poses several times a week. Depending on your child's attention span, you may wish to start with five poses or less. Asanas are body movements, or poses, associated with the body conditioning of yoga. Try to use complementary stretches that follow one another. For instance, forward movements are followed and complemented by backward movements and a twisting movement to the right should be followed by a twisting movement to the left, in order to balance the body.

Encourage your child to use diaphragmatic (belly) breathing with the movements. Generally, an upward body movement is accompanied by an inhalation and a downward body movement is accompanied by an exhalation.

Tip: Don't insist that children are quiet in their yoga poses; let them be free to hiss like a cobra or meow like a cat.

Tip: Never strain in any of the asanas (postures) and repeat each pose.

Between poses, or whenever they would like to rest encourage your children to relax in child's pose.

Child's Pose

DIRECTIONS:

Sit back on your heels with knees apart.

Stretch foreword and place your forehead on the floor.

You may stretch your arms in front of you,

or put them by your sides, palms up.

COMBINING STORYTELLING AND YOGA

It's Bedtime in the Rain Forest

PREPARATION:

It's bedtime in the jungle.

Pretend you're walking through the rain forest in the evening.

Many of the animals are getting ready to go to sleep.

You come upon a stretching tiger.

She sees you and asks you to stretch with her.

THE TIGER

DIRECTIONS:

Get on your hands and knees with your hands directly below your shoulders.

Arch your back as far as you can, letting your head and shoulders round.

Pull in your tummy and hiss like a tiger if you'd like.

Now release your back, drop it to curve as far as possible, head and chest lifted. (You and the tiger stretch a few more times.)

The tiger lies down and goes to sleep. (*Optional: child's pose.*)
You look down and see a friendly cobra slithering toward you.
He wants you to stretch with him.

THE COBRA

DIRECTIONS:

Lie on your belly with the palms of your hands under your shoulders,
forehead on the floor. (*Fingertips should be pointed away from the body.*)
Take a deep breath in and lift up your head, neck, and upper back.
(*Direct your child to keep the pelvic area firmly on the floor.*)
Keep your elbows bent. (*Hold.*) Stick out your tongue, if you'd like.
Lower your chest and head back down to the floor, letting out a long
hiss.
Turn your head to the side, lie your hands down by your side with
your palms up, and rest.
(*Repeat pose, resting head in the opposite direction afterward.*)

The snake hears the roar of a lion and slithers away.
The lion did not mean to scare the snake.
He just wants to show you his bedtime stretches.

THE LION

DIRECTIONS:

Sit on your heels.
Put your hands on your knees, keeping your arms straight.
Sit up straight and tall.
Breathe in and open your mouth wide.
Stick out your tongue down toward your chin.
Open your eyes wide. Look at the tip of your nose.
Stretch your fingers straight out and keep your hands on your knees.
Roar!
(*Repeat two more times.*)

Benefits: The Lion relaxes parts of the body that most asanas don't: the face, jaw, mouth, throat, and tongue. It is particularly good for children who grind their teeth.

Thank You, World
(Gratitude Sequence One)

DIRECTIONS:

1. Begin with feet hip-width apart. Your arms are rising like the beautiful round sun. Slowly bring both arms out to your sides, stretching and reaching out with your arms and fingers (palms up) as you slowly reach up toward the sky. Lace your fingers together (palms up) and stretch as tall as you can toward the sky. You can try to reach even taller by standing on your tiptoes. Hold it. Hold it. Hold it. As the sun sets you stretch your arms out as far as you can and slowly, slowly, bring them back down to your sides as you lower your feet to the ground. Feel the sun's heat in your fingers.

   "Thank you, sun!"

DIRECTIONS:

2. Again, slowly bring both arms out to your sides (palms up), stretching and reaching out with your arms, until your arms are reaching straight up toward the sky. As you breathe in, bend backward, stretching your arms back and looking up at the beautiful moon.

   "Thank you, moon!"

FORWARD BEND

DIRECTIONS:

3. Stretch your arms and fingers out as far as you can and begin to bring them down as you slowly bend forward toward the ground. Keep your legs straight, let your head hang down, and put your hands flat on the floor.

    Bend your knees if you have to, otherwise keep your legs straight. (*Hold.*)

    "Thank you, Earth!"

    Slowly, slowly, begin to uncurl your spine and stand up as straight and tall as a tree.

TREE POSE

DIRECTIONS:

4. Place your left hand on the wall. Place your right foot on your left inner thigh to make a branch. Put your hands together in the prayer position at chest level, or stretch them up like branches on a tree. Try to be as still and strong as a tree. (*Encourage your child to hold the pose. If your child is balanced, remove the hand from the wall.*) Bring your right foot back down to the ground. Bring your hands back down to your sides.

    "Thank you, tree!" (*Repeat on the other side.*)

> **Tip:** Focusing on a point a few feet away at eye level (a *drishti* point) can also help with balance.

SIDE BEND (PALM TREE)

DIRECTIONS:

5. Make believe that you are still a tree. Stand up straight and tall with your feet hip-distance apart. The wind is going to blow your branches but your legs are like the trunk of a tree, unmoving and strong. Take a deep breath in. Breathe out as you bend the upper body gently to the right. The right arm drops along the side of the

right leg. Dangle the head toward the right shoulder. The left arm stretches and drops over the head. *(Hold the pose.)* Take a deep breath in and stand up tall and straight, bringing your hands back down to your sides. Now the wind is blowing in the other direction. Take a deep breath in. Breathe out and bend to the left. The head bends toward the left shoulder and the right arm stretches over your head. *(Hold the pose.)* Now, slowly stand up straight and bring your hands back to your sides.

"Thank you, wind!"

Thank You, World
(Gratitude Sequence Two)

This sequence is a bit more difficult than the first one because it involves more balancing poses. For younger children, ages four to seven, start with the first gratitude sequence.

SIMPLE WARRIOR
DIRECTIONS:

1. Stand up straight and raise your arms above your head. Step forward on your right foot, putting your weight on it. Put one hand on the wall. Breathe in and lift your left leg while stretching forward. Keep raising your left leg and stretching forward. Bring your arms out to your sides if you'd like, as if they're wings. You're flying! *(Hold the pose.)* Lower your left leg and stand up tall and straight. *(Repeat on the other side. Your child is likely to need a hand on a wall for balance. As balance improves, have your child attempt to remove the hand from the wall. Try to have your child's head, torso, and back leg in alignment with each other, forming a ninety-degree angle with the standing leg.)*
   "Thank you, bird!"

Squatting

directions:

2. Slowly bend your knees and squat down like a frog. Place your hands on your knees, or put them in front of you to make balancing easier. (If you can, put your heels down on the ground.)

"Thank you, frog!"

(If you'd like to, do a "partner squat." Both you and your child squat, facing one another. Try to lower your heels and hold each other's hands.)

Head to Heels

directions:

3. Sit up tall with your legs stretched out in front of you. Bend your knees and put the soles of your feet together. *(The soles of the feet should be at about the spot where your child's knees were, when they were outstretched.)* Clasp your feet with your hands and bring your forehead toward your heels. *(Elbows should be bent outward.)* You are wrapped up in your little cocoon.

"Thank you, cocoon!"

Cobbler

directions:

4. Butterflies break free from their cocoons and become butterflies. Sit up tall, but keep the soles of your feet together. Bring your feet close to your body. Your knees and legs are butterfly wings. Gently, flutter your knees down toward the floor.

"Thank you, butterfly!"

Rocking

directions:

5. Stretch your legs out in front of you and gently shake them out. Now, bend your knees. Place your hands loosely under your knees. You are a roly-poly bug. Your body bends forward. Keep your back rounded. Rock back. Rock forward. Back and forward.

Back and forward. Make sure you keep your back rounded and your chin down. *(Rock back and forth five or six times.)*

"Thank you, roly-poly bug!"

(For older children, you can begin to teach them to inhale as they go forward, and exhale as they go back up. It is also more challenging for them to try to keep their balance without letting their feet touch the ground when they roll forward.)

Below, I'll list the directions to a few postures that children usually enjoy. The instructions are fairly specific; however, it would be best to use fewer words and do the asanas with your children, letting them follow your example. While you should encourage your children to hold the postures, they should never strain.

ADDITIONAL POSES THAT YOUR CHILDREN MAY ENJOY

AGAINST THE WALL
DIRECTIONS:
Put your bottom as close to a wall as you can. Lay back with your legs resting against the wall. Have your legs be windshield wipers. One leg at a time, slowly open your leg and then bring it back to meet the other leg. Then, slowly spread both legs apart, then bring them together, apart and then together.

WALKING UP THE WALL
DIRECTIONS:
Get on your hands and knees, facing away from the wall. *(Child's feet should be a few inches from the wall.)* Begin to walk your legs up the wall behind you, supporting yourself with your hands.

COWSHEAD

(This asana is useful for relieving tension in the upper back and neck.) Ask your child, "Can you have one hand go down your back while the other hand goes up your back and still hold your own hands?"

DIRECTIONS:

Stretch toward the ceiling with your right hand and bend the arm at the elbow, trying to touch the middle of your back. Place the left hand with the palm up in the middle of your back and clasp your hands together in the middle of your back. *(If your child cannot clasp hands, use a cloth held in the right hand and clasp the cloth with the left hand. Repeat on the other side.)*

BRIDGE

(While most children have limber backs, if you are doing the asanas with your child and have any back trouble, you may wish to eliminate the arch in your back and only raise your back to a forty-five-degree angle.)

DIRECTIONS:

You are going to make a bridge with your body. Lie on your back. Bend your knees, keeping your feet flat on the floor. If you can, clasp the ankles. If not, place the hands palms down by the side of your body. Lift your bottom and arch your back. *(At this point, the hands may be placed underneath the buttocks to increase the arch or they can remain clasping the ankles.)*

ROCK YOUR BABY

This stretch is a great hip opener. (It's also a great stretch during pregnancy for mothers to be.)

DIRECTIONS:

Sit up tall with both legs straight out in front of you. Pick up your left foot, (bending your left knee) and put it in the crook of your right elbow. Wrap your left arm around the outside of your left leg and join both hands together. Pretend your left leg is a baby, and rock it back and forth. Try to sit up tall. (*Switch sides and repeat.*)

The Bow
DIRECTIONS:
You are going to make a boat with your body. Lie on your belly with your hands at your sides (palms up). Rest your forehead on the floor. Bend both your legs at the knees and bring them toward your bottom. Reach back and hold each foot with your hands. (*If you cannot grasp both feet, reach one foot with one hand and alternately reach the other hand and foot.*) Raise your knees and thighs off the floor and raise your head and upper body off the floor. (Pull your arms and legs against each other.) Keep your head back and up as far as you can. You're a boat! Hold. Rock back and forth if you'd like to. Don't forget to breathe. Slowly lower yourself down. Straighten out your legs and rest with your palms up and head turned to the side. (*Repeat and rest your head on the other side.*)

Nose-to-Knee Pose
DIRECTIONS:
Have you hugged your knees today? Lie flat on your back. Place the hands by the side of the body and draw the right knee to the chest while trying to touch your knee to your nose. Give your knee a good-night kiss. (*The shin is clasped so that the stretch is even more pronounced.*) Lower your leg back down slowly. (*Repeat on the left side.*) Bring both knees in to your chest, holding your legs with both hands. Give them a hug. Gently rock from side to side, if you'd like.

The Spread-Leg Stretch
DIRECTIONS:
Sit on the floor and stretch your legs wide apart. Keep them straight. Put your hands on the floor in front of you and begin to walk your hands as far away as you can, while you bend forward with your body. Try to make yourself as flat as a pancake. (*Hold.*) Walk your hands back and sit up tall.

Then, keeping both hips down on the floor, walk your hands and upper body down your right leg. Sit up tall and repeat on the left side.

T-Twist
(*The T-twist is useful for freeing up the lower back and releasing tension in the area.*)

DIRECTIONS:

Make your body into a T by lying on your back with straight arms extending from your shoulders. Bend your knees toward your chest and begin dropping them to the left, toward the ground. Keep the shoulders, arms, and hands pressed toward the ground. Slowly bring the knees back to the center and then drop them to the right, toward the ground. Bring them back to center and stretch out your arms and legs. (*Repeat.*)

READING AND STORYTELLING

Bedtime stories and poems will reinforce the love of reading. It's not the time for dark stories or fairy tales with evil characters that may frighten your child. Also, be aware of the messages that children may be absorbing from fairy tales. For instance, in fairy tales, the ugly characters are almost always evil while beauty is a girl's most important attribute. When you read fairy tales, you may want to modify them so they're not so scary, change some of the stereotypes, or just be sure to comment on how silly some of the messages are.

BETWEEN US

Patti Teel

Between us, my daughter, the stories aren't true
The one where Prince Charming must come rescue you
Learn to be strong and do things on your own
Then you can choose what you'll do when you're grown

Between us, my sons, the stories aren't true
The ones where the conqueror has to be you
Don't start a fight to show you are strong
Or prove you're right and the others are wrong

The only time fairy tales really come true
Are when they are written and starred in by you
Rewrite your story in your own way
Each page of your life is a wonderful day

Storytelling

It's a shame that storytelling seems to be a lost art. Children often prefer to be told a story, rather than read one. When you tell a story, you create a special bond with your child. It's as if you and your child are dancing as you automatically adapt your tone, facial expression, pace, and length of the story in response to your child's reactions. As children listen to stories, they use their imaginations, "seeing" characters and scenes in their minds. Because children create their own pictures they are very involved in the story and more likely to remember the characters, sequence, and moral. As all parents know, children love repetition and the same story can be retold many, many times. The wonderful thing about storytelling is that, like visualizations, you can adapt them to your child's interests, teach specific lessons, and help your child solve individual problems. Don't forget to tell your children some of the fables and stories you enjoyed when you were a child. You can always adapt them to make them less scary. (Suggestions: *The Ugly Duckling, The Boy Who Cried Wolf, The Tortoise and the Hare, The Gingerbread Man, Goldilocks and the Three Bears, The Elves and the Shoemaker, Cinderella,* and *Jack and the Beanstalk.*)

Storytelling can be used for the following:

- Foster cultural appreciation.
- Expand knowledge.
- Sheer enjoyment.
- To build character and values.
- Inspire action and solve problems. It's very effective to help children solve real-life personal problems through storytelling. As mentioned earlier, some children like stories to be about themselves and others feel more comfortable when the story is about someone else.

If you're telling a story to help your child solve a problem the following steps may be helpful.

1. Introduce your characters.
2. Describe the problem that your character is facing.
3. Visit a wise animal or person who shares an insight or gives clues to help the character solve the problem.
4. Have the character solve the problem in a unique and imaginative way.
5. End the story by summarizing the lesson.

Storytelling may come very naturally to you, or it may be something new. Often, once you find a theme that your child enjoys, you can continue to build upon it. For instance, the stories may take place in a particular setting or you may create characters that become familiar and reappear frequently in the stories that you tell.

Stories with a Purpose

I wrote the following story to help children face their fear of monsters. I recommend it for children ages five and up. Be sure that your presentation is playful so that children don't find it scary. If your child enjoys the Willy Monster character, you may wish to have this brave and protective monster become a frequent character in the stories you tell. *If your children like stories to be about themselves, substitute Stephen's name with your child's name.*

Willy Monster
Bedtime Fears Go Away

Patti Teel

Theme: One step at a time, you can face your fears and overcome them.

Once upon a dream there lived a good and kind monster named Willy. This is a story about Willy and his friends. Perhaps you are one of them.

Willy Monster lives on a faraway planet. The children on Earth are Willy's friends. He watches over his friends and makes sure they are safe at night when they sleep. When a child on Earth needs him, Willy rides his lightning bolt down to Earth in a flash. Whenever Willy calls out, "*Thunder,*" Lightning Bolt appears and takes him wherever he wants to go.

Stephen is a little boy who lives on Earth. He likes to ride his bike, and practices sharp, skidding stops that leave black marks on his driveway.

One evening, while Willy is cruising through the sky on Lightning Bolt, practicing his 360s, Stephen is in bed, staring at the dark shadows in his room. He thinks that they look like monsters. Whenever he feels like this he asks his mother to tell him about Willy Monster. His mother sings him a song,

Once upon a dream, a monster brave and strong
Once upon a dream, he kept children safe from harm
So close your eyes and think of him, and he will appear
Child of mine, dream away your fear

Stephen's mother gives her son a kiss and tiptoes out of his room. Soon, Stephen begins to fall asleep. Suddenly, a boogey monster appears. Stephen jumps out of bed and the boogey monster begins chasing him in circles around and around his room. It is the same boogey monster that has scared him on countless other nights. The boogey monster keeps saying in a low, growly voice, "Boogey, boogey, boogey." Stephen runs as fast as he can. He hears the monster's footsteps behind him. The boogey monster is so close that Stephen can feel his breath. The voice only says, "Boogey, boogey, boogey."

Stephen remembers the song his mother sang.

He sings to himself, "Close your eyes, and think of him and he will appear."

There is a flash of lightning and the boogey monster disappears as Willy rides Lightning Bolt into Stephen's room.

"Willy, is that you?" asks Stephen.

"Of course it's me," answers Willy Monster. "You need me, so here I am. Was something scaring you?"

"There was a boogey monster chasing me in my room," replies Stephen.

Willy looks under Stephen's bed and in his closet.

"He's not here anymore. You're not scared of boogey monsters, are you, Stephen?"

"Everyone is afraid of the boogey monster," answers Stephen.

"Boogey monsters like to boogey and play at night, but they're not bad monsters," says Willy. "My best friend Beth is a boogey monster. Beth is the smartest, bravest monster I know. She could help you find the boogey monster who has been scaring you. Would you like to go to Boogeyland and meet her?"

"I'd like to Willy, but it's so dark," says Stephen.

"The moon and stars will light up the dark sky and show us the way. And, you'll get to ride on Lightning Bolt!"

Stephen thinks for only a minute before he answers.

"Okay, Willy, let's go!"

"Thunder!" shouts Willy.

Stephen and Willy climb aboard Lightning Bolt.

Willy puts on his pilot's hat and says, "This is your captain speaking. Welcome aboard Dream Flight 101 with nonstop service from Earth to Boogeyland. For your safety, keep your seatbelts securely fastened. Take a moment to notice that the emergency exits are on all sides, and safety clouds are located throughout the sky. Our time of departure is now 8:30 P.M. Enjoy your flight. Lightning speed ahead!!!"

Willy wraps his wings of protection around Stephen as they fly through the sky.

"My house looks like a toy! The cars on the street look like my match-box cars!" exclaims Stephen.

Stephen and Willy look down on the mountains, rivers, and forests of the Earth. The Earth looks like a beautiful ball. The ball gets smaller and smaller until it is just a tiny dot in the distance. Finally, they cannot see the Earth at all.

"Look at the stars," Stephen exclaims. "I've never seen anything so beautiful, Willy!"

"I told you the moon and stars would light up the sky," replies Willy.

As they whiz past hundreds of shining stars, they feel a cool breeze blowing on their faces.

"Look, Willy! We're getting closer and closer to a planet!" exclaims Stephen.

"That's Boogeyland!" answers Willy.

Lightning Bolt heads straight down toward the planet, then straightens out at the last second for a perfect landing. Willy unwraps his wings from around Stephen and they step down from Lightning Bolt.

It is dark on the planet, but they can hear the sounds of music nearby.

The singing boogey monsters and party animals, which are the creatures of Boogeyland, welcome Willy and Stephen. Even though they look strange, they are so friendly that Stephen is not scared.

"I thought the boogey monsters would be asleep this late at night," says Stephen.

Willy Monster laughs.

"What's so funny?" Stephen asks.

"All boogey monsters sleep in the daytime and are awake at night," Willy tells him.

Even though it is dark, there are three moons shining above Boogeyland, so Stephen and Willy have no trouble finding their way to Beth's house. Willy knocks on the door of Beth's house and a boogey mom answers. Her hair is orange, green, and red and it is sticking up in a lot of different directions.

"Any friend of Willy's is a friend of mine. Come on in," says the boogey mom.

She introduces Stephen to the boogey dad and to Little B, her baby boogey. Little B is crawling around on the floor. He crawls at full speed, back and forth, back and forth, across the room. The baby boogey has one little strand each of orange, green, and red hair that sticks straight up. When he finally stops his speed crawling, he looks at Stephen and says in a cute little voice, "Boogey, boogey, boogey."

"Beth, maybe you can help Stephen," suggests Willy.

"Tell me, Stephen, what does the boogey monster look like?" asks Beth kindly.

"He's very big, and he always says the same thing . . . 'boogey, boogey, boogey.' I would know his voice anywhere," says Stephen.

"It sounds like a nightmare boogey," says Beth thoughtfully. "I'm sorry to say, there are some nightmare boogey monsters in Boogeyland that scare children. They live in Nightmare Cave. Stephen, you should find that boogey monster and tell him to stop bothering you."

"I'm too scared," replies Stephen.

"I know," says Beth. "We all get scared sometimes."

"Will you and Willy come with me?" asks Stephen.

"Of course we will!" say Beth and Willy Monster.

Stephen thinks for a moment. "Okay, let's go."

Little B makes a beeline for the door but Beth quickly picks him up. "Sorry, Little B, you have to stay home." She hands her baby brother to her mom and tells her parents, "Don't worry, Mom and Dad, I promise I'll be back before it gets light." Beth kisses Little B on top of his little Boogey head. "Good-bye, Little B. You be good."

Little B waves good-bye with both his tiny paws. "Bye-bye, Beth. Boogey, boogey."

Then the friends are on their way. Beth tells Stephen which way to go, and he bravely leads the way as they head for Nightmare Cave. They follow a winding path through the trees toward the sound of a waterfall.

Behind the wall of falling water, Beth finds the secret entrance to an enormous dark cave. The friends enter the dark, shadowy cave. No longer can they see the light from the three moons. They know they have entered Nightmare Cave because of the scary sounds they hear from deep inside.

A nightmare boogey who sounds like a witch shrieks and laughs, "I'm your worst nightmare! Boogey, boogey, boogey."

Then Stephen hears the sound of the nightmare boogey that has been scaring him.

From far away they hear his voice saying, "Boogey, boogey, boogey."

"That's his voice," says Stephen.

They follow the sound of his voice through the dark passageway. They can hear the nightmare boogey, louder than before: "Boogey, boogey, boogey." Stephen stops. Dark shadows are everywhere.

"What's the matter?" asks Willy.

"It's so dark in here. I can't see anything," answers Stephen.

"How far can you see?" asks Beth softly.

"Just one step," says Stephen.

"Take it, Stephen," urges Willy.

Stephen takes one step and Beth asks, "Now how far can you see?"

"Just about one more step," replies Stephen.

"Go ahead and take it, Stephen," says Willy.

Step by step, Stephen gets closer and closer to the nightmare boogey monster until he is close enough to see him clearly. The boogey monster is looking in the other direction and does not see Stephen. Stephen takes a good look at the nightmare boogey monster. He sees that the boogey monster is not as big as he remembered. In fact, Stephen decides that he himself is bigger than the nightmare boogey. Stephen suddenly feels very brave.

In a clear voice he calls to the boogey monster. "Boogey!" The boogey monster is startled and screams. When he sees it is Stephen, he tries to scare him as he has on so many nights before.

"Boogey, boogey, boogey," says the nightmare boogey monster. This time Stephen is not frightened. The boogey monster doesn't know what to think. He clears his throat and tries again. "I said, boogey, boogey, boogey!"

Stephen says to him, "You don't scare me anymore." Before his very eyes, the nightmare boogey monster gets smaller and smaller. "Now go away, boogey, and don't bother me anymore!" says Stephen.

The nightmare boogey monster turns and runs away.

Stephen smiles as he proudly walks back to his friends. His friends smile back at him. No one talks as they follow the light from the three moons safely back out of the cave. Willy and Beth are thinking of Stephen's courageous steps. They understand that one step at a time they can do almost anything.

Stephen yawns. "I'm tired. Willy, will you take me home so I can go to sleep?"

"You've got it! Thunder!" calls Willy.

Beth, Willy, and Stephen enjoy the ride back to Stephen's house.

When Stephen is safely back in his room he says to his friends, "The nightmare boogey won't be bothering me anymore, but I'm going to miss all of you. Can I visit Boogeyland again someday?"

"I'll take you anytime. You know how to call me." Willy says, "Close your eyes and think of me and I will appear . . ."

"Now I know I'll sleep without fear," says Stephen softly.

"Thanks for taking me on a dream flight, Willy," Stephen says sleepily.

The friends say good-bye and in a flash, they are gone. Stephen feels safe in his warm, cozy bed. Soon, he falls asleep. From that night on, Stephen dreamed happily ever after.

THE SPIDER POEM

Dr. Peter Claydon

Theme: A playful way to approach a fear of spiders

Now some people don't like spiders, I really don't know why.

They're so friendly in bed as they hang by a thread, and look you straight in
   the eye.

Now don't think that you can fool them, by pretending to be asleep.

For as soon as it's dark, just for a lark, across your face they'll creep.

If they think you look cute and sweet, they'll dance with all eight feet.

Up on your nose, though I suppose, this might tickle a bit,

and cause you to sit, knocking them on to your sheet.

Now this is the start of my favorite part,

as you jump out of bed and search with such dread, as they play hide and go
   seek.

The Big-Hearted Giraffe and the Brave Tick Bird

Patti Teel

Themes: compassion and empathy, doing the right thing and not following the crowd, accepting differences.

Amani was a young giraffe who lived with her family as she grew up. When she was almost full grown, she left her herd to start a new life on her own. Although Amani no longer lived with her family, she carried the lessons they had taught her deep in her heart.

Amani wandered in a grassy Uganda savannah where there were lots of acacia trees, her favorite food. One day, she saw a group of zebras and antelopes and walked toward them to say hello. When they saw Amani, they stared at her. They thought Amani looked strange. Not only was her neck longer than anything they had ever seen before, it was crooked. A bold zebra named Gamba teased Amani:

"Too tall, too tall, you're a wreck; long, long legs and a crooked neck!"

Soon the other zebras, antelopes, and hippos joined in the teasing. To Amani, it felt as if every animal in the savannah was making fun of her. Amani tried to ignore them. She thought about sticking out her eighteen-inch tongue, but did not. She told them to stop. When they didn't, she turned and walked away. She didn't walk away because she was afraid. She left because she didn't want to be with animals that acted that way. A tick bird named Obi followed her. He sang, "Gamba really thinks he's cool. He needs to learn the golden rule."

Obi and Amani became good friends. Every day, Obi would hop on Amani's back and look for pesky ticks. He'd call to them, "Here ticka, ticka, ticka, ticka." Now many people don't know this but giraffes can snore like a person, moo like a cow, bleat like a calf, and bellow like a bull. Amani, like all giraffes, could also grunt, snort, cough, whistle, and growl. While giraffes are usually quiet by nature, when Obi and Amani were together they would make all kinds of weird and wonderful music. When ticks and other bugs would come out of Amani's fur to find out what all the racket was about, they would quickly be gobbled up by Obi. "Mmmmm, " said Obi. "Nothing like a tick for breakfast, lunch, or dinner." Obi always made Amani laugh and she was very glad to get the ticks off her back. Obi and Amani were best friends.

Amani grew taller and taller and by summertime she was a full-grown giraffe standing seventeen feet tall, which is as high as a two-story building. She weighed 2,600 pounds and could run thirty miles per hour. When Amani ran, none of the other animals, except Obi, could keep up with her.

That summer there was a terrible drought, which means there was no rain. The rivers were now dried-up mud. The green meadow turned brown as the grass and plants died. Animals were sick and hungry. There were still some leaves on the treetops, which Amani could reach with her long neck. She knew that the other animals couldn't reach high enough to get any food. Every day, she and Obi pulled leaves and fruit off the treetops and scattered them on the ground for the hungry animals to eat. Amani shared what little she had with the others. She fed the hungry animals until the rains came and the grass grew back. If it were not for Amani and her long neck, many animals would have died.

Gamba was sorry that he had made fun of Amani. The other animals knew that they had been just as bad by going along with Gamba's teasing. They apologized to Amani for teasing her and calling her "Too Tall." Amani accepted their apology. She had a very big heart.

After that, no one paid any attention to Amani's crooked neck. In fact they no longer even noticed it. They were, however, still amazed by the size of her heart.

Now, think about your own heart. Be very quiet. Put your hand on your heart and feel it beating. Think of someone that people aren't very nice to. Be as brave as Obi and think of ways you can be nice to that person. Now, feel your heart beating again. Feel its warmth. I do believe that your heart is as big as Amani's.

PRAYER

Science is catching up with something that many people have always known: prayer is powerful and it works. Prayer is a personal matter and your beliefs and religion are likely to determine whether you encourage your children to pray and what form the prayers take. I personally believe that everything we do, think, and say has an energy that affects others as well as ourselves and is, in effect, a prayer. Encouraging our children to send thoughts of love and kindness to others is indeed putting a prayer out into the world and teaching our children about goodness.

For example,

> Bless me, bless Mommy, bless Daddy,
> I pray they are happy and well.
> May I be safe. May Mommy and Daddy be safe.
> May I be happy. May Mommy and Daddy be happy.
> May I be healthy. May Mommy and Daddy be healthy.

Gradually, children can spread their loving thoughts further and further, to their entire family, extended family, friends, school, country, world, universe, and so forth. Eventually, encourage your children to pray for the very people who they are angry or unhappy with.

Prayers of gratitude and thankfulness help children to reflect on some of the blessings in their lives that may be frequently overlooked. For example,

> I see the moon and the moon sees me
> God bless the moon and God bless me.
> I see the stars and the stars see me.
> God bless the stars and God bless me.

APPENDIX

relaxation techniques

Breathing Techniques

ATTENDING TO THE BREATH
  THE TREE–201, THE WAVES–213 AND THE
  WIND–220
  FEELING THE AIR AS YOU BREATHE   187
DIAPHRAGMATIC BREATHING
  BELLY BREATHING (BASIC
    DIRECTIONS)   158
  BALLOON BREATHING   208
  BALL BREATHING   205
  SIGH BREATHING   190
ISOLATING THE PARTS OF THE
    BREATH
  ELEVATOR BREATHING   218

GUIDED RELAXATION

The guided relaxation routines from the *Floppy Sleep Game* program can also effectively help children to relax during quiet time. Rather than telling children to fall asleep, bring them back to a refreshed state by saying something like the following:

Take a deep full breath and gently stretch your body.
Lie on your side. *(Pause.)*
When you're ready, sit up and enjoy feeling relaxed.
You are ready to enjoy the rest of your day.

PROGRESSIVE RELAXATION

THE FLOP GAME   146

LET GO   159

QUIET BLESSINGS   291

RELEASE-ONLY RELAXATION

HEAVY AND RELAXED   173

VISUALIZATIONS

MAGIC WINDOW   150

WHEN YOU BELIEVE   155

YOU CAN FLY   162

THE DREAM TEAM   166

THE SOUND OF DREAMS   170

MOONSTONES   176

THE HIDDEN TREASURE   179

PLANTING SEEDS   188

THE FOREST OF DREAMS   191

WONDERING   195

IN SEARCH OF THE UNICORN   199

A CELEBRATION   202

FREE TO FLY   205

REMEMBERING   208

FUN STRESS BUSTERS

Quiet Blessings

Adapted from *The Inside Out Blessing Game* CD by Patti Teel

Although "Quiet Blessings" is written in rhyme, read it slowly, allowing time for relaxed movements and slow breathing. This whimsical routine focuses on blessings and combines progressive relaxation, imagery, and breath awareness. It is track 7 on the *Floppy Sleep Game Book* CD. (For ages three through eight.)

INTRODUCTION:

Thank you, fingers, thank you, toes.

Thank you, legs, and thank you, nose.

This game gives you one last stretch,

before you have a lovely rest.

It's time to play the Quiet Blessings game.

It is a relaxing game to play before you go to sleep

or when you want some special quiet time.

Follow the directions in the song unless you get too sleepy.

DIRECTIONS

Listen, listen, and you'll hear, blessings that are very near.

Your breath whispers from within, "Time to tuck our tootsies in."

Your toes stand for one last bow; stretch them up and bend them down.

Wiggle, wiggle, wiggle, squirm, one by one they bow in turn.

Feel your breath go in and out, slowly, slowly, round about.

Each breath is a special song; Ticklish Tootsies dance along.

Quiet, quiet, and you'll hear, blessings that are very near.

Your toes whisper from within, "Time to tuck our long legs in."

Lift your legs up to the stars; they are spaceships circling Mars.

Circle them around the moon; land them now, it's bedtime soon.

Feel your breath go in and out, slowly, slowly, round about.

Each breath is a special song, Daddy Long Legs dance along.

Hush now, shush now, and you'll hear, blessings that are very near.

Your legs whisper from within, "Time to tuck our belly in."

Your round belly is a ball; breathe in slowly, fill it all.

Breathe out; pull your belly in; now you fill it up again.

Feel your breath go in and out, slowly, slowly, round about.

Each breath is a special song; Belly Ball will dance along.

Be still, so still, that you hear, blessings that are very near.

Belly whispers from within, "Time to tuck our fingers in."

Bend your fingers one by one; don't forget to bend each thumb.

Make two fists with all your might; hold them, hold them, hold them tight.

Feel your breath go in and out, slowly, slowly, round about.

Each breath is a special song, Nimble Fingers dance along.

Silence, silence, and you'll hear, blessings that are very near.

Your hands whisper from within, "Time to tuck our shoulders in."

Give your shoulders a soothing rub; rub a dub, a dub dub dub.

Push your shoulders toward the ground; lift them up and drop them
 down.
Feel your breath go in and out, slowly, slowly, round about.
Each breath is a special song; Sturdy Shoulders dance along.

When you listen you will hear, blessings that are very near.
Shoulders whisper from within, "Time to tuck our own neck in."
Turn your neck from left to right; like a turtle, stretch good night.
Turn again from side to side; your head likes the lovely ride.
Feel your breath go in and out, slowly, slowly, round about.
Each breath is a special song; Turtle Neck will dance along.

When it's quiet you will hear, blessings that are very near.
Your neck whispers from within, "Time to tuck our own head in."
Lift your eyebrows toward the sky; drop them down and blink
 each eye.
Twitch your nose and make it hop; hippity-hippity, hop, hop, hop.
Open your mouth very wide; move your jaw from side to side.
Scrunch your face, your nose and chin; finish with a great big grin.
Feel your breath go in and out, slowly, slowly, round about.
Each breath is a special song; Sleepy Head will dance along.

In the silence you will hear, blessings that are very near.
Your head whispers from within, "Time to tuck our own heart in."
Beating, beating, through the night, loving is your heart's delight.
Caring for each part of you, you're a blessing through and through.
Feel your breath go in and out, slowly, slowly, round about.
Each breath is a special song; Loving Heart will dance along.

In the stillness you will hear, blessings that are very near.
Your heart whispers from within, "Finally, we're all tucked in."
Good night all and God bless you; thank you for the things you do.

Fun Stress Busters

The Noodle Game—Have children practice making their limbs and body as loose and limp as a spaghetti noodle.

The Melting Popsicle—Your child pretends that he is a melting popsicle.

The Jellyfish—Child pretends to be a jellyfish with all his muscle groups as loose and limp as jelly.

I'm Doggone Tired—Child pretends to be a sleepy dog, flopped on the ground.

Catnap—Stretch like a cat and take a short snooze.

The Sloth Slow-Motion Game— Children move in slow motion, like a sloth.

Feel your Pulse, or Your Heartbeat—Have kids be so quiet that they can feel their own heart beating.

index

Activities
  adult, 11
  at bedtime, 124–125, 143–144, 206–207
  family, 11–12
  overscheduling, 12
  for physical health, 12–13, 34
Acupuncture, for asthma, 61
ADHD. *See* Attention deficit hyperactivity
    disorder
Advair, for asthma treatment, 60
Affirmations, focus for, 33–34
Allergies
  analysis of, 113–114
  causes of, 61–63
  testing for, 62
Alone sleep
  progress in, 183–185, 221–222, 233, 249–
    250
  ritual for, 124, 136–139, 288
  rules for, 26–28, 221–222, 228–229
  theories about, 22–24, 35–36
  training for, 1–2, 26–28, 222
  transition to, 9, 25–28, 140–142, 233–235,
    238

Alpha waves
  music effect on, 129–130
  during wakefulness, 46
Alternative therapies. *See also* Nutrition
  herbs for, 87–88
  for neurobiological disorders, 64–65
  supplements for, 86–89
  types of, 82–85
The American Association of Naturopathic
    Physicians, 83
American Diabetes Association's 61st Annual
    Scientific Session, 21
American Holistic Medical Association, 83
Amino acids, 86–87
Analysis. *See also* Research
  of allergies, 113–114
  of arousal, 95–96
  of asthma, 113–115
  of bedwetting, 113–115
  of journal, sleep, 96, 98, 100, 102, 104,
    106, 108, 112, 114, 115
  of sleep disorders, 109–112
Anger
  anxiety-related, 247–248

Anger (*cont.*)
  expression of, 247–248
  during night terror, 51
  from overstimulation, 14–15
  from sleep deprivation, 17–18
  upon arousal, 43–44, 70
Annals of Internal Medicine, 21
Anxiety
  about co-sleeping, 21
  body response to, 245–246
  disorders from, 243–245
  management of, 237–241, 246–247, 249–252
  nutrition for, 68, 78, 86–87, 234
  related anger, 247–248
  risk of, 241–243, 246
  from sleep loss, 21, 68–69, 241–242
Arousal
  analysis of, 95–96
  anger during, 43–44, 70
  difficulty with, 69, 70, 90–91, 140–142
  routine for, 95–98, 231–232
Asperger's syndrome, sleep problems in, 71–72
Asthma
  analysis of, 113–115
  causes of, 61
  diagnosis of, 59–60
  nocturnal, 60–61
  treatment of, 60–61
Attachment parenting, 23
Attention deficit hyperactivity disorder
    (ADHD)
  bedwetting incidence in, 54
  diagnosis of, 19–20, 65
  homework for, 130–132
  RLS incidence in, 55–56
  sleep effects on, 18–20, 65–66
  stimulation effect on, 14–15
  subtypes of, 65
  with Tourette's syndrome, 67
  treatment of, 66
Autism, 71–72

Ball breathing, 205
Balloon breathing, 166
Bedtime. *See also* Fears; Relaxation; Yoga

  activities at, 124–125, 143–144, 206–207
  fears at, 132–133, 235–237
  reading at, 184–185, 276
  recording at, 184–185
  ritual at, 124, 136–139, 288
  routine at, 105–108, 133–136, 228
  worry at, 9–10, 131–136, 248–249
Bedwetting
  ADHD incidence of, 54
  analysis of, 113–115
  from bipolar disorder, 69
  sleep disturbances from, 50, 54–55
Behavior. *See also* Anxiety; Management
  angry, 14–15, 17–18, 43–44, 51, 70
  denial, 244–245, 247
  deprivation, sleep and, 17–20
  distracting, 245
  dumping, 245–246
  fearful, 235–237
  improvement of, 2–3, 19
  observation of, 92–94
  positive, 246–247
  related sleep disorders, 43–44, 47–48
  review of, 116–117
  rewarding of, 92, 210, 222, 229–230
  successful, 183–185, 221–222, 233, 249–250
  support of, child, 12, 246–247, 253–254
Bipolar disorder
  diagnosis of, 45–46, 68
  sleep phases in, 69
  sleep problems from, 69–70
Body, function of, 20–21
Books, reading of, 184–185, 276
Brain development
  exercise effects on, 12–13
  glucose for, 75–76
  of phobias, 235–237
  in sleep cycles, 46–47
  technology effect on, 14–15
  tryptophan for, 68, 82, 87
Brain disorders. *See* Neurobiological disorders
Brain waves
  during non-REM sleep stages, 48–49
  spindles, 48–49
  types of, 46–47

Breast-feeding, 35–36
Breath
    attending to, 187, 201, 213, 220, 237–
        240
    belly, 31–32, 144, 157–158, 165, 169, 178–
        179, 198, 214–215
    connection of, 31, 165
    diaphragmatic breathing, 158, 166, 190,
        198, 205
    focus on, 141, 144, 154, 183, 190
    isolation of, 218–220, 227
    journal of, 29–30
    shallow, 31–32
    with yoga, 265
Breath with the ocean, 194
Brown University, 19
Bruxism, 51–52, 113–114
Bush, Barbara, 126

Caffeine, 55
Carbohydrates, 76–77
Cataplexy, 58
A Celebration, 202–203
Cell salts, 85
Chamomile, 88
Chamomilla, 85
Chemical Sensitivity (Rea), 79
Christakis, D.A., 14–15
The Christmas Dream, 3, 162, 176, 195
Circadian rhythm disorder, 52–54
Co-sleep
    anxiety about, 21
    journal for, 28–30
    research on, 35–36
    theories about, 22–24, 35–36
    transition from, 9, 25–28, 140–142, 233–
        235, 238
Colic, 7
Concentration. See Focus
Conditions, for sleep, 124–125
Cravings, 76–77
Creativity
    development of, 32–34
    in visualization, 141, 162, 170, 176, 184–
        185, 191

Cycles, sleep
    in bipolar disorder, 69
    in brain, 46–47
    delayed phase syndrome of, 52–53
    normal, 45–46

Dawn simulators, 53, 69
Delayed sleep phase syndrome, 52–53
Democratic parenting, 8–9
Denial, 244–245, 247
Dependency, 28–30. See also Co-sleep
Depression. See also Mood
    nutrition for, 68, 78
    sleep problems from, 7, 16, 21, 67–68
    treatments for, 86–87
Deprivation, sleep
    in adults, 16–17
    behavior effects from, 17–20
    risks from, 20–22
Desire, of happiness, 33–34
Diabetes, risk of, 21, 75–76
Diagnosis
    of ADHD, 19–20, 65
    of allergies, 61–63
    of asthma, 59–60
    of bipolar disorder, 45–46, 68
    of neurobiological disorders, 63, 67–72
Diaphragmatic breath, 158, 166, 190, 198, 205
Diet. See Nutrition
The Dream Team, 166–169
Dreams
    discussion of, 231–232
    nightmare, 47, 69, 109, 112, 221
    in REM sleep, 46–47
    sleep paralysis with, 56
"Drive Down the Freeway," 261
Driving, drowsy, 16–17
DSI. See Sensory integration dysfunction

Eat. See Food; Nutrition
Education, special, 18, 20, 63, 76
An elephant steps on your stomach, 190
Elevator Breathing, 218–220, 227
Emotional health. See also Fears; Physical
        health; Self

Emotional health. (*cont.*)
    happiness in, 33–34, 250–252
    improvement of, 8, 12–13, 21, 250–252
    nutrition for, 68, 86–89
    review of, 116–117
    sleep effects on, 8–9, 9–10
Endangered Minds (Healy), 15
Environmental toxins, health effects from, 61
Exercise. *See* Physical health

Family, quiet time for, 11–12
Family bed. See Co-sleep
Fantasy, 198
Fatigue. *See also* Deprivation, sleep
    from RLS, 55
    from sleep apnea, 57–58
Fatty acids, 88–89
FDA. *See* Federal Drug Administration
Fears
    at bedtime, 132–133, 235–237
    brain development of, 235–237
    desensitization of, 240–241
    overcoming, 133–136, 237–241, 279–285
    research on, 235
    specific, 243–244
Federal Drug Administration (FDA), 67–68
Feel the air as you breath, 187
Fight-or-flight response, 238, 241
Fixed scene visualization, 32–33
The Flop Game, 146–148
Floppy sleep game program
    overview of, 142–143
    progress in, 183–185, 221–222, 233, 249–250
    questions about, 182–183
Focus
    for affirmations, 33–34
    on breath, 141, 144, 154, 183, 190
    improvement of, 8
    inability to, 19
    inward, 251–254
Food. *See also* Nutrition
    allergies to, 79–80
    carbohydrates, 76–77
    eating habits, 76–77, 80–81
    impact of, 74

    for sound sleep, 81–82
    sugar sensitivity, 74–78
The Forest of Dreams, 191–193
48 Hours, 2–3
Free to Fly, 205–206
Full-spectrum lights, 53

Give yourself a bear hug, 201
Glucose, for brain development, 75–76
Glycemic index, 76–77
Goals, visualization of, 33–34, 166
Good Housekeeping, 2–3
"The Great Big Cat," 260
"Great Big Elephant," 259
Green tea, 87
"Grow Garden Grow," 188, 191, 257
A growing seed, 186–187, 189
Guests, in house, 29
Guided relaxation
    progressive, 146–149, 159–162, 211, 224–
        225, 238, 291
    release-only, 145, 172–175, 207, 211, 215,
        226

Habits. *See also* Journal, sleep
    of eating, 80–81
    observation of, 28, 92–94
    self soothing, 27, 141, 144–145, 233–235,
        237–241
Head stretches, 263–265
Headaches, upon arousal, 90–91
Health. *See* Emotional health; Physical health
Healy, Jane, 15
Heart rate, during non-REM sleep, 49
Heavy and Relaxed
    breathing in, 175
    directions for, 173–175
Herbs, 87–88
The Hidden Treasure, 179–182
Homeopathic remedies
    efficacy of, 84
    safety of, 84–85
Homework, in routine, 130–132
Hormones
    anxiety effect on, 241

growth, 49, 57
melatonin, 53–54, 69
music effect on, 129–130
Hunt, Dr. Carl, 22
5– Hydroxytryptophan, for emotional health, 68, 82, 87
Hyland's Calms Forté 4 Kids, 85
Hypnagogic hallucinations
in narcolepsy, 58–59
in sleep paralysis, 56
Hypoglycemia, 75

IEP. *See* Individualized educational plans
I'm taking your picture, 207
Images
mental, 32–34
negative, 10, 14–15, 248
positive, 10, 34, 249
in visualization practice, 184–185
Imagination
development of, 32–34
in visualization, 141, 162, 170, 176, 184– 185, 191
Immunity
depressed, 16, 22
music effect on, 129–130
vaccination for, 22
In Search of the Unicorn, 199–200
Independence. *See also* Alone sleep
training for, 9, 25–26, 140–142
Individualized educational plans (IEP), 20
Inhalers, for asthma, 60
The Inside-Out Blessing Game, 3, 202
Internet
dawn simulators on, 53
glycemic index on, 77
natural medicine on, 83, 85
sleep information on, 2

The jellyfish, 206
Journal, sleep
action plan for, 117
analysis of, 96, 98, 100, 102, 104, 106, 108, 112, 114, 115
breath in, 29–30

importance of, 91, 94
observation in, 28, 92–94
routine in, 90–91
sample of, 95, 97, 99, 101, 103, 105, 107, 109–111, 113, 116
starting of, 37–40, 93–94
visualization in, 28–29
Journal of the American Medical Association, 22

Kali phosphorous, 85
Kaye, Dr. Gloria, 159, 265
Keeping the rain out of your eyes, 204
Kids World, 2, 155, 170, 199, 208, 258

La Leche League International, 35–36
Laxative, magnesium as, 86
Learning
sleep apnea and, 58
sleep effects on, 14–16, 18–20
Let go
breathing in, 161–162
directions for, 159–160

Magic Window, 150–152
Magnesium, 86
Management. *See also* Relaxation; Routine
of anger, 247–248
of anxiety, 237–241, 246–247, 249–252
of asthma, 60–61
of behavior, 2–3, 19
of emotional health, 8, 12–13, 21, 250–252
of mental tension, 31–32
of mood, 2–3, 34, 43–44
of neurbiological disorders, 64–65
of nutrition, 77–78, 81, 86–89
self-soothing skills for, 27, 141, 144–145, 233–235, 237–241
of worry, 248–249
Massage, 261–262
Media
attention from, 2–3
exposure to, 11
overstimulation from, 10, 14–15, 128
Medications. *See also* Alternative therapies
for ADHD, 66

Medications. (*cont.*)
  for asthma, 60
  for depression, 67–68
  for neurobiological disorders, 64–65
  for REM sleep disorders, 48
Melatonin, 53–54, 69
Mental tension, relaxation of, 31–32
Mind
  conscious, 32
  subconscious, 33
Minerals, 55, 82, 86
Mood. *See also* Bipolar disorder
  depressed, 7, 16, 21, 67–68
  improvement of, 2–3, 34, 43–44
  nutrition for, 68, 70
  observation of, 92–94
Moonstones, 176–178
Mother earth says, 204
"Motor Boat," 260
Motor skills, 22, 69
Movement. *See also* Yoga
  exercises for, 257–261
  music with, 256–257
  neck stretches, 262–265
Muddy toes, 204
Muscle groups
  massage of, 261–262
  relaxation of, 144–146, 157
  tensing of, 169–170, 172, 178, 182–183,
    186, 189–190, 193–194
Music, soothing
  effect of, 3–4, 129–130, 256–257
  songs, 188, 191, 257–261
Mutism, selective, 243

Narcolepsy, 58–59
National Center for Homeopathy, 85
National Center on Sleep Disorders
    Research at the National Institute
    of Health, 22
National Education Association, 130
National Sleep Foundation, 8, 144
Native Americans, traditions of, 136
Natural medicines
  healers with, 82–85

  herbs as, 87–88
  for neurobiological disorders, 64–65
  supplements as, 86–89
Nebulizer, for asthma treatment, 60
Neck stretches, 262–265
Neurobiological disorders, 63–65
Neurotransmitters, 12, 76, 82
NHTSA. *See* U.S. National Highway Traffic
    Safety Administration
Night terror
  analysis of, 110, 112
  from bipolar disorder, 69
  routine, 221
  types of, 50–51
Night waking, 27–28, 230–231
Nightmares
  analysis of, 109, 112
  in bipolar disorder, 69
  as REM disorder, 47
  routine, 221
Nocturnal asthma, 60–61
Nocturnal bedwetting enuresis, 50
Noises. *See also* Music, soothing
  negative, 10, 14–15
  positive, 3–4, 10, 129–130, 256–257
Non-rapid eye movement sleep
  disorders of, 49–52
  stages of, 48–49
Northwestern University, 18
Nutrition
  amino acid, 86–87
  for anxiety, 68, 78, 86–87, 234
  benefits of, 74
  for bipolar disorder, 69–70
  carbohydrates for, 76–77
  for depression, 68, 78
  diet types for, 78
  eating habits, 80–81
  food sensitivities, 79–80
  health tips for, 77–78, 81, 86–89
  magnesium, 86
  mineral, 55, 82, 86
  obesity and, 75–77
  for relaxation, 86–89
  for sound sleep, 81–82

sugar sensitivities, 74–78
vitamin, 82, 86

Obesity
    nutrition and, 75–77
    from sleep apnea, 57–58
    sleep loss and, 21–22, 73–74
Observation
    of behavior, 92–94
    of breath, 31–32
    in journal, sleep, 28, 92–94
    of mood, 92–94
Obsessive-compulsive disorder, 244
Omega-3 fish oil, 68, 70, 88–89
Orthodox sleep. See Non-rapid eye movement
    sleep
Outdoors, exposure to, 13, 53

Panic disorder, 244
Paradoxical sleep. See Rapid eye movement
    sleep
Parasomnia, 44–45
Parent Teacher Association, 130
Parents
    democratic, 8–9
    deprivation, sleep of, 16–17
    patience of, 17
    support of, child, 12, 17, 246–247, 253–
        254
Passionflower, 88
Path to Inner Peace (Bush), 126
Pediatrics, 14–15
People, 2–3
Phobias. See Fears
Physical health. See also Emotional health
    activities for, 12–13, 34
    effects on, 8–9, 12, 21–22, 61
    immunity and, 16, 22, 129–130
    nutrition for, 77–78, 81, 86–89
    review of, 116–117
Piaget, Jean, 235
Pineal gland, 53
Planting Seeds, 188–189
Poetry
    "Between Us," 277

"Slow Down, Don't Dance So Fast," 255
"The Spider Poem," 285
Post-traumatic stress disorder, 244
Prayer, 136–137, 288
Progress, in alone sleep, 183–185, 221–222,
    233, 249–250
Progressive relaxation routine, abbreviated,
    224–225
Proteins, 85–86
Protest, about routine, 153, 222
Psychologist, in school, 20
Psychology Today, 19

Quiet blessings, 291–295

Rapid eye movement sleep (REM), 46–48. See
    also Non-rapid eye movement sleep
Rea, Dr. William J., 79
Reactive airway disease, 59–61
Reading. See also Storytelling
    at bedtime, 184–185, 276
    difficulty with, 14
Recording, tape
    creating of, 211–212
    rules for, 209–210
    transitions to, 184–185
Relaxation. See also Breath; Guided relaxation;
        Visualization; Yoga
    for bipolar disorder, 69
    games for, 291–294
    herbs for, 87–88
    massage for, 261–262
    of mental tension, 31–32
    of muscle groups, 144–146, 157
    music for, 129–130, 257–258
    nutrition for, 86–89
    preparation for, 13, 142–144
    ritual for, 124, 136–139, 288
    self-soothing skills for, 27, 141, 144–145,
        233–235, 237–241
    for tooth grinding, 51–52
    transition exercises for, 238–240
Release-only routine, abbreviated, 226
REM. See Rapid eye movement sleep
Remembering, 208–209

Research
    on acupuncture, 61
    on aggression, 14–15, 17–18
    on co-sleep, 35–36
    on co-sleeping, 36
    on fear, 235
    on motor skill development, 22
    on negative images, 10, 14–15
    on negative noises, 10, 14–15
    on sleep loss, 8, 16, 21–22
    on violence, 14–15
Restless leg syndrome (RLS), 55–56
Reward system, for behavior, 92, 210, 222,
        229–230
Rinkel, Dr. Herbert, 80
Risk
    of anxiety, 241–243, 246
    of diabetes, 21, 75–76
    from sleep deprivation, 20–22
Rituals
    back-rub, 140–142
    in morning, 231–232
    personalized, 137–139
    in routine, 124, 136–139, 288
RLS. See Restless leg syndrome
Rogers, Dr. S.A., 80
Routine. See also Relaxation
    afternoon, early, 99–100
    afternoon, late, 100–102
    bedtime, 105–108, 133–136, 228
    consistency of, 123–125, 143–144, 229
    creating time for, 125–127, 130
    establishment of, 121–122, 124–125, 140–
        142, 184–185, 228
    evening, 103–104, 127–130
    for homework, 130–132
    importance of, 122–123, 137, 143–144,
        184–185
    for journal, sleep, 90–91
    morning, 95–98, 231–232
    problems with, 228–231
    protest about, 153, 222
    ritual in, 124, 136–139, 288
    rules for, 221–222, 228
    yoga in, 153–154, 159–162, 165, 169, 172

"Row, Row, Row Your Boat," 259
Rules
    for alone sleep, 26–28, 221–222, 228–
        229
    for democratic parenting, 8–9
    effect of, 9
    emotional health and, 9
    of physical health, 8–9
    for recording tape, 209–210
    for routine, 221–222, 228
Safety
    during sleep transitions, 23
    structure for, 12–13, 122–123
Schedule. See Routine
School
    education, special in, 18, 20, 63, 76
    performance in, 7–8, 20
    psychologist in, 20
    self-worth at, 253–254
Schuessler, Dr. William, 85
The Scientific Basis of Environmental Medicine
        Techniques (Rogers), 80
Selective mutism, 243
Self
    knowing of, 33–34, 250–252
    positive image of, 34, 249
    soothing skills for, 27, 141, 144–145, 233–
        235, 237–241
    worth, 208, 253–254
Sensory integration dysfunction (DSI),
        70–71
Sensory processing deficit, 69
Separation anxiety, 243
Seratonin, 76, 82
Show me how small you can be, 197
Show me how strong you are, 207
Simon says, 197, 214, 219
"Sky so Blue," 258
Sleep apnea
    fatigue from, 57–58
    obesity from, 57–58
    obstructive, 56–58, 113–114
    RLS in, 55–56
    symptoms of, 57–58, 90–91

Sleep disorders
    analysis of, 109–112
    behavior related, 43–44, 47–48
    during non-REM sleep, 49–52
    non-stage, 52–59
    REM, 48
Sleep journal. *See* Journal, sleep
Sleep level. *See also* Deprivation, sleep
    amount of, 94, 144
    conditions for, 124–125
Sleep loss effects
    on ADHD, 18–20, 65–66
    on anxiety levels, 21, 68–69, 241–242
    on Asperger's syndrome, 71–72
    on driving, 16–17
    on DSI, 70–71
    on emotional health, 8–9, 9–10
    on learning, 14–16, 18–20
    on neurobiological disorders, 63–65
    on obesity, 21–22, 73–74
    on physical health, 8–9, 21–22
    on seratonin, 82
Sleep paralysis, 56, 69
Sleep talk
    analysis of, 111–112
    during non-REM sleep, 49–50
Sleep terror, 50–51
Sleep walk
    analysis of, 110, 112
    during non-REM sleep, 50
    routine, 221
Slow wave sleep. *See* Non-rapid eye movement
        sleep
Snoring, 56–58, 113–114
Solve Your Child's Sleep Problems (Ferber),
    35
Songs. *See* Music, soothing
The Sound of Dreams, 170–171
Sour lemonade, 194
Special education, 18, 20, 63, 76
Spindles, brain wave, 48–49
Sports team, 13
Squeeze a lemon, 193
Squeeze through the fence, 212–213

Stimulation
    anger from, 14–15
    limits of, 127–130
    from technology, 10, 14–15, 128
    from television, 10, 14–15, 127–128
Storytelling
    about dreams, 231–232
    *The Brave-Hearted Giraffe and the Brave
        Tick Bird*, 286–287
    poetry, 255, 277, 285
    with purpose, 279
    themes for, 279, 286
    uses of, 277–278
    Willy Monster, 279–285
    with yoga, 266–268
Stress. *See also* Emotional health; Relaxation
    about sleep transitions, 26–28, 30
    games for, 291–294
    increase of, 3, 64, 67, 229–230, 233–235
    nutrition for, 68, 78, 86–87, 234
    pressure and, 9–10
    related disorders, 243–244
    self-soothing skills for, 27, 141, 144–145,
        233–235, 237–241
    worry and, 9–10, 131–136, 248–249
Stretch and relax, 217
Stretching. *See* Yoga
Subconscious mind, 33
Success, with alone sleep, 183–185, 221–222,
        233, 249–250
Sugar
    metabolism of, 75–76
    sensitivity to, 76–78
Support, of children, 12, 246–247, 253–254
Symptoms
    of ADHD, 19–20
    of allergies, 62–63
    of anxiety, 242–243
    of Autism/Asperger's syndrome, 71–72
    of bipolar disorder, 68–69
    of depression, 67
    of DSI, 70
    of food sensitivities, 80
    of sleep apnea, 57–58, 90–91
    of Tourette's syndrome, 66–67

Tantrum, crying and, 3, 7, 26–28
Technology, overstimulation with, 10, 14–15, 32, 128
Tel Aviv University, 19
Television
    falling asleep with, 73
    overstimulation from, 10, 14–15, 127–128
Tension, mental, 31–32
Theanine, 87
There's a fly on my nose, 215
Theta waves
    music effect on, 129–130
    during sleep, 33, 46
"Tick Tock," 258
Tighten the whole body at once, 220
Toe tensing, 216
Tooth grinding, 51–52, 113–114
Tourette's syndrome
    with ADHD, 67
    characteristics of, 66–67
    sleep problems from, 67
Toxins, environmental, 61
Training
    for alone sleep, 1–2, 26–28, 222
    for independence, 9, 25–26, 140–142
Transitions
    to alone-sleep, 9, 25–28, 140–142, 233–235
    to recording, 184–185
    relaxation exercises during, 238–240
    safety during, 23
    stress about, 26–28, 30
    trauma during, 26–28
Trauma, during sleep transitions, 26–28
The tree, 201
Tryptophan, 68, 82, 87

University of Chicago, 21
U.S. National Highway Traffic Safety Administration (NHTSA), 16

Vaccinations, 22
Valerian, 88
Violence, research on, 14–15

Visualization
    fixed scene, 32–33
    of goals, 33–34, 166
    imagination in, 141, 162, 170, 176, 184–185, 191
    journal for, 28–29
    negative, 248
    partnered, 223–224
    personalized, 212
    questions about, 183
    themes for, 34, 149, 154, 162, 166, 170, 176, 187, 191, 194, 198, 201, 205, 208, 224
    types of, 32–34
Visualization exercises
    A Celebration, 202–203
    The Dream Team, 166–169
    The Forest of Dreams, 191–193
    Free to Fly, 205–206
    The Hidden Treasure, 179–182
    Magic Window, 150–152
    Moonstones, 176–178
    Planting Seeds, 188–189
    Remembering, 208–209
    In Search of the Unicorn, 199–200
    The Sound of Dreams, 170–171
    When You Believe, 155–157
    Wondering, 195–196
    You Can Fly, 162–164
Vitamins, 82, 86

Waking, night, 27–28, 230–231
Walk, sleep, 50, 110, 112, 221
Wall Street Journal, 2–3
The waves, 213
Weil, Dr. Andrew, 76
When You Believe, 155–157
Will Monster, 279–285
The wind, 220
Wondering, 195–196
Worry, bedtime
    effects of, 248–249
    elimination of, 133–136, 249
    problems with, 9–10, 131–133

Yoga
    bow pose, 274–275
    breath for, 265
    bridge pose, 273–274
    child's pose, 266
    cobra pose, 267
    cowshead pose, 273
    importance of, 13, 265
    lion pose, 51–52, 267
    music with, 256–257
    neck stretches with, 262–265
    nose-to-knee pose, 275
    rock your baby pose, 274
    in routine, 153–154, 159–162, 165, 169, 172
    spread-leg stretch pose, 275
    storytelling with, 266–268
    t-twist pose, 276
    thank you, world sequence one, 268–270
    thank you, world sequence two, 270–272
    tiger pose, 266–267
    for tooth grinding, 51–52
    walking up the wall pose, 273
    against the wall pose, 272
Yoga Therapeutics (Kaye), 159–162
You Can Fly, 162–164